Start Your Own

e-BUSINESS

Additional titles in *Entrepreneur's Startup Series*

Start Your Own

Arts and Crafts Business	*Hair Salon and Day Spa*
Automobile Detailing Business	*Home Inspection Service*
Bar and Club	*Import/Export Business*
Bed and Breakfast	*Information Marketing Business*
Blogging Business	*Kid-Focused Business*
Business on eBay	*Lawn Care or Landscaping Business*
Car Wash	*Mail Order Business*
Child-Care Service	*Medical Claims Billing Service*
Cleaning Service	*Net Services Business*
Clothing Store and More	*Online Coupon or Daily Deal Business*
Coaching Business	*Online Education Business*
Coin-Operated Laundry	*Personal Concierge Service*
Construction and Contracting Business	*Personal Training Business*
Consulting Business	*Pet Business and More*
Day Spa and More	*Pet-Sitting Business and More*
e-Business	*Photography Business*
Event Planning Business	*Public Relations Business*
Executive Recruiting Business	*Restaurant and More*
Fashion Accessories Business	*Retail Business and More*
Florist Shop and Other Floral Businesses	*Self-Publishing Business*
Food Truck Business	*Seminar Production Business*
Freelance Writing Business and More	*Senior Services Business*
Freight Brokerage Business	*Travel Business and More*
Gift Basket Service	*Tutoring and Test Prep Business*
Grant-Writing Business	*Vending Business*
Graphic Design Business	*Wedding Consultant Business*
Green Business	*Wholesale Distribution Business*

Entrepreneur
MAGAZINE'S

startup

Start Your Own

3RD EDITION

e-BUSINESS

Your Step-by-Step Guide to Success

Entrepreneur Press and Rich Mintzer

Ep
Entrepreneur
PRESS®

Entrepreneur Press, Publisher
Cover Design: Beth Hansen-Winter
Production and Composition: Eliot House Productions

This publication is designed to provide accurate and authoritative information in regard to the subject matter covered. It is sold with the understanding that the publisher is not engaged in rendering legal, accounting or other professional services. If legal advice or other expert assistance is required, the services of a competent professional person should be sought.

Library of Congress Cataloging-in-Publication Data
    Mintzer, Richard.
      Start your own e-business / by Entrepreneur Press and Rich Mintzer.—3e [edition].
        p.   cm. —(Start your own)
      Revised edition of: Start your own e-business : your step-by-step guide to success / Entrepreneur Press and Lynie Arden, 2nd ed., published in 2009.
      Includes index.
      ISBN-13: 978-1-59918-530-9 (alk. paper)
      ISBN–10: 1-59918-530-X (alk. paper)
      1. Electronic commerce. 2. New business enterprises. I. Arden, Lynie, 1949– Start your own e-business. II. Entrepreneur Press. III. Title.
    HF5548.32.M37785 2014
    658.8'72—dc2   2014006562

18 17 16 15   10 9 8 7 6 5 4 3 2

Contents

Preface xiii

Chapter 1
The Internet Gold Rush 1
    A New Set of Rules 2
    Reaching Their Peak. 3
    Sweet Dreams 4

Chapter 2
Ten Reasons You Should Be Online. 7
    The Downside 9

Chapter 3
Dotcom Dreams and Disasters 11

Chapter 4
**Should You Shut Down Your
Brick-and-Mortar Store?**. .15
    Moving Out 16
    Having It Both Ways. 17
    It's All About the Business. 17

Double Vision 20

Chapter 5

Website Building 101 . . . . **21**
    Know Your Purpose 22
    Getting Started 23
    Be a Savvy Shopper 24
        Functionality 24
        Growth Potential 25
        Site Design 25
        Support—HELP! 25
        How Much? 26
    Leading Factors When Building Your Site 26
    Photo Options 28
    Testing, Testing 30
    Keep It Fresh 31
    Hosted Ecommerce Solutions 31
    Free Online Store 34
    Web Developers 34

Chapter 6

Making Your Site Special **39**
    Video 40
    Polls and Surveys 41
    Blogs 41
    RSS Feeds 42
    Podcasting 43
    CGI Scripts 43
    JavaScripts 44
    Forums 44
    Daily Content 45

Chapter 7

The Ten Most Deadly Mistakes in Web Design **47**

Chapter 8

Echat with Headsets.com's Mike Faith **51**

Chapter 9

Cheap Tricks with BlueSuitMom.com's Maria Bailey **57**

Chapter 10

The Nuts and Bolts of Web Hosts and Domains..........61

What to Look for in a Web Hosting Service.................62

Storage 62

Bandwidth 63

Support and Customer Service 63

Backup 63

Add-On Domains 63

Email 64

Languages 64

Blogging...64

Web Sharing 64

Master of Your Domain............................65

What's In a Name? 66

Choosing a Name 66

Chapter 11

The Scoop on Business-to-Business Ecommerce 69

Taking Care of Business 70

The Many Faces of B2B 71

Liquidity Services Inc..............................72

Marketing Still Matters 73

Adding "C" to B2B 74

A Slam Dunk? 75

Chapter 12

Echat with Autobytel's Jim Riesenbach..................77

Chapter 13

Echat with Zappos' Tony Hsieh 81

Chapter 14

Secrets of Funding Your Business.......................87

Fund It Yourself! 88

Banks and the SBA 89

Venture Capitalists 91

Big Winners......................................91

Inside Information 92

Your Presentation 94

Your Business Plan 95

Chapter 15
Why Financial Angels Fund Startups **97**
Later On. 102

Chapter 16
Echat with Corporate Toner's Kapil Juneja. **105**

Chapter 17
Cheap Tricks with Redwagons.com's Tony Roeder **109**

Chapter 18
Cashing in on Affiliate Programs **113**
It All Clicks 114
Google AdSense Makes Sense. 115
Solid Links. 116
Pros and Cons of Affiliate Marketing. 117
The Positives 117
The Negatives 117

Chapter 19
Teaming Up with Big Brick-and-Mortar Companies. **119**
Risky Business 121
Forging Ahead 123

Chapter 20
Echat with eBags.com's Peter Cobb **125**

Chapter 21
Cheap Tricks with Blinds.com's Jay Steinfeld **129**

Chapter 22
Website Traffic Builders. **133**
Baiting Your Hook. 134
The Most Bang for Your Buck 136
The New World of Online Advertising 136
A Direct Approach. 138
News Flash 138
Special Delivery. 140

Stick It to Me 142

Chapter 23
Echat with GiftTree's Craig Bowen 145

Chapter 24
Secrets of Search Engines **149**
Improving Your Ranking 150
Getting Listed 151
Engine Trouble 152
Rank and File 152
Homespun SEO 152
Directory Assistance 155
Paid Placement 156
Spider Webs 158
Are You Ready? 158

Chapter 25
Echat with Drugstore.com's Dawn Lepore 161

Chapter 26
Cheap Tricks with eHolster.com's Scott Quarterman 165

Chapter 27
Accepting Credit Cards and PayPal 167
Taking Credit 168
Small-Business Pal 169
Secure Horizons 170
So, Which Is Better? 171

Chapter 28
Echat with Newegg.com's Bernard Luthi 175

Chapter 29
Cheap Tricks with Bowling Connection.com's
Gary Forrester 179

Chapter 30
Tapping International Markets 183
Foreign Affairs 184

All Aboard 185
Tips for International Business 187

Chapter 31
Echat with ProFlowers' Jared Polis 189

Chapter 32
Cheap Tricks with Fridgedoor's Chris Gwynn 193

Chapter 33
Knowing Your Customers 197
Web Analytics 198
Getting to Know You 200
Going to the Polls 201
Private Eyes 202
Be Careful 202
Confidence Boosters 203

Chapter 34
Customer Service for Success. 207
Aim Higher 210

Chapter 35
Echat with ICanHasCheezburger.com's Ben Huh 213

Chapter 36
Cheap Tricks with FrugalFun.com's Shel Horowitz 219

Chapter 37
Security Holes, Fraud, and More Bad Stuff 223
Security 224
Outages and Other Problems 225
Fraud 226

Chapter 38
A Tour of the Web 229
River of Dreams. 230
Beautify Yourself 232
Pushing the Envelopes 233
It's in the Mail 234
The Right Dose. 235

In Plain Sight 236
Start Your Engines. 237
Keeping It Fresh 237
Get Connected. 240
If the Shoe Fits 240

Chapter 39
The Future of Ecommerce **243**
Time Is Relative 244
Loyalty 244

Appendix
e-Business Resources **253**
Blog Software 253
Competitive Intelligence. 254
Consumer Websites. 254
Direct Marketing and Mail Order 255
Domain Name Registrars 255
Ecommerce Solutions 255
Global Commerce. 256
Miscellaneous Ecommerce Information. 256
Online and Offline Publications. 257
Payment. 257
Search Engines 257
Shopping Bots 257
Social Networking. 258
Software 258
Statistics and More 259
Traffic Reports and Ratings 259
Venture Capital and Angel Information. 259
Web Art. 260
Web Hosts 261
Website Building Tools and Help. 261
Wireless Web. 262

Glossary **263**

Index **267**

Preface

Like the mythical phoenix, the internet rose from the ashes after the 2000 dotcom crash. Today, over a decade later, online sales in the United States alone top $250 billion with no decline in sight. People, consumers in particular, are accessing the multitude of available websites in numerous ways, including mobile technology, led by smartphones. In fact, according to Pew Research Center's Internet & American Life Project, 56 percent of U.S. adults own a smartphone, which means that they are able to access the web from any place where they can get a connection. This makes it much easier to access an e-business today as opposed to the early days of the internet and online retail where most customers were sitting at their desktop or just discovering a laptop.

While venture capitalists (VCs) and angels are more prudent about offering funding for dotcom startups, driven entrepreneurs with good ideas are still devising ways to build solid businesses that utilize the power of the internet to reach millions of people worldwide.

Still, for every dotcom business that flourishes, hundreds—maybe thousands—go bust. What does it take to build a dotcom that will succeed? In this book, you will find out. We offer recipes for success, road maps that pinpoint the hazards, and dozens of interviews with dotcom entrepreneurs who have proved they've got what it takes to survive in this sometimes fickle marketplace.

What separates the losers from the winners? Poor ideas, poor execution, poor marketing, and poor funding.

Good ideas and smart business practices aren't always enough, though. The internet has become overcrowded with both internet-only businesses and the websites of millions of traditional businesses from the brick-and-mortar world. In some cases, launching a national, full-scale, consumer-oriented site today may require millions of dollars to cover detailed web design and navigation systems, marketing, hardware, software, and staffing costs. Gulp! That's a big leap from the graduate school project days that gave rise to Yahoo!.

However, numerous low-cost websites are still launching and making it to the big time. Consider that Facebook was born in a college dorm room. The modern e-business requires a unique combination of customer insight, business understanding, technical know-how, financial resources, marketing, and social media savvy as well as entrepreneurial drive. The possibilities of success remain enticing, even when wallets are thin—if your ideas are smart and your execution persistent.

The goal of this book is to give you the tools and knowledge you'll need to emerge among the victors in a crowded market. In these pages we'll cover building your site, hosting servers, funding, building partnerships, attracting visitors, and hopefully laughing all the way to the bank. This is not a technical book. It's a book about business and consumer psychology.

While the internet's roots are in technology, that technology has become much more accessible to a wider group of entrepreneurs through the efforts and investment of many companies and people. Today, there are better software tools that make it easier than ever for anyone, even technophobes, to build and manage a website.

Some words about how this book is organized: Interspersed among the chapters are "Cheap Tricks," mini-interviews with low-budget website builders. The book also features interviews, called "Echats," with CEOs of big-budget name-brand sites, among them Drugstore.com, Proflowers.com, Autobytel.com, eBags.com, and Zappos.com.

You'll also find three kinds of tip boxes designed to hammer home key points:

- *Smart Tip*: bright ideas you want to remember as well as online opportunities
- *Beware!*: pitfalls and potholes you want to avoid
- *Dollar Stretcher*: money-saving ideas and practices

Read on to find out how to make your internet dreams a reality.

1

The Internet
Gold Rush

Before you embark on your foray into starting your e-business, you might benefit from knowing a little about the previous gold rush, way back in the early days of the internet.

The first dotcom gold rush occurred roughly between 1995 and 2001. It began when a little startup named Netscape introduced a web browser. Amazon, eBay, Yahoo!, 1-800-Flowers.com,

Drugstore.com, Priceline.com, WebMD.com—they staked their claims to a piece of cyberspace and became billion-dollar businesses. Others, like Pets.com, WebVan, and eToys, flamed out spectacularly when the bubble burst in 2001. Many wondered if the internet would ever amount to anything more than a few pie-in-the-sky ideas.

But today, ecommerce is back in a big way. The market continues to thrive and websites come and go all the time.

Just as dotcom giants of the first wave did, over a decade ago, websites like Skype, YouTube, Facebook, Twitter, Pinterest, and a new breed of online retailers, such as Zappos and Nasty Gal, have taken off and become the standard go-to sources.

The influx of e-business sites worldwide has become increasingly evident over the past decade. Window displays have been replaced by branded Pinterest boards and traditional advertising has given way to inbound marketing through the social media sites.

The new e-businesses are succeeding because the new rules favor companies that are innovative, smart, and ultra-quick to react to changing consumer interests. It also helps that today's entrepreneurs have been able to learn from the mistakes and successes of the original dotcom pioneers.

The internet is for real, and in the 21st century, if you're not on it, you're not in business.

That being said, you need not go into your business with the idea that you will create the next eBay or Amazon. While we look at these and other hugely successful sites to glean knowledge, it is important to understand that building a business is not about becoming a worldwide phenomenon, since the odds are highly against that happening. The reality is that you want to stake out your own claim in your market and build a successful and profitable business. If it takes off and you become very wealthy, that's wonderful, but keep in mind that people have gone bankrupt overextending themselves and trying too hard. Start a business, nurture it, and it will grow. How big it gets will depend on many factors, but you can't force success.

A New Set of Rules

On the web, the advantage is yours—it belongs to the entrepreneur. Why?

Consider the story of Compaq computers, now a brand under the Hewlett-Packard umbrella since 2002. It makes fine computers—maybe no better than its competitors, but certainly no worse.

So why did Dell long ago surpass Compaq in market leadership? Dell jumped feet first into full-steam web retailing. It yanked its merchandise out of retail stores and threw the dice, betting the company's future on direct selling (via catalogs and the web) to corporations and individuals. Compaq, meanwhile, faltered at every step because it didn't want to alienate its established retail channels, convinced they would be irked if suddenly the same computers were available for less on the internet. So Compaq dithered during the infancy of the web, and that indecisiveness made it lose momentum and leadership while competitors grabbed market share.

Today, the web *is* an established manner of doing business. It is no longer new and "innovative." But unlike the brick-and-mortar world, which remains intact, the web evolves very quickly. For example, the banner ads of a decade ago gave way to pay-per-click advertising and internet marketing

 Beware!
Venture capital funding, billions of dollars' worth, is out there, but be prepared before you try to accumulate any of it. Venture capitalists want to know that you have thought out every possible aspect of the business and left no stone unturned. You need an air-tight business plan that defines exactly what you are planning to do and have all of your ducks in a row, from your costs to your management team, before approaching a venture capitalist.

has largely morphed into social media marketing. Sure, a store can add a new wing or open another outlet, but it takes time and a lot of funding. An e-business, however, can rearrange its inventory with a few clicks of a mouse and add pages of new products with a little bit of webpage designing. It's time and cost effective. The internet can, and does, change more quickly than the brick-and-mortar world, thanks to new technology coming out all the time.

Another great advantage of the internet is that it puts the squeeze on pricing. Not having inventory in warehouses all over the country, or all over the world, is one among many reasons why online pricing has been a boon to business.

Reaching Their Peak

Before embarking on how you can get started in your own online business, let's check out a few of the many successful e-business models that have preceded your endeavor.

If you're willing to expand your horizons a little, as two entrepreneurs discovered, the sky's the limit. Consider Jim Holland and John Bresee, who in 1996 founded Backcountry.com, a West Valley City, Utah, online retailer of outdoor gear for all things backcountry.

Holland, a two-time Olympic ski jumper and six-time national champion Nordic ski jumper, and Bresee, a former editor of *Powder* magazine, founded the company with the purpose of providing outdoor adventure gear to the hard-core recreational athlete. Holland and Bresee's online store has seen triple-digit average annual growth for the past ten years. Pretty amazing, considering the fact that they began the company without any outside investment.

"We developed the site ourselves and banked about $2,000 of our own money to get started, which we used for inventory," says Bresee. "We took a risk but knew there was an interest out there for what we were doing."

What's the company's secret to success? There's not one answer to that question, but a key reason is that the company decided to focus on a narrow niche—selling gear to hard-core sports enthusiasts—instead of competing with mass-market retailers like REI that might sell the same items, but without the same knowledge.

Backcountry.com, for example, populates its call-center staff with hard-core skiers and trekkers who are out there using the equipment the site sells.

Therefore, when customers contact Backcountry.com with their questions, the customer solutions team, known as "Gearheads," can answer by drawing on their own unique personal experience.

Excellent customer service, in fact, is the company's mantra. "We make it very easy for our customers to communicate directly with real people at Backcountry.com, whether they have a question or want to make a purchase. Our phone number is on every page of our site, and people can just as easily opt to IM a Gearhead if they prefer," says Bresee.

Other reasons for its continued growth? The addition of other successful niche sports gear sites (Tramdock.com, Dogfunk.com, SteepandCheap.com, WhiskeyMilitia.com, and BackcountryOutlet.com), cost-effective online and word-of-mouth advertising, and the company's philosophy that the risky way is the safe way.

"If it's safe, we're not interested in pursuing it," says Bresee. "To successfully grow a business, you have to take risks. In the case of Backcountry.com, we're lucky that the risks we've taken are working out pretty well."

Sweet Dreams

Sometimes even when your dreams aren't so lofty, the internet can save the day, as Barbara McCann found out. She and her husband, Jim, owned The Chocolate Vault, a store in Tecumseh, Michigan, a village about 60 miles west of Detroit. They'd watched traffic—and customers—veer away from little towns, and they'd watched their cash flow all but disappear. Then they decided to give the internet a whirl.

On a skimpy budget of a few thousand dollars, Barbara McCann personally built her website, ChocolateVault.com, and then she watched an amazing thing happen.

The Ecommerce Quiz

Think you're ready to become a "netpreneur"? Prove it. Before moving on to the next chapter, take this quiz. Answers are true or false.

1. I'm comfortable in an ever-changing world with new rules popping up often.

2. I see inefficiencies, such as waste and delay, in many current business practices.

3. I'm willing to delay this year's profits to potentially make more money next year.

4. Customer satisfaction is the most important thing a business can deliver.

5. I recognize that the internet can reach far more people than opening a local business.

6. I am prepared to deal with customers from anywhere.

7. I see opportunity where others see risks.

8. I'm not intimidated by technology and know that if I don't know the high tech solutions to problems that I can find others who do know such answers.

9. I am willing to work hard and learn as much as I can while launching a business.

10. I recognize the potential of owning an internet business but also understand that as a business there are always some risks and there are no shortcuts.

Scoring: Guess what? "True" is always the right answer for any netpreneur. But you knew that already because you're ready to compete.

"People from all over the country found us, and they started buying our chocolates!" she says.

McCann says the internet business has grown so much that she decided to close the retail store. In 2005, she moved her internet business, and home base, to another small town in southeastern Michigan and built a small factory-type facility that allows the company more space. McCann says the move was the best decision she could have made.

McCann doesn't have the money to buy major advertising space and instead puts all her energy into offering exceptional customer service. "We are trying to give our customers the kind of personal service online that they would receive if they walked into our store," she says. "We've also found ways to customize our products. For example, we make custom molds for our corporate clients."

McCann also says that most of her customers are return customers who keep coming back because the site is understandable and easy to maneuver.

Will The Chocolate Vault rise to the top and challenge the biggies in that space, such as Godiva and others? "Never," says McCann, who knows her budget and her ambition. But the big miracle is that "the internet has been a lifesaver for us," she says. "We would've closed our shop without it."

You can set the scale of your internet ambitions based on how much you can deliver to your customers. If you have a limited amount of time, or a limited budget, you can remain small. If there is a great demand for what you sell, then you can grow, merge with a larger company, or even sell your business and walk away with a profit. The choice is yours, but you need to get the ball rolling first.

Ten Reasons
You Should
Be Online

Still need convincing that the web is the place for your business? It would be no sweat to list 25 reasons, even 50 or 100, but to get you started, here are 10 reasons you have to be online.

1. *It's cheap.* There is no less expensive way to open a business than to launch a website. While you can spend many millions of dollars getting started, a low-budget site, starting with as little as a few hundred dollars, remains a possibility when you have an online business.

2. *You cut your order fulfillment costs.* Handling orders by phone is expensive. There's no more efficient—cheap, fast, and accurate—way to process orders than through your website.

3. *Your catalog is always current.* A print catalog can cost big bucks, and nobody wants to order a reprint just to change one price or to correct a few typos. A website can be updated in minutes.

4. *High printing and mailing costs are history.* Your customers can download any product information you want them to have from your website. You can focus your marketing efforts on the social media, email newsletters, and online advertising. Sure, you'll still want to print some materials, but you can save a bundle on printing costs.

5. *You cut staffing costs.* A website can be a one- or two-person operation until it grows. With just a few free, easy-to-use tools, you can put your business on autopilot. If you do need help with web development, design, marketing, or content, you can find freelancers or other online business owners working from their home offices and hire them as independent contractors. This is a much easier option than hiring regular, full-time staff.

6. *You can stay open 24 hours a day.* And you'll still get your sleep because your site will be open even when your eyes are closed.

7. *You're in front of a global audience.* Ever think what you sell might be a big hit in Scotland or China? Review your metrics and your site log, and you'll see visitors streaming in from Australia, Italy, Japan, or Malaysia. You never know where your products will be a big hit.

8. *There are typically no city permits and you'll have minimal red-tape hassles.* This could change, but in most of the U.S., small web businesses can be run without permits and with

Beware!
Not only can online catalogs be updated in seconds, they must be! A sure way to frustrate online shoppers is to take them through the buying process only to annoy them at the last moment with a "Sorry, out of stock" message. Never do that. If merchandise is out of stock, clearly note that early in the buying process. Customers can accept inventory problems, but they'll never accept you wasting their time. Keep your site up-to-date.

little government involvement. As you expand and add employees, you'll start to bump into laws and regulations, but it certainly is nice to be able to kick off a business without first filling out reams of city, county, and state forms.

> **Dollar Stretcher**
>
> On a really tight budget? Hire local college students or interns and have them work part time. Many young people are willing to work for low or no pay in exchange for getting in on the ground floor of an e-business startup. And many are very technologically adept!

9. *It's fast.* You can build a website on Saturday afternoon, open a Google AdWords account on Sunday, create a viral ad campaign to reach millions on Monday. It's not usually that simple, of course, but the potential for overnight results is always there.

10. *It's easy to get your message out.* Between your website and smart use of social media, blogs, email, and online advertising, you'll have complete control over when and how your message goes out.

You can't beat a website for its immediacy, and when a site is designed well and has a well-conceived marketing campaign, it's hard to top its ability to grab and hold the attention of potential customers.

There is also the interactive component of "getting your message out there and receiving responses." The internet lets your customers comment, review your business, ask questions, or reach out to your customer service representatives 24/7. It provides a fast and easy way to talk to your demographic audience and find out what they like and what they do not care for. In-person focus groups take time and money to organize and customer surveys found in brick-and-mortar stores often end up on the floor of the mall. Getting feedback is so much easier online and you can hone your sales strategies according to the feedback you receive.

You have other reasons for wanting a web business? Fair enough. The key is knowing your reasons and understanding the many benefits of doing business online, and being persistent through the launch. This isn't always an easy road to take, but it's definitely a road that has transported many to riches, with much less upfront cash, hassle, and time required than for similar, offline businesses. And that's a tough value proposition to top.

The Downside

OK, nothing is perfect. Yes, there can be drawbacks to a web-only business. First, you are 100 percent dependent on technology. If you are living in a region frequently

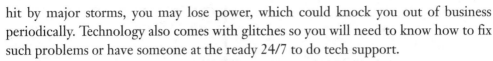

hit by major storms, you may lose power, which could knock you out of business periodically. Technology also comes with glitches so you will need to know how to fix such problems or have someone at the ready 24/7 to do tech support.

You also have to recognize that there is a lot of competition, so having a website is not enough without doing regular marketing and/or advertising. Even the best website won't succeed if nobody knows it's there. Remember, people won't simply be "driving by your store."

If you are not good at self-motivation, you will have a hard time running an e-business, or any business for that matter. An entrepreneur needs to be ready to put in long hours and focus on the business constantly, especially in the growth stages. With luck, you will have a team to help you once your business is successful. But, as any entrepreneur will tell you, it takes persistence and the ability to get up each day and get to work. Some people are good at this while others have a hard time self-motivating, which is not a good attribute for a business owner.

Dotcom Dreams and Disasters

The number of startups getting seed funding in 2012 jumped by 65 percent over the previous year to a total of 1,749, according to a report by CB Insights. This included funding from either angels or VCs, or both. The leaders of the pack were, guess what? Internet companies!

▲

But before getting your startup off the ground, it's worthwhile to look back and see why so many dotcoms have fallen by the wayside.

- *Bad balance-sheet math.* At no point did the companies that crashed and burned generate financial statements that indicated any reasonable relationship between income and expenses. Too many startups have simply spent money before they earned it. You need to recognize that you have to crawl before you can walk and then take small, baby steps. Yes, you may need a good team around you, but they need to believe in the business and understand that there will be some lean years. That being said, you don't need the ritzy office, the high-powered law firm, or the overpriced consultants. With all sorts of financial software programs on the market, you should be able to keep your expenses in some kind of rational alignment with your income. Hint: Do the math from Day One and never stop doing it until you've earned enough to have accountants and financial analysts doing it for you. And you should still double-check what they do regularly.

- *No revenue model.* The core question for dotcom startups is "What is your revenue model?" This is shorthand for "How do you envision bringing in income? What will be your revenue streams? How do you expect to make a profit?" Potential investors will ask this, as will would-be employees, partners, and anybody considering a financial future with your dotcom. In the early years of dotcoms, entrepreneurs could get away with a lot of vaguely explained responses that involved a mix of advertising dollars and ecommerce, and in most cases, the answer was accepted. It was a mistake because, as the failed dotcoms proved, nobody had ever really put flesh on the revenue models. Today, despite the fact that investors are savvier, simple business logic prevails. You need a clearly defined source of revenue. In most cases you'll actually need more than one revenue stream before you can launch your business website.

- *No clearly defined exit strategy.* Every well-conceived business startup comes equipped with an exit strategy for investors. An exit strategy is how investors will get their money out of the business, and when. Founders with

> **Beware!**
> Of course you'll start off in the red, which is the norm when launching any type of business. But when can you honestly project seeing black ink? You need to have a very realistic forecast based on a solid business plan to know when you will be profitable. So many dotcoms have shut down because they never had honest forecasts of when investors could expect to see black ink. Don't let that happen to you.

hands-on roles in the business should also have a plan for getting out (selling, passing it on to your family, etc.), but angels, VCs, and such want to know how and when they'll see a return on their investment.

What are possible exit strategies?

1. Going public: a prime choice for many dotcoms
2. Getting acquired by a bigger fish
3. Bringing in new investors to buy out others

Dollar Stretcher
When you start out, do as small businesses have always done: Operate on a shoestring. Dell Computers, for instance, got its start in a dorm room. Apple started in a garage. Your quarters needn't be that humble, but never, ever spend money you don't have to for the sake of "making an impression." Spend wisely.

There is no saying which exit strategy is best, but what can be said is that no CEO needs anxious investors calling every few minutes to ask when they might cash out. And that happens all too often when there's been a lack of clarity—even realism—about the investment. This means that in early talks with investors (even if it's your folks who put up the money), you need to be honest about how you see them getting their money back and when. Be as realistic and conservative in your estimates as possible.

- *Having no marketing plan.* Too many dotcom businesses started with great ideas, terrific products or services, and the mistaken notion that if they built the website, visitors would simply appear. Brick-and-mortar businesses base a lot of their future dreams of success on the old adage *location, location, location.* For a retailer, being in the right location would generate foot traffic and that could make the difference between success and failure. Websites, too, need to generate visitors who will hopefully be converted to customers. Marketing is essential, and it must be well conceived and implemented even before you launch your site.

- *Being blinded by technology.* You need technology for your online business to exist. BUT, technology cannot, and will not, handle all of your concerns. It is a tool with which you run your business, not the brain trust behind your company. Too many e-business owners are so overwhelmed by the possibilities of technology that they forget that there is always a human element to business that even the best technology cannot replace.

The sad fact about many failed dotcoms is that they could have been successful, maybe not on the lavish scale hoped for by the founders, but profitable nonetheless.

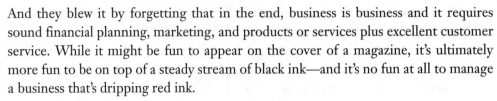

And they blew it by forgetting that in the end, business is business and it requires sound financial planning, marketing, and products or services plus excellent customer service. While it might be fun to appear on the cover of a magazine, it's ultimately more fun to be on top of a steady stream of black ink—and it's no fun at all to manage a business that's dripping red ink.

The message for you: Learn from the many mistakes of failed dotcoms.

Should You Shut Down Your Brick-and-Mortar Store?

If you are already in business, and not starting from scratch, we have a question for you: Is it time to lock the door of your brick-and-mortar store to focus exclusively on your online business? That's a question many small-business owners have asked. The web and its many opportunities are certainly exciting, often more exciting than Main Street. Ecommerce and offline retailing can coexist and, in many cases, the result is greater than the sum of the parts. Sometimes online retailing turns out to be the far better way to go, but not always. Every business is different, and you'll have to decide for yourself if it's a good idea to shut down your storefront.

Etailer Sherry Rand has a definite opinion on the subject. "The smartest thing I've done in business is shutting down my store and going exclusively as an online retailer," she says. "Now I have a really neat business. I love it." Rand has an online store that focuses on a very specific niche—gear for cheerleaders. You want pompoms in various styles and colors? You want megaphones for leading cheers? Then you should know about Pom Express (pomexpress.com), where Rand has conducted e-business for more than a decade since she shut the doors of her brick-and-mortar store.

"Online, I don't have to carry the great overhead of a store, and from a quaint town, North Hampton, New Hampshire, I'm selling globally," says Rand. "We get lots of orders from Europe, where cheerleading is really picking up." Rand, herself a cheerleader from fourth grade until she graduated from college, sold cheerleading supplies as a manufacturer's representative until she opened her own store. Now that she's operating solely on the web, she says, "This is a great niche. And on the internet, I can conduct business wherever I want to be."

Moving Out

The temptations are potent. Close a brick-and-mortar operation, go strictly cyber, and whoosh—you've distanced yourself from monthly rent payments and dealing face to face with grumpy customers, not to mention that you've positioned your business to sell globally. At least that's what it seems like in theory. But can you count on it happening for you?

Probably not, says Jackie Goforth, a partner for PricewaterhouseCoopers who focuses on retail and ecommerce companies. While she says a great example of an industry that has shifted to online is antique and collectible retailing, "I would say for the average retailer, this is not the time to shut down your shop. I think retailers can use their online presence as a great complement to their stores. It may actually drive in traffic by allowing the customer to do some online browsing."

Additionally, she says the appeal of being able to return merchandise purchased online at the local brick-and-mortar store gives shoppers confidence in their online purchases. "There still appears to be some fear that online purchases are difficult to return," she says. "The retailer who carries unique and exclusive merchandise could potentially tap into a much larger market by utilizing the web to reach a broad customer group."

"You have to keep in mind, though, that for every dotcom that thrives, there are more that flop," says Mark Layton, author of *.coms or .bombs . . . Strategies for Profit in e-Business* (Cornerstone Leadership Institute). "Many dotcoms will become dot bombs—they'll fail. Online or offline, you need a sustainable business model. If you don't have that, you don't have a business."

Having It Both Ways

Experiencing second thoughts about burning the lease on your storefront and going strictly virtual? Consider Vino! (vino2u.com), the online complement to a Winter Park, Florida, wine store, both owned by Rhonda Gore-Scott. Built around the tasty proposition that all the wines it sells are rated 85 or higher by a prestigious publication (such as *Wine Spectator*), both the storefront (opened in 1998) and the online store (launched a month later) are profitable, according to Gore-Scott. "Once you do a little foundation work," she says, "the website offers a very convenient and efficient way to manage another arm of our business."

But she has no intention of shutting down the brick-and-mortar store, for a flock of reasons. For starters, an online operation still needs some real-world warehousing for merchandise such as hers, and the brick-and-mortar store provides that. But it's the second reason that's the clincher: The site sells to many customers outside the area, but there are also many locals coming into the store with shopping lists they've printed out on the web. For those customers, the combination of the website and the store offers a great convenience—they hunt for wines they want online, at midnight or 6 A.M., and then they can get in and out of the brick-and-mortar store in a matter of minutes. "I enjoy the brick-and-mortar portion very much because of the face time with our customers. The two parts are very complementary," says Gore-Scott. "They combine the human element with the efficient, quick 24/7 element."

It's All About the Business

The type of business you run will largely determine whether you should be an e-business, a brick-and-mortar business, or both. Travel agencies—the ones you used to see on many street corners—are very hard to find these days because travel agents recognized that they could do all the work online. Conversely, there is no such thing as a real cyber dance studio. You can sell lessons online, but you still need a place to teach your hoofers their steps. Restaurants still need tables and chairs and customers, while small catering businesses can thrive by simply taking the orders online and doing the cooking in their home kitchens.

For many retailers it's a matter of what you sell, to whom you are selling it, and how well established your business has become.

A store with a steady walk-in clientele has no need to shut down. Why mess with success? People still enjoy browsing, talking with knowledgeable salespeople, and getting a feel for the products they may be buying. This explains why so many brick-and-mortar businesses continue to expand with new locations dotting the map. A web presence can be beneficial for marketing purposes, posting sales information, special holiday hours, and maps to those new locations.

What makes having both brick-and-mortar and online sales work is that you can:

- Accommodate orders from around the corner and around the globe
- Sell products that people want to "feel or smell" in the store and less touchy-feely goods online thus expanding your inventory
- Cross-promote your website from the store, for those times when people cannot get to you in person, AND market your store on the site hoping people will come in and see for themselves what you offer

Many stores have found that certain niche items which may not sell in their own town, city, or region are popular in another part of the country or even overseas. Much to their surprise, dress store owners in Maryland found that some of their line was very popular with customers in parts of Europe. Other store

Smart Tip

What's a click-and-mortar? This internet term describes a store that exists both online and in the physical world. It's also known as clicks-and-bricks, as well as bricks, clicks, and flips (the "flips" refers to catalogs that customers flip through). Classic examples of numerous click-and-mortars include Walmart, The Gap, and Best Buy. Click-and-mortars allow consumers to initiate or finalize transactions either on the website or at the physical location. Exchanges or refunds for items bought online can also be processed at a local store to avoid extra shipping costs. Although, following Zappos' trend-setting return policies, many other e-businesses have streamlined their return policies, making it easier to shop online without the "fear of returns" stigma.

owners have enjoyed similar success in other parts of the world. Of course the products need to be easy to ship to make online sales worthwhile.

The two questions are whether going online can enhance your business and whether it can replace your brick-and-mortar business. Sometimes having an actual business location gives you more credibility in your local region or neighborhood. It also gives you more face time with customers.

While many travel agents have found that the web business has rendered their walk-in business unnecessary, many other retailers have benefited from having both, to serve both customers who like the in-store shopping experience and customers who prefer to shop from the comfort of their home or from their smartphones while commuting to and from work or waiting to pick up their kids from soccer practice.

Fortunetelling

Want a manner of assessing how your business might fare online? College of William & Mary business professor Jonathan Palmer shares the three factors that shed a green light on this decision:

1. You sell a product line that can be delivered economically and conveniently.

2. You have both a desire to market to customers outside your own geographic location and a product with broad appeal.

3. There are significant economic advantages involved in going online.

Chew especially hard on points one and two because if they are on your side, the profits implied in the third point will likely follow.

Let's add a couple more items to that list, such as:

4. Your demographic group is largely the "under 40" crowd that has been weaned on web shopping.

5. You have the time and manpower to build awareness for the site by using the social media platforms and you have the budget to use traditional marketing.

Double Vision

Still, isn't this dual-channel strategy an unnecessary complication that forces an entrepreneur to focus on two distinctly different venues? The experts don't think so, and in fact, it has worked exceptionally well for many business owners. "A [brick-and-mortar store] can be a billboard for your website," says Bentley University ecommerce professor Bruce Weinberg, who points to The Gap as an example. It already has massive brand awareness, and whenever a customer walks in—even walks by—a storefront, there's a reinforcement of the URL, gap.com. Your business might not be a Gap, but even so, says Weinberg, the fact that you are in a physical location with signage and various advertising campaigns to promote the store will mean that you are also building awareness for your website.

> **Tip...**
>
> **Smart Tip**
>
> With smaller, nonbrand-name sites, a big consumer worry is that your ecommerce site is less reliable. When you have a brick-and-mortar storefront, you also have solidity in the minds of consumers. Don't hide it. Put up a photo of it on your website, and definitely show the street address. Consumer worries will vanish.

"Some products are ideal for online; others just work better in a brick-and-mortar store, where customers want to test the look, feel, and fit," says College of William & Mary business professor Jonathan Palmer.

The bottom line is that if you are already a business owner, having a web presence is almost mandatory in today's competitive market. It may just be a place for marketing or a billboard since people are always looking up businesses on the internet. For some businesses it may be a place to order gift certificates, tickets, or get coupons that can be redeemed when visiting the brick-and-mortar location. For other businesses, the website can be a place for customers to shop when they cannot get to the store or if they are out of the area. Only you can determine what direction your website will take.

5

Website Building 101

What's stopping you from putting up a website for your business? A big and persistent hurdle is the belief that doing it is hard, technically demanding work. The truth of the matter is that today, building a website is very easy.

Places like Wix.com, BuildYourSite.com, GoDaddy.com, and Web.com make it a very simple, cost-effective process.

"Even the smallest businesses can afford to be on the web," says Mary Cronin, a business professor at Boston College and editor of *The Internet Strategy Handbook* (Harvard Business School Press).

However, if you don't have time to spare, a small outlay of cash will buy you the services of a local college student or even an outsourced programmer from another country fluent in HTML.

For those of you who want to do it yourself, this chapter provides step-by-step tips for producing your website—from picking the right tools and putting them to use to testing your creation. Set aside a few hours, follow the steps, and you, too, will be in business on the web.

Know Your Purpose

The technical aspect of your site is the easy part. Knowing what you want, and making the site enticing to visitors so that they will make purchases, is the bigger challenge.

The key is to create and utilize the website for one or more specific purposes. You can use it to draw people to your company or so that people can find your basic information (address, phone number, hours, etc.) or make it part of, or all of, your business . . . which is the focus of this book.

There are clear advantages for a web business. On the web, for instance, "distance means nothing," says Jerry White, director of the Caruth Institute of Owner-Managed Business at Southern Methodist University in Dallas. A small business in the United States can use the web as a low-cost tool for reaching customers in other states, even other countries.

The clock, too, no longer matters. "On the web, your business can be open 24 hours a day, seven days a week," says Gail Houck, a consultant and web strategist. Another reason for building a web presence: The web lets you serve customers in ways that would be unimaginable in a traditional retail environment. On the web, it's easy to offer far deeper product selection, for instance, and—with clear thinking on your side—prices, too, typically can be driven down.

All good reasons? You bet, and you may have many more. Whatever your motivations, the single most important step you can take is this one: Define your goals and expectations. Do that, and the rest—including the mechanics of site design—will fall into place.

Where so many small businesses (and a few very large ones, too) go wrong is that they haven't taken this clarifying step. The resulting sites are fundamentally confusing because nobody ever took the time to specify their purpose. It's perfectly fine to erect a site that amounts to a company information brochure, but that site cannot be expected to function as a retail platform.

Getting Started

The first thing you want to do is find a website builder. These are easy-to-use software programs that make it simple for anyone to create a website on their own. Previously, websites were written manually by computer programmers in complicated computer code. This required anyone creating a website to understand computer code and code editing. If you didn't know all of that, and most people did not, you had to hire someone who did.

Today there are plenty of website building programs that make manual computer code and computer editing unnecessary. These programs make it simple to build a fully functional site with exactly what you need to market your business and sell products or services. Most of these tools integrate a reliable hosting package as well.

Note: The web builder helps you create a site, while the hosting service puts it out there on the internet. It's not unlike a production company and a TV network. One (the production company) creates the TV show and the other (the network) broadcasts it out for you to watch. We will talk about web hosting a little later, but for now, you need to focus on web building.

Among the more popular website builders are:

1. BuildYourSite at buildyoursite.com
2. Fatcow at fatcow.com
3. Hub at webhostinghub.com
4. GoDaddy at godaddy.com
5. Network solutions at networksolutions.com
6. Squarespace at squarespace.com
7. Web.com at web.com
8. Webs at webs.com
9. Wix at wix.com
10. Yola at Yola.com

There are many others, such as Dreamweaver, Joomla, Yahoo!, or Web Easy Professional 8. A Google search will provide you with even more options. Today, most web builders can be downloaded online. You'll find some site builders for a few dollars

▲

a month in conjunction with web hosting. You'll also find more elaborate web hosting suites that will run $500 or even over $1,000 with a variety of software programs, such as Photoshop, included.

As you look at various website building tools, you'll need to determine what features you are looking for. Since most of the major website building programs accommodate either PC or Macintosh computers, that should no longer be an issue.

Be a Savvy Shopper

There are several important things to look for when creating your e-business. There are numerous applications that can meet your needs, as well as plenty of extras, many of which you don't need and do not want to spend extra money on. First, you may look at some, to do side-by-side comparison shopping. Take a look at http://www. websitebuilderexpert.com's comparison chart, which is one place to get a look at some of the best options when it comes to web building.

Functionality

First and foremost, you need a site to accommodate your needs. Of great importance should be ease of payment if you plan to sell products or services online. People do not want to jump hurdles to pay for what they want, nor do they want to be interrogated with a slew of unnecessary questions. Checkout should be very smooth and simple. If you will be selling products internationally, you will also need to choose an ecommerce site builder that allows you to manage payments from multiple countries (and convert currencies).

If you have many products to sell you'll need a shopping cart so customers can browse the site and purchase as they go. You'll also want to have many display pages with products and easy landing pages to provide more detail on that which you are selling.

Landing pages are those pages that come up when you click on products and services that you are interested in learning more about. Amazon.com has great landing pages that offer all the details and then link to check out, where you purchase an item. And speaking of Amazon, they also save your relevant information so that each time you shop at their site you do not have to enter everything from scratch.

The point is simply you need to think very carefully about what it is you want the site to be able to do. Walk through the experience of each visitor, map out your site on paper, and then look for the functions you will need to make the site as user friendly as possible. Functionality, more than anything else, is where you will want to be selective.

Before you choose an ecommerce site builder, carefully list the "must haves." You can then decide whether or not you need many other features. It's not unlike buying a home. You know you need the fourth bedroom, the two-car garage, and a large enough kitchen for your family. You might not, however, need a fireplace, a third or fourth bathroom, or a view of the lake.

Growth Potential

While you may remain a small business or grow very slowly, it's nice to have a website that can accommodate growth, or "scalability," as it's called today. Look for site builders that allow you to add features and have the capacity to grow with you as your business expands.

Site Design

Look at some of the finished products of a site builder. Do you like the navigation of the websites? Is the navigation easy or difficult? Do the sites from a particular web builder all look the same? Once upon a time, site building was all about filling in a few templates. The result was that so many sites all looked the same. Today, most site building tools have the ability to create nice looking, original sites that are easy to use. BUT, this is your baby, so be discerning and choose one that can create pages that you like. You want a design that is easy to create, update, and re-do when necessary. Today's most engaging sites, unlike the early days of the web, are also clean and uncluttered, with some white space. The objective is no longer to wow people with bells and whistles, or cram as much on a page as possible. You just want to get your point across, letting people know what you do and what you sell in a clear, effective manner. That being said, you also want to know that loading photos and videos is easy, since both are an integral part of web success today. Blogs are also something you will want to be able to easily infuse into your site.

Look at many other websites and decide what you like and what you do not care for. Make a list of sites you would like yours to look like. Then look at the design capabilities of the site builder and see if features like easy photo uploading are included.

Smart Tip

Tip...

Make sure your site design fits the tone of your business. A yellow background with balloons and clowns is less likely to fit an esteemed law firm that specializes in wills and estates than it is to be appropriate for a children's party planning business. Design accordingly.

Support—HELP!

Technology is great when it works. When it doesn't, you want to pull your hair out. You

▲

NEED a site builder that comes with excellent support from real people, with more than a list of FAQs that may not fit your problem. You want reliable tech support and customer service from representatives that are knowledgeable and patient. The best companies have such people available 24/7 by phone or online chat.

Read reviews and look for other people who have used the web builder you have in mind. Find out what experiences they have had when trying to get technical help.

Your goal is to find a support team that can easily understand and answer your question without any language barriers. You want prompt responses.

How Much?

Now comes the tricky part, comparing and contrasting the costs. As is the case with most anything you purchase today, there are features that are included and extras. Since you will likely need to customize your site to fit your needs, you'll have to look closely at the cost and how much more such customization will cost. You'll also want to see if you need to pay extra for tech support of any other services. Some site builders are also part of web hosting services. Others include hosting, while some are strictly site builders. Find out ahead of time whether your chosen ecommerce site builder includes a hosting service and if you are required to use it. Again, see if you are saving money or will be spending more if you need to get an outside web hosting service.

Somewhere in between the rock-bottom prices and the super-duper deluxe package with a myriad of features, you will probably find the site builder that is right for you.

Leading Factors When Building Your Site

For an internet business, your website is your storefront, your office, your command center. Therefore, you want to consider all the possibilities, including:

1. *Preview option.* This lets you see what your site will look like after you make changes and before you publish it.
2. *Ease of mobile use.* Millions of people are using their mobile devices to access the web. Make sure your site is designed to work on mobile platforms and also looks great!
3. *A dashboard.* Like the dashboard in your car, this lets you monitor your site operations from one location.
4. *Drop-and-drag editing.* This is the latest and easiest way to move items around on your site. It allows for quick construction and easy updating.

5. *Emails.* You should be able to set up multiple emails.

6. *SEO.* Search engine optimization is crucial to being found through web searches. Some web builders include features to make SEO easier.

7. *Easy social media accessibility.* Make sure you can add links to Facebook, Twitter, Pinterest, and all the social media sites you want.

8. *Easy payment options.* You want your customers to be able to easily use credit cards or PayPal to purchase goods or services on your site.

Smart Tip

To have a professional looking site, you need to maintain control. Avoid any site building platform that puts someone else in control of your website. Also, try to avoid ads which will make your site look cheesy. If you want to sell advertising, that's your choice, but don't use a platform that will stick ads on your web pages.

9. *Photo galleries.* Your site should include photos and videos which should be easy to upload and download.

10. *Videos.* Like photos, videos are very popular. Your site should be able to easily accommodate videos.

11. *Access to forms.* If you are providing forms for visitors to download and/or fill out, that too has to be a simple process.

12. *Groups, forums, and interactive experiences.* The web is interactive and your site should allow for visitors to comment, share in discussions, or even start, and participate in, groups.

13. *Support other programs.* Integration with Flash, Photoshop, Adobe, and a wealth of other popular platforms is essential today. Make sure this is part of your site building process.

Puttin' on the Glitz

The web is a graphical medium, which means words matter, but images are just as important in attracting and holding viewers. In fact, images and videos increase your page views and your search engine ranking.

Image Boosters

While most site building platforms include image uploading and some offer more, there is also specialty software that will let you do a lot of image enhancement. A top choice is Adobe Photoshop (adobe.com/products/photoshop/family/), which offers several marvelous products that give you "everything you need to bring out the best in your digital images, transform them into anything you can imagine, and showcase them in extraordinary ways," as they put it!

You might also consider Corel's PhotoImpact (photimpact.com), formerly from ULead. It's easy to use, versatile, powerful, and will allow for creative reshaping of images to suit your website.

You can create quality web pages without owning image-editing software, but you can do so much more with the right tools. For most of us, less than $500 will buy all we need.

14. *Membership capabilities*. Is yours a membership site? Make sure your site builder can help you meet your membership needs

15. *Music*. Music and sound are a huge part of many sites. Consider your audio needs when selecting a web builder.

These are just some of the many possibilities that you will consider when building your site. We can't stress it enough: Make a list of all the things you want your site to be able to do and then seek them out in the site builder you choose. Also seek out some features that you may not use now, but expect to use in the future. Factor growth into your plans.

Photo Options

If you are not very happy with your own photography for your site, you have some options:

- *You can hire a photographer.* This can mean spending the big bucks on a pro, especially someone who has product photo experience. This is a great idea, but may be costly.

- *You can also look for young talent hoping to make a name for themselves.* Many young graphic artists are happy just to get their work in the public view and gladly let others download their images. Others may help you get the images you need in exchange for college credits as interns. You can start enhancing a web page's graphics with a visit to FreeGraphics (freegraphics.com), where you'll find hundreds of buttons, bars, photos, clipart, and things that spin, wiggle, crawl, and fly (animated graphics). There is even free graphic viewing and editing software and a list of websites where you can create your own buttons, logos, and 3D art—all without downloading or purchasing software. Most, but not all, of the graphics can be used free for commercial as well as personal websites. However, there are a number of different sources, so you'll want to be sure and check the guidelines for each.

- *There is always stock photography.* How about this great source? You can get very high-quality imagery at iStockPhoto (istockphoto.com). You'll find royalty-free stock photography, vector illustrations, Flash files, and videos for usually no higher than $20. It's a small price to pay for enhancements that will make your site much more polished. Among the many other stock photo image locations online are: FreeRange Stock at freerangestock.com, The Open Photo Project at openphoto.net, and Stockvault at stockvault.net.

Typically you become a member and pay a low fee for the photos you need. And yes, some are free!

You can spend many days downloading images, because the web is swamped with terrific free art. But be careful not to overdo it with graphics and/or images, or you can slow down your site, causing people to get impatient waiting for the pages to download. You want a clean, uncluttered site that not only loads easily but looks professional. So use images that are not too large for downloading easily.

You also want to size the photo accordingly so that it is clear. Typically sizing the photos to be at least 300 dpi will give you the best resolution for print media. For the web, 72 dpi was thought to be the standard, but today, programs can adjust and there is no real standard dpi. You can

Smart Tip

Tip...

Don't go crazy with colors—this is one of the biggest goofs of new web page designers. Stick with maybe two colors for fonts (words) and use a simple, basic color for the page background (white, off-white, and pale yellow are good choices). Always test your page on a laptop and on mobile devices since what you see on your monitor will differ on other people's screens. If it doesn't look good on a small screen, it's bad page design.

manipulate the size to make sure the photos look sharp but do not take too long to load. It's important to work with the photos to make sure they are clear and properly cropped to fit the intended space. Online photos are typically in jpeg or gif formats.

- *Another caveat.* Before uploading any images you didn't create yourself to your website, carefully read the fine print on the artist's page. Some prohibit use on commercial sites. If in doubt, ask for permission. That is a sure cure against future complications. Always assume an image is copyrighted, unless there is an explicit statement that says it can be used for free. You need to ask the owner of the photo to please sign an agreement that it is okay for you to use it for your site and for how long; never take chances. If he or she is looking for payment, determine if the amount is worthwhile for you to pay. Then make sure you have a signed agreement that you have paid for use of the image. Logos are typically protected by a trademark or copyright. Again, you need permission to use a company's logo on your site.

- *Something to keep in mind.* Simple is best with a web page. Better an unglamorous page that loads rapidly than a state-of-the-art page that causes your visitors to go elsewhere. When a mania seizes you and you want to design pages with fancy looks and the newest bells and whistles, put that stuff on a personal page, not your business site. All those toys are fun to play with—but web visitors hate them.

- *A reliable rule of thumb.* The more times you say "wow" as you design your web page, the worse it is. You want to create a page where the wow factor is minimal in terms of design but high in terms of functionality.

Testing, Testing

Gremlins often play tricks with web pages, and that's why no professional webmaster announces a new page to the public before testing it. Surf the web enough, and sooner or later you'll stumble into a test site mounted by a brand-name business that has put it online in a "beta" version so that insiders can find the bugs before the public does. Do the same thorough testing before publicizing your page.

A crucial test: Make sure pages work equally well in Microsoft Internet Explorer, Mozilla's Firefox, and all other popular browsers for PC and Mac. Ignore this advice at your own peril. If you're a Windows user and you don't have access to a Mac, or vice versa, find a friend who has one to test for you.

If, while testing your own site, you find bugs, don't fret. Few pages get put up without at least some kinks, and a good place to start is to pinpoint things that show

---

Smart Tip

Tip...

When updating pages, always go through your testing procedure as soon as you put up the changes. It's tempting to neglect this, but don't. Too often I've put up updated pages that, somehow, turned out to be bug-ridden. And never do page changes during your peak traffic periods! That's inviting calamity. Make your changes at the quietest times when your pages are getting the fewest hits.

---

up on your screen offline but don't work online. One standard problem is that an image (or two or three) isn't displaying, caused by a botched hyperlink. Strip down any web page to its essentials, and you'll find a little text interspersed with many hyperlinks, which are web directions to images and other files stored elsewhere. Put in the wrong hyperlink and the online page will show up as a jumble. Review all of your links carefully and retrace your steps. The slightest error when putting something onto the page will throw everything off.

Keep It Fresh

A sure way to go wrong with a website is to put it up and leave it there. To keep viewers coming back, a page needs regular updating. "If your page is aging, static, it says, 'I don't get it,' " says Boston College's Cronin.

How often does a site need updating? For an e-business, you need to update at least several times a week with new products, comments, and questions for your visitors and customers and much more. If you are running a content-driven site, such as a news or entertainment site, you will need to update several times a day. "Updating takes time, but the investment is warranted," says White at Southern Methodist.

Hosted Ecommerce Solutions

Pssst. Want to know a shortcut that eliminates much of your need to know how to build a website and still puts you in an ecommerce business? Then you want to know about Yahoo! Merchant Solutions, a service that allows you to easily create an online store (smallbusiness.yahoo.com/ecommerce).

As opposed to doing it yourself, Yahoo! Merchant Solutions allows small businesses to get major league ecommerce capabilities in an easy-to-use and affordable solution.

Here's the promise of the service: Within a short period of time, you will have an online store that looks good—and all you have to do is follow a form-driven set of instructions. Think of it as akin to cooking with a recipe. If you follow the instructions that Yahoo! provides, the result will be a credible, attractive site. A plus is that Yahoo! helps customers obtain a merchant account so they can accept credit card payments online.

Keep in mind that while Yahoo! does everything it can to make it easy to create an online store, it still takes a few hours, or if a customer needs to set up a merchant account for online credit card payments, several days.

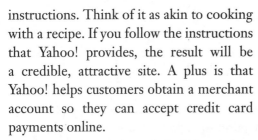

Dollar Stretcher

A Yahoo! location in particular may be real gold because of how it promotes its stores. Search for "Turkish coffee" on Yahoo!, for instance, and it's a fast hop into a couple of small etailers selling that brew as well as pots, cups, and so forth. Just as a suburban mall brings its merchants traffic, Yahoo! attracts shoppers to its stores.

Basically, when you purchase a Yahoo! Merchant Solutions package, you get web hosting and a full suite of ecommerce software to build a product catalog, create a custom checkout process, manage orders, and track your performance. Another important plus—you get featured on Yahoo!

Other etailers turn to eBay (ebay.com) for their online storefront services—especially those etailers who are already experimenting with eBay. If you visit pages. ebay.com/storefronts/start.html, you'll find eBay Stores that allow you to sell your fixed-price and auction items from a unique destination on eBay. You can build your own eBay Store through an easy series of steps: Create customized categories, include your own logo or choose one of eBay's online images, and list item descriptions and policies.

Your eBay Store is promoted to more than 250 million eBay users in several ways:

- All your listings will contain an eBay Store "red door" icon inviting buyers to visit your eBay Store.
- The eBay Store icon is attached to your user ID for extra visibility.
- Buyers will be driven to your store through the eBay Store Directory, which is designed to promote all stores.
- You will receive your own personalized eBay Store website address to distribute and promote.

For more information on eBay Stores, visit pages.ebay.com/storefronts/start.html.

Another storefront option is Amazon, featuring Amazon's WebStore at webstore. amazon.com. You will get your own branded web business backed by the support, selection, and expertise of Amazon. It's so easy to set up, you can start selling online in minutes. WebStore comes with a number of great marketing features like product recommendations, customer reviews, and recently viewed items for your own store.

Because your WebStore is associated with Amazon, existing Amazon customers can use their Amazon customer account to buy products from your WebStore. If customers don't have Amazon accounts, they can simply create one as they place an order on your site. Your customers get the safety and protection of the Amazon shopping cart and you get the fraud protection of Amazon's checkout system.

There are other options as well: Small merchants can use hosted ecommerce solutions from companies such as Volusion (volusion.com), Affinity Internet (affinity. com), 1 & 1 Internet Inc. (1and1.com), Big Commerce (bigcommerce.com), or Shopify (shopify.com). In general, like the Yahoo! and eBay solutions, these sites provide everything you need to do business online, but without taking a bite out of your profits. They offer a combination of shopping cart technology, merchandising, payment, shipping, marketing smarts, and, of course, hosting.

The advantages of using hosted ecommerce applications are:

- Easy setup with simple templates to choose from
- Cost effective
- Typically wizard driven, which means you don't need to know anything about computer language or codes.
- You can automatically receive application upgrades as they are developed by the provider, essentially receiving the latest tools for your site.
- Payment services (for customers) are typically provided, but there is a fee.

The disadvantages include:

- Less creativity. You are limited by the available tools and templates of the provider and have less freedom to design and customize the site as you might like (many, however, do have customization).
- Sites may take a percentage of your sales, which is not unlike a car rental company charging you for the miles driven (most of which no longer do that).
- The host might run advertisements on your site.
- Hosted ecommerce sites typically have limited search engine optimization or marketing tools.
- You may have a hard time using outside applications or software programs that are not offered by the provider, and the tools and updates the provider gives you may not benefit your site.

Free Online Store

Another option for etailers is osCommerce (oscommerce.com), a free, open-source online ecommerce solution used by more than 260,000 store owners, developers, and service providers. It allows store owners to set up, run, and maintain their online stores with minimum effort and with no costs, license fees, or limitations involved.

The services provided on the network of osCommerce support sites are continually improved to match the growing community the project has attracted in its seven years of operation. Today, this community consists of more than 12,800 registered online stores around the world, and numerous community members and project enthusiasts who help make the project succeed.

For more on web hosting, see Chapter 10, and for more on payment options, see Chapter 27.

Web Developers

When the job is too big or too time consuming, you can hire a professional web developer. But, it will cost you. Depending on the developer's experience, your specific site design needs, and your budget, you can bring in a pro for anywhere from a few hundred dollars to many thousands of dollars. If you are not particularly web savvy or get easily frustrated, you may be best served by having someone handle this important part of your business for you.

In fact, if you are financially able to do so, and are launching a somewhat complex business, you should definitely start looking for a web developer, also referred to as web designer or webmaster. The point is, you want someone with experience that can get your site built to your liking and get it up and running for your business.

You'll find many web developers by doing a Google search, but you should also ask around to find names of designers and developers that other people have used and liked. Personal recommendations are always advised so you can get a feel for what the person was like to work with. Even if you call someone that you find online, you should ask for some references.

You should also always ask to look at a portfolio, and visit the sites that were created by the web developer, particularly for ecommerce sites. Ask if you can speak to at least one or two of these site owners as a reference.

Here are a few things to look for in a web designer:

- *Experience.* You want someone with knowledge in various web design techniques and the ability to build a site using the latest utilities.

- *Custom design and creativity.* Some web builders can design a site the way the client wants it, while others use a cookie-cutter approach. Look at their portfolios and see if the sites all have the same pattern or look like they are all from the same template. You should be able to get a web design that fits your specific needs and sense of design. Look for someone who can share YOUR vision (since it's your website) or has the creativity to come up with something that you like. Don't settle: This is your business.

- *Availability.* Does he or she have time to build your site? How long will it take? Can the developer commit to a date in writing? Too many business owners have hired site developers only to wait and wait for the job to get done. Find out how long it will take and check with references to see if they finished previous jobs in a timely manner.

- *Customer service.* Not only do you want someone who is available to design and build the site, but you also want someone who is available to answer questions, make changes, and help if you have a problem. You are the customer and you should expect good, prompt service. That being said, don't expect a small site design business, or a one-person business, to be available 24/7, BUT, you should get responses quickly.

- *Mobility.* Is the developer on top of the latest in mobile technology and can he or she make sure your site will look good and work well on these mobile devices? Things are changing rapidly and more people are accessing the web from their iPhones or other devices. Make sure they can access your site without any problems.

- *Graphics and content.* Not all web developers provide graphics or content, and in many cases that's not a bad thing. Many site designers are marvelous at creating

Techies Aren't Necessarily Good Writers

Some site developers are very creative, and many excel at the technical aspect but are not writers. Content is important, so look for web writers and don't leave an important aspect of your site to someone who specializes in another area, like technology.

a site, but they need your input, your photos, and your words to input onto the site. In some cases the site developer may know a writer or photographer that can be of help. Don't anticipate that the web developer will be the driving force behind the creation of the content or graphics; it's not typically what they do (or do well) and should come from you or someone with strong graphics or writing skills, but he or she should be able to make both content and graphics look great on the site.

- *Ecommerce.* If you are selling on your site, make sure that credit cards, PayPal, a shopping cart, and whatever else you need, including landing pages, are all within the realm of your developer's abilities. These are crucial elements and ones that must work seamlessly. Some developers handle all of this while others do not: Ask beforehand.

- *SEO.* Some developers offer it and others do not. It may cost more, but if they are knowledgeable and can optimize your site to come up higher in search engine rankings, that's a big plus.

- *Updating.* Does the web designer help you make changes to the site or simply leave you with the password to get in there and make your own changes? Some people have the technical know how to go in and revamp the site on their own. In other cases it's a matter of what the change entails. You may be able to add a new blog for example, but if you need a major redesign, you'll have to contact the designer. In other cases, you'll want someone who can handle all of your changes and updates for you. Inquire, because updating your website is crucial to your success. Hint: Try to learn how to do the simple updates since you will most likely be making them on a daily basis to stay competitive in the ecommerce market.

- *All the extras.* Can they help you register a domain name? Find a good hosting service? Help with marketing? Many web designers offer additional services. Ask and you shall find out what they can do for you.

- *Price.* Considering all of the above, shop around and compare prices.

> **Smart Tip**
>
> Provide examples. Visit websites, keep track of the links, and use them to show your web developer the style of sites you like. Let the designer get a feel for what your site should look like. Also take specific notes, or even draw pages, to clarify your ideas. The more you can explain to the web developer, the closer the site will be to what you really want. Of course, if certain things are not practical or your developer thinks they may detract from your site, listen to what he or she is saying. Sometimes, you'll benefit from the experience of a good web developer.

Your website is crucial, so be discerning when choosing a web developer. See if they have a good reputation, a quality portfolio, and references that have good things to say about their work. It's very important to see if they listen carefully to what *you* want. Communication is extremely important. This is your site, so make sure it meets *your* needs and not those of the site designer. Be smart and shop around.

In the end, your website is your "business" home, and it's not unlike finding your own home. You can rent, which is like having an ecommerce hosted site. You spend less and have a lot provided for you but you don't get very much freedom to do as you wish.

Buying a home is costlier, but gives you more options, as does building your own site through a site builder.

You can also have a home custom built from the ground up. This is very expensive but it can be built to your specifications.

Making Your Site Special

Now that your site is up, how do you make it special and filled with content that attracts visitors and keeps them coming back? For one thing, we know it is important to keep it simple.

Case in point: The website for a luxury hotel chain based in India features a soundtrack of classical music, which is just annoying. Other sites open with lavish introductions.

Most people click to shut them off or leave the site entirely if they encounter such over-the-top graphics.

It is simply bandwidth-hogging craziness. Resist the temptation to put something on your site just because you can. Never put up content that slows access to a page, especially if it doesn't improve your users' experience on your site.

What works? Content that gives users reasons to linger and absorb more of what you're offering. You'll find there are many, many ways to introduce this content, and you are going to have to exercise discretion here. Pick a few tools, try them out, monitor user responses, and then delete the ones that don't prove to be valuable. Be ruthless here, and never forget that simple is better.

That understood, here are many tasty tools for you to consider using to beef up your site.

Video

Companies of all sizes are taking advantage of the YouTube phenomenon and so should you. Although there are other video-sharing sites where you can upload and share videos (like Vimeo and Flickr), YouTube is the place to be if you want to go viral and reach a potential audience of millions.

You could put your videos on your own website, but YouTube can save you valuable storage space on your own web server while delivering all those viewers. Plus, you don't have to worry about all the bandwidth that's being used when visitors watch your videos. Also, if you're lucky enough to have a video go viral, you don't risk having your servers overload and shut down—YouTube's servers will handle the load. If you want, you can still display the video on your own site by embedding a short snippet of code provided by YouTube. This is also free of charge. YouTube then serves the video from its site to appear on your web page. It's a good compromise.

If you already have a business-related video, you're about five minutes away from sharing it with the world. Uploading is free and easy—just follow the simple YouTube instructions.

The key to a successful video is to be entertaining, enlightening, informative, or all of the above. People won't watch a boring video, not when there are so many YouTube videos to choose from. Therefore, you need a unique, creative manner of making your point.

For example, Blendtec, a blender manufacturer, ran a hugely popular viral YouTube campaign called "Will It Blend?" In the campaign they tossed all sorts of items into their blenders to see what results they would have. From a Big Mac to credit cards, ice, golf balls, and cell phones, they tested out whether or not these items would blend to the delight of millions of viewers and a significant increase in brand popularity and sales. In short, the blender videos were far more interesting than listening to the CEO or a spokesperson rattle off statistics. Take a look on YouTube at which videos get millions of hits. You want to go "viral," which means thinking out of the box and giving your audience the "wow" factor.

While you do not want to entertain for the sake of it, you do want to present the benefits of your products or services in a visually entertaining manner.

Polls and Surveys

Polls and surveys let visitors register their opinion on an issue. These are at the heart of the net because this is interactivity in its most basic form. You can use surveys to improve any aspect of your business, or you can survey people on topics that relate to your site. Perhaps you are selling flooring. You might ask which type of flooring people would choose for their kitchens. If you are selling sporting goods, you could take a survey of people's favorite brand of golf clubs or tennis racquets. You could simply ask something about a sports topic in general. The point is, get your visitors to be active on your site.

Thinking about launching a new product? Conduct a survey to find out if anyone is interested, what benefits they'd like to see, and how it could beat the competition. For existing products, survey your customers to learn how your products rank with similar ones and what they think could be improved.

A particularly effective (and popular) survey uncovers interesting new ways to use products—you can't ask for a better marketing tool than that!

Writing a survey from scratch is a tricky bit of coding, but free polling templates are readily available for insertion into your site. All you have to do is fill in the blanks in a template and copy and paste a bit of code into your site, and you're in business. Sources of such templates are plentiful, but good ones are available from SurveyMonkey.com or FreePolls.com.

Blogs

At its most basic, a blog is a frequently updated, timed, and dated online journal. That may not sound like much to get excited about, but blogs have gone beyond a fad to become a full-fledged internet phenomenon. The elements of interactivity, community, and collaboration are key as growing businesses adopt blogs for customer relations, advertising, promotion, and even internal communications.

There has been an explosion of blog marketing since 2006. Companies ranging from IBM to Stonyfield Farms are using blogs as effective marketing tools. They've realized this simple method of getting their message out can increase exposure, generate buzz, and even elevate their website's position on search engines. Most web hosts today provide blogging tools, but you can also pick one up for free from WordPress (wordpress.org). And, if you are not a good writer, or have no time to turn out a weekly or biweekly blog, hire a freelancer with blogging experience (not your nephew who just got an "A" in seventh grade English) and pay the going rate. It can be well worth it! Remember, this is your business and you want to make it look good.

RSS Feeds

Originally built to distribute syndicated news, RSS instant notification promises a host of other uses—including innovative marketing for your business.

The fast-spreading internet standard lets you instantly publish or receive bits of text and graphics. While it's currently used to show the latest news and blog updates, there's no limit to what it could be used for. RSS—originally created by Netscape as a simple way to swap news headlines between consenting languages, and later picked up and improved on by UserLand—stands for "Really Simple Syndication." (RSS, in earlier versions, also stood for "Rich Site Summary" or "RDF Site Summary.") RSS is based on XML, which XML.com defines as "a markup language for documents containing structured information," which really just means a language that allows you to easily mark up, sort, and display data.

To see RSS in action, either download and install an RSS reader (also known as an RSS aggregator) from the web or use a web-based service. Open the reader, and you'll see a few sample RSS "feeds" with the latest headlines for each. Depending on the reader, the headlines may appear in your browser, in a separate application that looks much like an email application, or within another application such as Microsoft Outlook. Simply click on a headline to bring up its associated web page.

Smart Tip

Tip...

Use web tools sparingly. Best advice: Introduce one, and only one. Monitor the hits. If it proves popular, leave it up and add a second. If users ignore it, put up another but take down the unloved tool. Always keep it simple, and you'll invariably do better.

While this will appeal to the news junkie in you, RSS marketing skill may prove more powerful for your firm. In the simplest example, you could spiff up your website by adding RSS feeds from news services or blogs that will intrigue site visitors. More strikingly, in the future, RSS may handle marketing tasks where email now falls flat. For example, as with email, visitors can sign up for marketing alerts (for instance, useful product news plus discount coupons). Unlike email, visitors can rest assured that they can't be spammed. If you don't like what you're getting via RSS, just pull the plug.

Where do you get RSS feeds for your website? There are several good sources of free RSS feeds, such as rssfeedlist.com. You can always Google "RSS Feeds" and start browsing. Look for the RSS feeds that will match your site. One caveat is that when you feature RSS feeds from other sites and they don't include the full text of the news or blog item, readers may click out to that site to view the full item. If you worry about people leaving your site and not returning, outside RSS feeds may not be for you.

An RSS feed can be especially effective as a marketing tool if you create your own messages rather than republish someone else's content. Creating RSS feeds from scratch is not really that difficult and you don't need a degree in XML programming. There are many tools available for do-it-yourselfers, including free internet tools and low-cost software with wizards that walk you through the process. Most blog programs also have RSS feed creation functions. RSS Feed Generator Program from Software Garden at www.softwaregarden.com/products/listgarden is an example of such a program.

Podcasting

A podcast is an effective method of publishing recorded audio and video presentations through the internet in a way that will automatically tell your listeners when your new material is available. With a podcast, you can have your own radio show heard around the globe. Your listeners can tune in at their convenience on their own iPhones.

You don't have to know anything about RSS or learn any programming code to create your own podcast. There are many free and low-cost websites and software that will help you easily create your podcast, host your files, and distribute them. If you can click a mouse, you can create a podcast.

CGI Scripts

These are easy-to-use scripts (prewritten code) that you simply pop into your page to create a guest book, display images in different ways, add tests and quizzes, or gain

▲

the ability to track visitors. CGI (or "Common Gateway Interface," a programming tool that lets many small applications run within a web environment) is one of the web's oldest resources. Newer, slicker ways to do much of what can be accomplished via CGI are plentiful, but the real plus is their price tag and simplicity: Scripts put together by enthusiasts are free and available for anyone to use. Always test any CGI script thoroughly before going public with a page, however. Because they're free and created by hobbyists, they may contain errors or not be up to snuff for the latest browsers.

Thousands of free CGI scripts exist, and one of the best resources for finding the scripts you need is The CGI Resource Index (cgi.resourceindex.com). If you can't find the script you want here, it probably doesn't exist.

JavaScripts

Feeling patriotic? Add a flag waving in the breeze. Want your customers to know what time it is? Add a clock that ticks away in real time.

You can add just about anything—calculators, interactive games, security passwords, email forms, ticker tapes, and special effects with a JavaScript. It's an easy-to-use programming language that can be embedded in your web page's code. You don't have to be a programmer to come up with one. There are thousands of free JavaScripts on the net. Just browse through the categories on JavaFile.com (javafile.com) to find what you want. Adding the code to your page is very simple; unless you want to change any background colors, text colors or images, it's a basic cut-and-paste job. Visit JavaFile.com's "Help" section (javafile.com/help.php) for basic instructions.

Forums

These are a great way to get feedback and encourage interactivity with your visitors. CreateMyBB (createmybb.com) is a free forum hosting service that's easy to set up and administer; simply fill out a short series of forms. You can even customize the appearance and features of your message board to match the style of your website.

> **Smart Tip** *Tip...*
>
> If you decide to offer original content in your site's email newsletter, be sure to archive that content on your website—otherwise, you're just letting that information go to waste. Giving visitors a taste of what your newsletter offers may also entice newcomers to sign up as well. For more information on email newsletters, turn to Chapter 22.

At least in the beginning—and possibly long after that—you'll have to nurture discussions on your forums. After all, someone has to post first, and someone has to police the forums and monitor inappropriate discussions or heated arguments. If your forums get really popular, you may be able to hire a local college student to manage them or give your most trusted users administrative status so they can do the policing for you.

Daily Content

Many websites offer a "tip of the day," "quote of the day," "joke of the day," or any other daily tidbit that can get your visitors into the habit of dropping by your site on a daily basis. Often visitors will check in early in the day to glean the daily message. Or they subscribe to a daily newsletter full of tips, and advertising. Some companies, such as Daily Candy (dailycandy.com), were originally founded just on the premise of providing free daily tips via an email newsletter. JokeOfTheDay.com started off quite simply and expanded to include photos and more. You can hook people with daily content and then build as you go.

Popular types of daily content include philosophical tips, household hints, obscure word definitions, recipes, religious verses, or poignant quotes or puzzles. To start, you don't have to come up with 365 of them; instead, work on a few months' worth of tips. Just be sure you're committed to your project. You don't want to get customers addicted to your daily dose of wisdom or fun, only to leave them high and dry when you run out of ideas. (For more on ways to make your site sticky, see Chapter 22.)

> **Smart Tip**
>
> *Tip...*
>
> Have you ever visited a website, intending to grab a quick bit of information only to look up and realize two hours have passed? You've landed on a "sticky" website. A sticky website is one that has somehow managed to grab and hold your attention so you "stick around" a while. Top websites invest a lot of money and effort to get sticky. Why? Because the longer surfers stick around, the more likely they'll become a paying customer.

The Ten Most Deadly Mistakes in Web Design

This chapter could probably be called the 100 most deadly mistakes in site design—there are so many goofs site builders make—but let's narrow the focus down to the most disastrous ten. Avoid these gaffes, and your site will be far better than much of the competition.

1. *Disabling the back button*. Evil site authors long ago figured out how to break a browser's back button so that when a user pushes it, one of several undesired things happen: There's an immediate redirect to an unwanted location, the browser stays put because the "back" button has been deactivated, or a new window pops up and overtakes the screen. Our advice: Never do it. All that's accomplished is that viewers get annoyed and do not return to your site.

2. *Opening new windows*. Once upon a time, using multiple new frames to display content as a user clicked through a site was cool—a new thing in web design. Now it only annoys viewers because it ties up system resources, slows computer response, and generally complicates a surfer's experience. Sure, it's easy to use this tool. But don't. With tabbed browsing common in browsers like Firefox users who wish to open links in new tabs can do so if they wish.

3. *Failing to put a phone number and address in several easy-to-find locations*. If you're selling, you need to offer viewers multiple ways to contact you. The smartest route is to put up a "Contact Us" link that leads to complete info—mailing address, phone, fax number, and email address. That link should be on each and every page of the website. Even if nobody ever calls, the very presence of this information adds real-world legitimacy and transparency to your site and comforts some viewers.

4. *Broken links*. Bad links—hyperlinks that do nothing when clicked or lead to "404" error pages—are the bane of any surfer. Test your site—and do it weekly—to ensure that all links work as promised. Include a "Contact the Webmaster" link in your site's footer (the area at the bottom of each page of your site) so users can quickly let you know if they find a broken link or other mistake on your site—and fix those errors immediately.

5. *Slow server times*. Slow times are inexcusable with professional sites. It's an invitation to the visitor to click away. What's slow? A recent study by Akamai Technologies, commissioned through Jupiter Research, showed that online shoppers, on average, will wait only four seconds for a site to load before clicking away. If your site is loading significantly slower than this, put it on a diet—images may be too large or special add-ons, like a Flash introduction, may be slowing things down.

Dollar Stretcher

Check your site for broken links, automatically and free, with a stop at Keynote NetMechanic (netmechanic.com). Type in your URL, and—whoosh!—you will get a report on broken links and page load time, and even a freebie spell check. It can also give a free report on browser compatibility on the spot.

6. *Outdated information.* Again, there's no excuse, but it's amazing how many sites include old, dated content. Make sure to keep your site fresh and updated daily for best results. You cannot afford the loss of credibility that can come from having dated content. Also, make sure your content is accurate, and if you should find a single error, fix it immediately.

7. *Poor navigation.* The internet promises speed. If surfers can't figure out where to go next quickly and get there easily, they'll simply surf on to the next website—your competitor's! It's very frustrating to be forced to go back two or three pages to get to other areas of a site. It's also a waste of time. There should be a navigation bar on every page that guides visitors to other areas of the site. Position the bar along the top of the page or along the left side so that it will always be visible regardless of screen resolution. Add an easy-to-find site map in your main navigation bar and/or footer to provide visitors with an at-a-glance view of every page on your site.

8. *Too many font styles and colors.* Pages ought to present a unified, consistent look, but novice site builders—entranced by having hundreds of fonts at their fingertips, plus dozens of colors—frequently turn their pages into a garish mishmash. Use two or three fonts and colors per page, maximum. The idea is to reassure viewers of your solidity and stability, not to convince them you are wildly artistic.

   And be wary of font size for older viewers and those with weak eyesight. A 12-point font is good if you're targeting that audience; a 10-point font is good for a general audience. Remember to make sure your font and colors look good on all possible devices from desktops to tablets to iPhones, etc.

9. *Orphan pages.* Memorize this: Every page in your site needs a readily seen link back to the home page. Why? Sometimes users will forward a URL to friends, who may visit and may want more information. But if the page they get is a dead end, forget it. Always put a link to "Home" on every page and make your site logo (usually found near the top left side of the screen) link back to your home page—that will quickly solve this problem.

10. *Failing to link with your social network sites.* Most businesses have their own Facebook pages, others use Pinterest with boards full of photos, while

Smart Tip

Tip...

OK, there are exceptions to the "no orphans" rule. If you want a special page set aside only for invited viewers, send out the URL, but offer no links to the page from any of your other pages. When might you use it? For instance, if you're offering big discounts to a special group of customers, that price list might be put on an orphan page.

some broadcast their latest activities on Twitter. The point is that social media is here to stay and businesses are benefitting from having a presence in it. Forgetting to link to your social media platforms is a big no-no. People should be able to go from one to the other effortlessly. Using the social media to market your business and to drive customers to your website will only work if you make it easy for the web users to move from one to the other. If done right, you can drive a lot more traffic to your site; consider that along with Google, Facebook is one of the two most used sites in the world.

Echat with Headsets.com's Mike Faith

Headsets.com

Mike Faith, CEO and President
Location: San Francisco
Year Started: 1998

Time out. So far, you've absorbed the theory of building a website, but to really understand what is going on, you need to hear from the experts, the entrepreneurs who have done it successfully.

▲

Throughout this book, you will find two types of interviews, some with top executives at the internet's most distinguished sites and others who are running their own smaller businesses and are still successful in their own right. Why both types? The top execs offer their perspective on how successful online businesses are run, but it's the lesser-known yet still successful entrepreneurs who give us insight into the nitty-gritty of the process. Remember, small businesses are at the heart of American business.

Meet Mike Faith of Headsets.com, a leading provider of headsets that has been consistently successful online for more than 16 years.

Entrepreneur: *Tell me about your background. Why did you start Headsets.com? When was it founded?*

Mike Faith: I immigrated to the United States from England, where the business climate is so stifling that it felt like "entrepreneur" was a dirty word. I wanted the freedom to do business in a way that supported my creativity, and the United States seemed like the perfect place. So in 1990, I jumped on a plane and never looked back. I started a few ventures that were moderately successful. They taught me some of the fundamentals of running a business and generated enough capital for me to start Headsets.com in 1998. Those early companies were call-center based, so we used a lot of telephone headsets. Finding good quality units at a reasonable cost and with decent supplier support turned out to be harder than it should have been—impossible, in fact—and that tripped my opportunity radar.

Entrepreneur: *With how much money did you start Headsets.com? Did you get venture capital money? Was it self-funded?*

Faith: Six weeks after realizing the opportunity, and with $40,000 of my own money, we were in business selling headsets. It was 1998, and we had a single product. The simplicity and cost of our offering was an instant hit, and we quickly grew revenues to the point that I was comfortable putting up the shutters on my other businesses to concentrate on the opportunity. Two years later, in 2000, our competitors were slashing prices and their margins. We were losing our differentiator. We looked at our business and the original opportunity and realized we had only served two of the three needs of the market. [We offered] a good product at a low cost, [but] we were missing that vital third part—service. So in 2000, as we incorporated from an LLC, we accepted a small round of funding, and that allowed us to fund a cultural shift in the organization to deliver what we think is world-class customer service.

Entrepreneur: *Where did you open up shop? Why?*

Faith: My wife and I were living in San Francisco when I started the business, so naturally that's where we opened shop. The Bay Area is a wonderful region with a near endless pool of world-class talent and an attitude [about] business innovation that, for me at least, captures all the reasons I moved to the United States. Many times over the years people have questioned the premiums we pay running a call center in the middle of one of the most expensive cities in the country, but every time it comes up, we can't help but see it as a strength. If you want the best, you have to pay for it. We want the very best!

Entrepreneur: *What's been the biggest challenge you've had in building your company?*

Faith: The biggest challenge we've faced, I'm proud to admit, has been my own growth. I'm an entrepreneur—I make decisions like you'd expect me to—and I've had to learn to involve others, think longer term and more strategically, and deal with a lot more formality and "corporate stuff" than I'm used to. It took a while before I built a team that I could trust to share the load, to execute my vision and my passion.

Entrepreneur: *How have you broadened your offerings or diversified your company since starting out? Why is this important for etailers to do?*

Faith: I'm going to give you an answer that perhaps will go against conventional wisdom. The world's greatest marketer, Al Ries, taught me about ruthless focus years ago—and it's been an invaluable lesson. We sell headsets, and we sell only headsets. Because of this, we know more about selling headsets than anybody else, and we sell more headsets than anybody else. The more headsets we sell, the better we get at it. It's a wonderful virtuous cycle. I believe that other etailers would do well to stay focused, do less, do it better, and reach deeper into a narrower market. Of course, we've been tempted to diversify—we have this fantastically efficient, high-service model for selling business-to-business productivity tools. Why shouldn't we apply that to as many products that fit the mold as possible? Well, we dabbled in a few areas but found that even trying to pick up incremental sales in similar categories like audio

Secrets to Success

What is Headsets.com's secret weapon against some of the bigger companies that sell headsets? For one, they're experts; headsets are all they sell. In addition, they offer great prices, unbeatable guarantees, a solid reputation, free product trial, and it's all backed up by knowledgeable, smart, professional reps offering what Faith calls the "world's best customer service." These are all weapons any small etailer or online business owner can use to compete against the big guys—and win.

headphones and teleconferencers complicated our business to the point that the whole became less than the sum of the parts—not more.

Many people warn us of disruptive technologies and saturated markets, and we aren't cavalier or arrogant enough to believe that these risks aren't real—they are, but for us to tackle these risks through diversification means abandoning our core strengths, and that's just not an acceptable trade.

Entrepreneur: *Who is your competition? Are they big guys? If so, how do you find your niche against them?*

Faith: You can get headsets from lots of places, but it's almost always part of a diverse offering of products. A headset is still for the most part a consultative sale, despite their widespread adoption and the simplicity of the product relative to other things on the corporate desktop. So we make sure we remain true to our company tagline "America's Headset Specialists," and we serve the market's needs better than generic telecom suppliers or office equipment suppliers who try to bolster volume by slashing margins and the all-important expert knowledge and service. For the longest time, we were the little guys, carving out a niche with the small companies and new headset users, while our big rivals squabbled over the large call-center market. But now we look around the competitive landscape and find the call-center market dwindling as it moves increasingly offshore and new headset adoption in the small-office sector driving all the growth in the industry, with us leading the charge and the historic big guns standing eerily silent.

It's exhilarating.

Entrepreneur: *Have you thought about going public? Why or why not?*

Faith: I've often thought of taking Headsets.com public, but I usually talk myself out of it the same day. Then a month later, I'll think of it again. The shift to a public company would change our business and our ability to compete on the terms that I know will win. Public companies maintain their stock price by focusing on growth. But like success and happiness, growth is a byproduct of doing something to the best of your ability. The pursuit of growth for growth itself will always come up short. As a private company, we are free to focus on delivering what the customer wants—the best product at the best price, and with the best service. The irony is, of course, that by not focusing on growth, we are enjoying it in abundance, around 50 percent annually.

Entrepreneur: *How do you market your site? What works? What doesn't?*

Faith: We don't market our site specifically. Our website, as proud of it as we are, is nothing more than a way for our customers to place an order as quickly and efficiently as possible. We do market our products, of course (which ultimately drives traffic to our web servers and our call center), and we do that through a pretty significant business-to-business direct-mail program using a catalog and solo product offerings. We also use pay-per-click online advertising and do phenomenally well in natural search rankings and have a lively affiliate program. Of course, it helps that our company name (Headsets.com) and 800 number (800-HEADSETS) say pretty much everything you need to know to find us and what we sell. But above all of our marketing efforts, we've found that we've reached a critical mass, with repeat and referral business now becoming our largest source.

Entrepreneur: *How do you up your look-to-buy ratio?*

Faith: We simply remove all the barriers to buying our products. I know that sounds trite, but it's true. We offer great prices, unbeatable guarantees, a solid reputation, free trial of our products, all backed by knowledgeable, smart, professional reps offering the world's best customer service. I challenge anyone who needs a headset to not buy from us—why would you go anywhere else? Hey—even I want to buy a headset from us, and I'm a skeptic!

Smart Tip

Tip...

You don't have to spend a lot of money on a big, traditional mass media advertising campaign to be successful. Look at Headsets.com: It sends out targeted, business-to-business direct-mail catalogs and uses search engine marketing. It helps that the company also has a memorable name (Headsets.com) and 800 number (800-HEADSETS) that say pretty much everything you need to know about them.

Cheap Tricks with BlueSuitMom.com's Maria Bailey

BlueSuitMom.com

Maria Bailey, President and Co-founder
Location: Pompano Beach, Florida
Year Started: 2000

The ability to carve out niches on the web is amazing. Just ask

Maria Bailey. A onetime marketing executive with AutoNation, she

launched BlueSuitMom.com on Mother's Day 2000 with the aim of meeting the needs of executive working moms. Her take on the net was that there were sites geared for working moms in general—but none aimed specifically at executives who also happen to be moms. So she decided to build one to offer networking opportunities, news geared for executive moms, and tips (how to manage time, for instance).

What started as a single website and a big dream has now grown into BSM Media (bsmmedia.com), a full-service marketing firm specializing in marketing to moms. Bailey has launched several other media properties as well since she began BlueSuitMom.com. She started Mom Talk Radio, which is the number one nationally syndicated radio show for moms, and hosts Mom TV, the largest online TV show for moms. Bailey is also the author of *Marketing to Moms: Getting Your Share of the Trillion-Dollar Market* (Prima Lifestyle), *Trillion Dollar Moms: Marketing to a New Generation of Mothers* (Dearborn), *Mom 3.0: Marketing WITH Today's Mothers by Leveraging New Media & Technology* (Wyatt-MacKenzie), and *Power Moms* (Wyatt-MacKenzie).

Today, BSM Media and its media properties connect some of America's most well-known brands such as Disney, HP, and Precious Moments with the mom market, and enjoys sales of more than $2 million.

Brilliant as the idea for BlueSuitMom was, the ramp-up of Bailey's site wasn't smooth. Read on for her candid—and helpful—comments on building a site.

Entrepreneur: *How much funding did you start with? Where was it raised?*

Maria Bailey: We started with a commitment for $1 million from a former boss—but, unfortunately, the money did not become a reality. So we truly began with $100,000 raised from personal savings and a few friends.

Entrepreneur: *What were the first big obstacles you encountered in building a web business?*

Bailey: Our biggest obstacle has been getting interested investors to actually write the check. That stems from a historical obstacle: Career women have done such a good job at proving to the wealthy/powerful men they work with that they have obtained work and family balance that it is difficult to help my potential investors understand the needs of our market. And on top of it, these men are most likely not married to a

---

Smart Tip

Building a web business is a road filled with ups and downs for any entrepreneur, but a wonderful thing about it is that it provides a space of genuinely equal opportunity. Color, race, gender, creed—none of it matters because all cybercitizens are created equal. Better still, whatever you are, if there are others like you, that's the basis for creating an internet community that just may become a profitable business.

woman who is a vice president or CEO. So you say "mother," and they envision their spouse, who is [usually] a stay-at-home mom.

There has been a bit of challenge in learning to manage the young technology pros you need to grow your site. There is little loyalty, and they convey an attitude that they have you by a leash and without them you wouldn't be able to execute your business plan. They realize that their talents are in demand and are used to changing jobs often. Also, their confidence in technology has led many of them to believe that they also know how to run a business based on that technology. There is a short learning curve to adapt your management style to the new breed of employee you find in the web world.

Entrepreneur: *How do you promote the business?*

Bailey: We promote our business mainly by creating very strategic partnerships. For instance, we have a partnership with Stork Avenue, the largest retailer of birth announcements. They were willing to put our logo on five million catalogs in exchange for driving traffic to their site. We are relying too on the strong word-of-mouth network moms and businesswomen create and networking within women's professional organizations, HR departments, and parenting organizations. We have also been featured in the media, including *The Wall Street Journal* and *USA Today*. Also, we are sponsoring events such as parenting conferences and distributing our content to other websites to build brand recognition, and we have been very lucky in creating great press.

Entrepreneur: *What's the business's goal? What's the end game?*

Bailey: Our exit strategy is not to go public. Our goal is to create a prequalified niche market that may be attractive to content aggregators, such as iVillage, or a search engine. Because there is no one out there exclusively targeting our market, we feel we have a good shot at it. We monitor the women's market regularly and watch the internet strategies of others so that we can identify possible acquirers.

Entrepreneur: *What unique advantages do you have vs. other websites?*

Bailey: We felt the best advantage we could have was to be the first to market—and we

Smart Tip
Consider marketing to a large buying demographic, such as moms. According to PunchTab 2013, 84 percent of moms (in the USA) go online when looking for product/brand recommendations and 74 percent of moms have purchased products as a result of mentions they've read in a blog. Some 64 percent of moms read online reviews before making a purchase, and 65 percent of moms learn about a product of service through social media. That's a lot of moms!

Tip...

were. We have used this as our strategy for every one of our media properties. With Mom Talk Radio, we were the first radio show for moms. Because BlueSuitMom.com was the first site aimed at executive working mothers, it allowed us to create all the great press we received. The other advantage we have is that anytime we are working with a woman to make deals or create partnerships, we almost always get what we need because the woman on the other side of the phone relates immediately to the elements of our site.

Entrepreneur: *What's been your biggest surprise in building this business, and your biggest disappointment?*

Bailey: The biggest surprise has been how quickly the company has grown and morphed into other businesses with even greater opportunities. The response we have gotten from other internet companies and offline retailers, marketers, and associations has been overwhelming. We can't keep up with the people who want to do business with us. Also, the international response we have received has been incredible. In addition to the growth of our marketing business, it's always rewarding to receive emails from women all over thanking us for our vision to create something that is valuable to them. It is personally fulfilling to know that your business is touching so many lives.

The biggest challenge is managing our growth. We have so much growth opportunity now. One of the biggest challenges is not going after every single opportunity, but selecting the smart opportunities.

The Nuts and Bolts of Web Hosts and Domains

With your website designed, you need a place to stow it so that visitors can access it, and the best way to do this is to hook up with a web hosting company.

There are many out there; you need to just research them online and do some comparison shopping.

Through a Google search or by going to a site like WebHostingFreeReviews. com or Web-hosting-review.toptenreviews.com, you'll find plenty of possibilities, including Hostway, IPage, Fatcow, Web.com, HostMonster, HostGator, or Bluehost. There are also many small local hosting companies, and many small etailers swear by them. Why? Because they are usually available any time of the day if there is a snag and offer excellent customer service.

When picking a host, you first and foremost want to know if a host can handle ecommerce activities. Some of the most bare-bones companies simply are not equipped. Other criteria that are important to most users: setup and monthly fees (a typical range for basic web hosting is $3.99 to $29.95 monthly, but the price usually goes up when adding ecommerce functionality, with a setup fee equal to one month's fee) and the capacity of the server to handle the amount of traffic you anticipate.

What to Look for in a Web Hosting Service

You need to put your website in good hands and feel comfortable knowing that people can access it 24/7 and that if there is a problem you can get help fixing it promptly. After all, this is your business, and you need to make sure it's operating at full strength. Remember, a few minutes of downtime can cost you sales, so you need to know your business is open even if you're sound asleep.

In short, choosing a reliable web hosting service has become a critical mission for most business owners. Here are some areas to consider.

Storage

You want to know how much data you can store. Typically, with a small business, you'll find that several gigabytes will suffice. However, the more storage space you need, the more you will have to get some clear numbers, such as a maximum of 100 GB as touted by Yahoo!, or 150 GB listed by Go Daddy. Many companies will tout "unlimited," which is fine until you reach a limit. For most small businesses, this will not become an issue unless you expect to grow rapidly. However, it never hurts to talk with a representative and review your needs and make sure the space you are allotted can handle what you need.

Bandwidth

Like storage, you want to make sure the bandwidth will handle the traffic to your site. Essentially, bandwidth is the amount of data that your host will let you and your visitors upload and download in a given month.

Here too, you will see the term *unlimited*. This will suffice for a typical small-business website. But, in case your business suddenly takes off or your video goes viral, you should get an idea of how much traffic the site can handle before it shuts down or before you get charged more money.

Support and Customer Service

You need tech support. I don't care how reliable any host service claims to be, there will be glitches and you will want 24/7 support. While some hosting services may claim 100 percent uptime, it's hard to assure such a claim.

You want to make sure that you can get questions answered promptly without long waits or leaving messages that are returned days later.

Backup

Most hosting services today provide backup on a regular basis, meaning that if the server goes down, your data is safe. Backup can make a world of difference when something like a hurricane or another such act of nature hits a region, as was the case in 2005 when Hurricane Katrina hit the Gulf Coast, or in 2012 with Superstorm Sandy pelting the Northeast. Businesses with backups in place had a much easier time of re-opening than those that did not have their data and their sites backed up. Look for a service that has off-site and/or cloud backup.

It is also important for you to back up all of your own data, including all business files, documents, addresses, and permits you have. Back up everything having to do with your business in the cloud and off-site. Hard copies of documents, such as contracts, stored in a safe place are also highly recommended. Sometimes a paper trail is very important, so take the time to make hard copies of your most important documents and data.

Add-On Domains

Many businesses own more than one domain name, such as Google, where you can type in Google.com, Google.net, or you can even misspell it as Gooogle.com and get to the same place. Can your host server accommodate variations on your main domain name with other similar domain names? It's always a good idea to buy a few close names. That way, if someone types .net instead of .com, you'll still get their business. It also keeps competitors from having a domain name that is too close for comfort.

The same holds true for adding other domains, should you do micro sites or launch new sites as your business grows and expands. It would be advantageous to use the same hosting service and not have to set up a whole new account for each new site you open. Can that be accomplished and how many domain names can you have on an account?

Email

You'll find that most hosting services offer email accounts. See what they offer and how many email accounts you get in their various packages before having to pay extra. Also find out if you can get your emails from various locations. Are they in the cloud or downloaded to your computer?

Languages

There are a lot of languages used in programming today. For your purposes, you want to know what is offered to support various computer languages and the latest versions thereof. PHP is very popular and used on many platforms. Consider what else you may be using for graphics or blogs.

Blogging

Speaking of blogs, you will likely want to have a blog for your site(s). WordPress is the most popular blogging platform. Make sure your server can support this or any other blogging platform you wish to use.

⚠ Beware!

Don't get locked into an agreement that you cannot get out of. If you are unhappy you should be able to move your site to another server when your contract runs out or at some point along the way. A confident web hosting company will let you know how to get out should you need to.

Web Sharing

Keep in mind that most often you will be sharing a web server with many other businesses. Web sharing is very common and works for most small businesses. The upside is that the price is affordable. The downside is that the multitude of other sites can sometimes cause trouble. Servers can be overloaded because of activity on one site and it can cause problems for everyone; infrequent, but possible.

The alternative is to have a virtual private server (VPS)—also called a virtual dedicated server (VDS). A VPS is somewhat more complicated and will cost a little more, perhaps $40 to $60 a month, but you will have a higher quality web server and faster performance. Many host servers offer this as an option. For most small businesses a shared hosting server will be sufficient, but if you anticipate rapid growth, or are starting a fairly large business, this is something to inquire about. Again, you'll need to review what is included, such as support, customer service, email accounts, and so on.

Take your time when host server shopping and read any contract very carefully.

Master of Your Domain

Before setting up your site, you also need to stake out your domain name, which are the words between "www." and ".com" or ".net" in your web address. So what name suits you? Come up with some possibilities, then head over to any number of web hosting companies—many offer CCTLD (country code top-level domain) registration.

There are many places from which you can get a domain name such as Register.com, Domain.com, DomainNames.com, Networksolutions.com, and GoDaddy.com, which is the largest but not necessarily the best. Domain names are very cheap to own, often around $9.99 per year.

Keep in mind, however, that if you are working with an ecommerce hosting provider to set up your online business, it will most likely be able to offer you domain registration as well. The drill is simple: You type in a name, and the host service or domain registration site will let you know if it's available. Of course you can simply seek it out on your own by typing in the address, but this doesn't mean that the site is available, because people often buy names that they may launch at a later date. Typically one of the domain registration sites can find out whether or not the name is available. If the name you want is taken, you can go with

Smart Tip

Tip...

Want a fast take on comparative features of web hosts? Log onto Compare Web Hosts (comparewebhosts.com), where a few mouse clicks let you specify what's important to you and check out which hosts likely will serve your needs best. For a second opinion, head to TopHosts (tophosts.com), a site with a bit less functionality but more layers of detail—meaning it's not the easiest resource to use, but it has lots of information.

another option besides .com, such as .net or perhaps .biz. If your business is part of an organization, you could try .org.

What's In a Name?

There's wide agreement that nothing matters as much as a good name. Yet who would have thought Amazon was one? What most matters in a name is that it's easy to spell and easy to remember. For my money, that's an argument against using a catchy name with an unorthodox country code suffix. Most U.S.-based computer users just automatically type ".com," ".net," ".edu," or ".gov." Throw a weird ending at them, and you may lose them. So I would recommend a clunky name with a ".com" or ".net" ending over a catchy name with an unorthodox ending.

How do you buy a domain name? Sedo.com's model is an offer-counteroffer model. This means that you negotiate directly with the domain's owner until you both agree on a price. This system takes away the uncertainty of an auction model, reduces the potential for fraud, and gives you control over how much you pay. Also, try GoDaddy, which offers auction sales of domain names in addition to its domain registration and web hosting services.

> **Beware!**
> Can you "park" a domain name for free? When you park a domain, you reserve it but haven't yet mounted a site. Many outfits tout that they offer free parking, but that's not exactly true: You still have to pay the registration fee. Free parking only means they'll put up an "under construction" sign that anyone who hunts for your domain will find. Be aware that some companies will also place copious amounts of advertising on your parked site.

Choosing a Name

Here are a few tips on choosing your domain name.

- Think of something catchy
- One to three words should do it.
- Keep it as close to your company name or the products or services you provide as possible. If you can include something that makes you unique, include it, such

as the folks at FastCarpetCleaning.com did: The name says what they do and what makes them special; they're fast!

- Clever spelling can set you apart, such as Pantz.com if you own a business selling pants, but don't make it too confusing or people won't remember the spelling (or you can also purchase the correct spelling if it's available).

Smart Tip

Check out similar domain names. You don't want people to misspell the name and land on your competitor's site or a site that may be inappropriate.

- Sometimes you can benefit from having the name of your location. This can work if you have a prestigious location, as it does for NewYorkCupcakes.com, or if you anticipate doing mostly local business.
- First names can work; using them personalizes the business, such as Charleyscheesecakes.com.

The Scoop on Business-to-Business Ecommerce

It used to be, the dream was starting the next McDonald's, or maybe inventing a new widget everybody would need, putting you on the fast track to wealth so immense it could scarcely be counted. Today, of course, the dream is to come up with the new Amazon or Yahoo!—but that might be the wrong dream.

Isn't this book all about launching the Next Big Thing? Nope. It's about building viable businesses on the internet. Nowadays, a very good argument can be made that there's a smarter way to go than scouting around for the idea that will spawn a new Amazon.

Taking Care of Business

Consider Walt Geer. It was in late '98 that Geer, a partner in an Atlanta promotional products company, faced up to reality. His little business—which sold logo merchandise such as pens and coffee mugs to companies to distribute to employees and customers— was chugging along OK, but it was just one of 19,000 promotional products companies in the country. Plainly put, Geer's company was lost in the mob. So he decided to take the plunge. He cut the cord on his traditional company, dumping his existing customers and putting his business online as eCompanyStore.

After some time, he left eCompanyStore, which no longer exists, and formed another company called Phenix Direct (phenixdirect.com), an overseas importer that serves larger promotional product distributors.

Geer says that in Phenix's early days, there were a couple months of hard swallowing: "We had no revenue coming in," recalls Geer, "but we had to focus our energy on the internet. We didn't have the resources to do it and run our traditional business." But, he says, "in just a few months, the internet let us move from being a small company to a national player. Before, we serviced lots of little accounts. Now we have Microsoft, for example. The internet lets us go after big accounts." In addition, Phenix grew at an average annual rate of 55 percent in 2006 and 2007. Today, the Atlanta-based business also has an office in Hong Kong and imports promotional items directly from factories in Southeast Asia. The company has also become particularly adept at assisting distributors in landing and filling large-quantity orders.

Phenix Direct is just one of hundreds of business-to-business (B2B) enterprises, where companies sell not to consumers but to other businesses. These internet companies may not be winning wide press attention by dazzling people with their Facebook pages, but they are creating a real buzz in big-money circles.

Today, businesses are realizing that using the internet allows them to drive down costs. How much? One statistic says that when shifting purchasing to the web, a business can eliminate about 90 percent of the cost of a transaction. But more than just cost savings are propelling this mushrooming of business trade on the net, says Geer. "The real drivers are speed and efficiency," he says. "And besides, our web store is always open. These advantages are as attractive to our customers as the savings. The internet is a better and faster way for businesses to shop."

In addition, B2B transactions can take place globally. Without travel back and forth, businesses on either side of the globe can review inventory online and make deals in hours that would have taken days of travelling not that long ago.

The Many Faces of B2B

Just who is making it in B2B ecommerce? Beyond big-name B2B players like Staples.com, OfficeDepot.com, and ThomasNet.com, the web is filled with enticing companies that illustrate the breadth of this marketplace. That's because B2B ecommerce offers diverse opportunities, with some players seeking to establish marketplaces where buyers and sellers meet to do deals, while others are positioning themselves to provide services and products to business customers in a wholly new, web-based way. The bottom line: B2B ecommerce entrepreneurs are limited only by their own imaginations.

In the Know

What industry do you know, and know well? Substantial expertise is needed to create a viable B2B company. If you are considering B2B as an option, ask yourself the following questions:

- ○ What industries have you worked in?
- ○ Which ones interest you enough that you'll enjoy the long hours of hard work and research that you'll need to put in? Do you know how the back end of the industry works?
- ○ Which industries are currently underserved on the internet?
- ○ Which industries offer a cost-effective business opportunity?

Marketing glitz doesn't go as far in a B2B context as getting down to the nuts and bolts of what you have to offer businesses that will positively affect their bottom line. Business executives tend to be more cold-blooded about these things, so show them where they will save time and money, and they will follow you.

Liquidity Services Inc.

The success of eBay, online discount retailers such as Overstock.com and Amazon. com, and click-and-mortar discount shops have proven that consumers and businesses want high-end products but want to pay less-than-high-end prices. As the market for less-than-new items grows for both consumers and business purchasers, those with an entrepreneurial heart are eager to capitalize on selling to these markets. The challenge, though, is where to find this type of inventory for prices low enough to make a profit on the resale.

Liquidity Services Inc. (LSI) in Washington, DC, is a business that helps organizations shed unwanted inventory through online auction marketplaces, and has amassed more than 700,000 registered buyers of wholesale and surplus goods. LSI provides a consistent flow of new and used assets, including overstock, returned, refurbished, and seasonal items, on its online auction marketplaces Liquidation.com and GovLiquidation. com. The merchandise comes from LSI's contracts with Fortune 500 companies, public sector agencies, top retailers, manufacturers, wholesalers, and distributors.

Buyers often resell the merchandise as individual units or in multiple quantities to small retail chains, through eBay, to small businesses, and even in export markets. "Our business model is very simple and transparent for both sellers and buyers," says Bill Angrick, chairman and CEO of LSI. "Not only do we convert surplus assets to cash for large and medium-sized organizations, but we enable buyers to find and purchase this inventory through secure online marketplaces."

The LSI marketplaces offer buyers a total solution to source inventory in bulk through an online auction process. The sites have thousands of auctions to bid on at any given time in more than 500 categories, including consumer electronics, computers and networking equipment, clothing and accessories, general merchandise, building and do-it-yourself hardware tools, vehicles, and many others.

LSI has contracts with major domestic and international shippers that enable significantly reduced shipping costs. This means buyers are able to resell the merchandise at more competitive prices while still maintaining a profit margin. Liquidation.com also allows buyers the opportunity to arrange their own shipping for inventory that is stored in LSI's six warehouse facilities located throughout the United States.

Smart Tip

If it can be sold by phone or by mail, it can be sold, probably better, on the web. Ecommerce may never completely replace face-to-face selling since you may not want to rent, or buy, an office space or your new home over the web, but it has taken a huge bite out of telemarketing and direct-mail sales.

Dedicated to providing excellent customer service, LSI also offers a Buyer Relations team that is available to assist buyers throughout the buying process. On the seller side, LSI offers a full range of value-added services, including reconciliation of surplus, de-labeling, auction creation, marketing to current and potential buyers, buyer assistance, payment arrangements, and complete and transparent tracking.

"The overall goal of our asset remarketing activities is to provide a solution that maximizes the recovery value of surplus property," says Angrick. "We have more than 724,000 registered buyers that consistently use our marketplaces to source bulk and wholesale inventory, which ensures a competitive market price on the surplus inventory we handle for our sellers. Our buyers have confidence bidding on these items and know that they will receive winning purchases in an easy and trusted manner."

According to Angrick, sellers can obtain 20 to 200 percent higher recovery using LSI's marketplaces, as well as save a significant amount of time, resources, and money associated with traditional liquidation options.

LSI has focused on bringing the right services and expertise together in a single offering. "We provide the technology, buyers, product sales knowledge, compliance expertise, and value-added services to maximize revenues and reduce overall costs," says Angrick.

Marketing Still Matters

Launching a B2B site can be significantly less expensive than trying to create a winning consumer site. Usually it's cheaper to target an audience and pursue it in B2B because you have narrowed down a business niche and know how to cost-effectively target it. That being said, you still need to market yourself because there is stiff B2B competition going after these same niche customers.

Therefore, if you are going to enter the B2B market, you need to know a little something about what you are getting into and what B2B clients are all about. After all, you always need to know your demographic market.

First, consider that B2B marketing is about meeting the needs of other businesses. However, it is often very likely that these demands are driven by the consumers that frequent these businesses.

You should also consider that many, if not most, B2B decisions are made by committees, teams, and those in the chain of command. Therefore, unlike selling to a consumer who is making his or her own decision, it is up to you to learn the process, know who the decision makers are, and build relationships with them. B2B sales are largely about establishing relationships. After all, your buyers are representing their businesses and putting their reputations (and perhaps their jobs) on the line. They need to have some trust and faith in you to sell them quality products or services.

In situations where you are selling more complex B2B products, you need to be well versed in how the product works. Consumers may be sold on how something looks, feels, and tastes, and whether it is fashionable or has sex appeal. In the B2B world, the buyer needs a more detailed

---

Dollar Stretcher

Do you buy anything for your business that could be more efficiently purchased on the internet? That thought alone can be the trigger to launch a B2B website. Start thinking about what you buy and where—and whether the net would make the process cheaper and faster.

---

understanding of the product, the quality, what makes it work, and how to fix it if something goes wrong; remember, the business needs to stand behind what they sell. If they are not selling products, but using them for manufacturing or for business purposes in their own offices, they will also need to know the nuts and bolts of what you are selling. Therefore, marketing to B2B customers is much more about the technical aspects of a product than the look, feel, or flavor.

And finally, if you are looking to establish a long-term relationship in the B2B market, keep in mind that having a few good long-term customers is more important than many short-term customers. You will have fewer clients than you will have when targeting a consumer market. Therefore, you want to build a connection that will keep you in business together for years to come. This means:

- Being transparent
- Listening to your clients' needs
- Being able to solve clients' problems with practical solutions

B2B is about sound business practices and win-win situations that benefit both parties. You will find that B2B clients are more demanding, with greater expectations, but you will also find that they are more loyal clients and even somewhat predicable once you get them on board.

Adding "C" to B2B

As these examples show, there are many small B2B web companies thriving despite the current economy. Some traditional B2C (business-to-consumer) companies are also entering the B2B ecommerce fray. Consider eBay. At any given time, there are approximately 102 million items available on eBay worldwide, and approximately 6 million new items are added each day. To make business buying easier for small- and midsize businesses (SMBs), eBay provides a section on its site called eBay Business Seller Information (www.pages.ebay.com/sellerinformation) that includes a business-oriented search engine bringing together all of eBay's business and industry listings under one easy-to-browse destination, focusing heavily on office technology products, such as computers and networking devices, as well as lots of consumer goods and services (think insurance and shipping) at wholesale prices.

A Slam Dunk?

Hold on, the sailing for new B2B entrants won't be entirely smooth. In key respects, the bar may be higher in B2B ecommerce than it is in B2C, and the requirements for succeeding will likely be stiffer. "B2B is different from B2C," says John J. Sviokla, vice chairman of Diamond Consultants, a global management firm that helps companies develop and implement growth strategies. "To succeed in this space, you will need deep domain knowledge." You don't need to know much about farming to successfully peddle peaches to consumers, but to build an exchange for farmers, you have to grasp the fundamental issues in that industry. Lack that, and there will be no trust on the part of your target audience.

Another hitch: B2B involves long selling cycles, and you may need to do some face-to-face selling. It is one thing to buy $20 books with a mouse click. It's an entirely different matter to buy $400,000 worth of antiques. Sometimes, you will need to put in face-to-face time as well after setting up all the preliminaries. Remember, B2B is very much about establishing relationships, some that can last for many years.

Echat with Autobytel's Jim Riesenbach

Autobytel Inc.

Jim Riesenbach, CEO and President
Location: Irvine, California
Year Started: 1995

Do you wish you could get a glimpse into the mind of a CEO at

the helm of a dotcom that has evolved into a diversified and suc-

cessful automotive marketing services company? Read on. Below,

▲

Jim Riesenbach, president and CEO of Autobytel Inc., offers an in-depth look at the world of internet car buying and selling.

When Autobytel® (autobytel.com) was founded in 1995, the internet and ecommerce were still relatively new, unproven concepts, and the word "tel" in Autobytel's name stood for telecommunications, which included fax and internet communications. Within the first year of business, the internet became the dominant means of communication. Consumers all over America began logging on to Autobytel and asking, electronically, for the vehicles they wanted to buy—say, a dark green four-door sedan with a six-cylinder engine and ABS. This electronic "Purchase Request" was routed to a local dealer based in the car buyer's ZIP code. The dealer was trained to get back to the consumer with a firm competitive price usually aimed below the sticker price.

A major goal of the company is to enable the dealer to make a better profit from online sales because its advertising/marketing costs (a big expense for dealerships) are often much lower for Autobytel-generated customers. In addition, a steady stream of incremental business can be generated through Autobytel—i.e., customers whom dealers likely wouldn't have seen otherwise. So it's "win-win-win" for Autobytel, the dealer, and the consumer.

A veteran of online and digital media, Jim Riesenbach was named president and CEO of Autobytel in 2006. When he first joined Autobytel, Riesenbach was struck by how similar and limited the consumer experience was at the leading third-party automotive sites—all of which were built around new and used "buying funnels" that effectively push consumers to the transaction moment while walling out relevant information. Having witnessed the shortcomings of this "walled garden" approach during his tenure at AOL, he recognized that Autobytel's future should be guided by its pro-consumer past—and set out to create a more convenient, open, flexible, and comprehensive consumer resource.

As a result, the company launched its flagship site, MyRide.com, under Riesenbach's leadership. Riesenbach says, "Myride.com combined original content with the first fully integrated vertical search experience for the automotive marketplace." In time, MyRide merged with the Autobytel site.

To put Autobytel's impact on the automotive industry in perspective, since

> **⚠ Beware!**
> Success breeds nearly instant imitation on the net. That's the irony: The more you prosper, the tougher you have to fight. How will you stay a step—better still, two steps—ahead of those who will follow? Keep on being creative and forge new ideas, use trademarks and copyrights to protect yourself from thieves, as much as possible, and always have your eyes and ears paying attention to what your competitors are up to.

1995, millions of car shoppers have visited Autobytel, generating billions of dollars in vehicle sales for Autobytel member dealers.

Entrepreneur: *As the CEO of Autobytel, what is your goal for the company?*

Jim Riesenbach: My goal is to continue what has been our mission since 1995, empowering consumers with the information they need to make smart, well-informed vehicle ownership and buying decisions while also offering automotive dealers and manufacturers marketing services that help them sell more cars efficiently.

Entrepreneur: *What's been the biggest surprise you've experienced since coming on board as CEO?*

Riesenbach: I think that the stall in innovation in the online automotive space was the biggest surprise, especially in the face of the dramatic migration of automotive marketing dollars from traditional media to the internet in what is arguably the largest industry in the world.

Before I came on board, it was clear to me that the market opportunity was huge. With 90 percent of all car buyers using the internet to shop for a vehicle, it was profoundly obvious to me that the internet was the place for automotive marketers to find their customers. This was borne out by the hunger among automotive marketers for more and more online inventory and leads. To enter a space as a marketer where there is such a high demand for exposure is very exciting.

In the early days, with perhaps the most compelling market opportunity in any industry, it was very surprising to me that online automotive sites had barely innovated since the auto dotcom glory days of 2000. In fact, if you stacked the leading automotive sites next to each other, Autobytel.com included, and removed the branding, you would not be able to tell them apart.

Entrepreneur: *What's your biggest challenge?*

Riesenbach: I think it is—and will always be—to keep ahead of the rapidly evolving online automotive consumer. This is why it is so important to me to have people on our team who are both veterans of online automotive media as well as marketing innovators who know that looking one step ahead of not only our industry but the digital industry as a whole, is what's going to keep us on top of today's consumer. And

> **Tip...**
>
> **Smart Tip**
> One reason Autobytel is a market leader is that the company hasn't fallen in love with how it does things. As market conditions change, Autobytel quickly adapts. That way of thinking and acting is essential for any dotcom. So once you've launched a site, prepare to continually retool your site and, perhaps, even your business model. Adaptation is the only way to survive on the web, or, for that matter, in business in general.

the consumer comes first at Autobytel. While it can be challenging to balance the many different needs of all our constituents—automakers, auto dealers, and auto consumers—by providing a superior consumer experience, we firmly believe that the results will be more site traffic, better lead volume and quality, and more valuable and diverse ad opportunities.

Entrepreneur: *What's your strategy for coming out ahead of competitors?*

Riesenbach: The strategy is to focus on providing the best consumer site and the best dealer programs in the industry. I think there are some glaring automotive consumer needs—namely the ability to quickly find information beyond the confines of a single site, via search and user-generated information, and to provide an experience that, while incorporating the buying funnel, is also about every automotive need and experience.

It's the Place to Be!

Clearly, the internet is now where auto marketers want to be. For example, according to *DigitalAge*, as of 2013, 90 percent of car buyers continue to do their research online. It is also estimated by *DigitalAge* that $142 is the average price spent per car sold through online display advertising by the three largest automakers.

Today Autobytel continues motoring along. The business has helped tens of millions of automotive consumers research vehicles and has connected thousands of dealers nationwide with motivated car buyers. The company now runs a network of automotive sites, including Car.com℠ and MyGarage.com®.

They also continue as a dedicated provider of top-quality automotive internet programs to provide consumers with a comprehensive and positive automotive research and purchasing experience. In addition, they serve auto dealers and manufacturers with cost-effective customer referral and marketing programs.

Echat with Zappos' Tony Hsieh

Zappos.com

Tony Hsieh, CEO
Location: Las Vegas
Year Started: 1999

It's surprising what you can sell on the web. Ask Tony Hsieh. When

Zappos founder Nick Swinmurn approached him with the idea of

selling shoes online, Hsieh was ready to hang up the phone. Then

Swinmurn mentioned the size of the shoe market at that time, which was $40 billion in the United States. What's more, $2 billion of that was sold by mail-order catalogs. If shoes—a highly personal and tactile item—could be sold through mail order, why not over the internet?

It was 1999, the heady days of dotcom dreams. Anything seemed possible, even an online shoe store. Convinced that the nonexistent ecommerce market for shoes would someday be even bigger than the $2 billion mail-order market, the pair started Zappos.com.

Today, online footwear is a multibillion-dollar business, and Zappos is the undisputed leader in footwear retailing on the web. The Las Vegas company has been featured in many publications, including: *The New Yorker*, *USA Today*, CNN, *The New York Times*, CBS News, *The Los Angeles Times*, *The Chicago Tribune*, and *Forbes*.

Smart Tip

Today, many CEOs keep in touch with customers through corporate blogs. Want to start your own blog? Go for it. But first do your research and understand what you're getting yourself into. Blogs can be fun, but they can also be demanding. A great resource is *The Rough Guide to Blogging* by Jonathan Yang (Rough Guides). The book is an excellent reference for anyone who wants to know more about blogging, whether you're a casual reader or an experienced professional blogger. Another good (and quick) read comes from Amazon and is called *How to Write Great Blog Posts that Engage Readers*.

How did they do it? It's all about service. In fact, according to the company's philosophy, Zappos is a service business that sells shoes, not a shoe retailer that provides service. The company's service policies would make most etailers cringe. The call center, with its staff of more than 1,300 people, is open 24/7 and services an average of over 5,000 calls per day, sometimes more during the end-of-year holiday season. The warehouse is also open 24/7. But the clincher that turns browsers into customers for life is the 365-day return policy with free shipping—both ways! That's right, you can shop till you drop and send back anything that doesn't fit or doesn't look just right with that new outfit. No harm, no foul.

Entrepreneur: *You've built Zappos on great customer service, but how?*

Tony Hsieh: Part of it is the very fast shipping. We run our warehouse 24/7. It's not the most efficient way to run a warehouse, but it gets the shoes out to our customers as quickly as possible. We also run our call center 24/7. We're unlike most websites where it's hard to find a phone number to contact the company. Our 800 number is on the left corner of every single page of the website. And when you call a member of our customer loyalty team, they really strive to go above and beyond, making the experience very different from calling most other call centers. Our call center isn't outsourced either. It's right here at our headquarters in Las Vegas. As an example of what we believe is service, imagine a customer is looking for a specific pair of shoes. Now let's say we're out of stock in their size or that particular style. We will actually search other online retailing websites and if we find them there, we'll direct the customer to that competitor.

Entrepreneur: *Zappos started out as the first online shoe retailer. Who are your competitors now?*

Hsieh: We don't think of our main competitors as anyone online. It's really more about getting customers used to the idea of buying shoes online. When most people hear that, it's a scary concept because of fit issues. So our biggest challenge is educating customers on how easy and quick it is to get the shoes. Some people order 10 pairs of shoes, try them on with 10 different outfits, and then ship back the five that don't fit or don't look good. They've got 365 days to return them and we pay the shipping back to us. A lot of people don't know or realize that when they first hear about Zappos. We try to do everything we can to minimize the perceived risk for the customer.

Entrepreneur: *How do you attract new customers to your site?*

Hsieh: In terms of paid advertising, we do buy key words on search engines and we also have an affiliate program. We've enjoyed fast growth, and the vast majority of that growth has been from repeat customers and word-of-mouth. So our philosophy is that all the money we might have otherwise spent on marketing, let's instead put it back into the customer experience. Things like offering free shipping both ways is very expensive. Things like running the call center and warehouse 24/7 is very expensive. But we really view those as our marketing expenses, and let our customers tell each other about our service.

Entrepreneur: *You received several rounds of venture capital along the way. How important was venture capital to your success?*

Hsieh: It allowed us to accelerate our growth because as our sales grew, our inventory requirements needed to grow as well. Funding that inventory growth was the

> ## Tip...
>
> ### Smart Tip
> If you offer extraordinary service—like 24/7 customer service via a toll-free number or free shipping and returns—announce it prominently on your site. Let customers know how great your service is! On Zappos. com, you can find their 800 number and free shipping and returns declaration right below their logo and navigation on every page of their site. Also, make sure you have a significant presence on social media that lets people "like" what you do on Facebook and follow you on Twitter. Social media has spread the word, like wildfire, about Zappos and their great customer service.

reason we needed to raise the money. If we hadn't done that then we would have continued to grow, but just at a slower rate because we wouldn't have been able to warehouse as much inventory.

Entrepreneur: *Do you have any advice for entrepreneurs wanting to attract venture capital?*

Hsieh: Generally, VCs are looking for a business that is growing at a rapid rate and is in a large market. Plus, they want to see that the people in the company are passionate about whatever the company is about, that they're not in there just to try to make a quick buck.

Entrepreneur: *Why did you expand into other merchandise besides shoes?*

Hsieh: We got into handbags several years ago and then started selling apparel. Our plan was always for the Zappos brand to be known for great service, and not necessarily for shoes. In fact, hopefully 10 years from now people won't even realize we started out selling shoes online.

Entrepreneur: *If you had to pinpoint one thing, what would be the secret to your success?*

Hsieh: The company culture. Our number-one priority as a company is to make sure that, as we grow, we continue to maintain a really service-focused culture. When we hire people, for example, we do two sets of interviews. One set is a standard set that the hiring manager's team does. Then, our HR department does another set of interviews to assess culture fit. And they have to pass both in order to be hired.

Then after they are hired, everyone in our Vegas office, regardless of their position (accountant, lawyer, or whatever you do) go through the same four-week training program. We go over our customer service philosophy, company history, the importance of company culture, and then they get on the phone and talk to customers for a couple of weeks. After that, we send them to our warehouse in Kentucky to spend a week picking, packing, sending, and receiving. So it's a total of five weeks of training, being immersed in company culture, before starting as an accountant or lawyer or whatever you're hired for. It's pretty hard to go through that five weeks without understanding our focus on customer service and company culture. It gets everyone on the same page. I think when everyone's moving in the same direction, it moves the company forward that much faster.

Entrepreneur: *What's next on the horizon for Zappos.com?*

Hsieh: We're just going to continue what we've been doing. On an ongoing basis, we look for ways to improve service and slowly experiment with adding other product categories based on what customers tell us they'd like us to sell.

In July 2009, Zappos was acquired by Amazon in a $1.2 billion deal. Very little has changed within the business model of the company. The primary sales come from

Zappos' Ten Core Business Values

These help maintain the company's culture, and success:

1. Deliver "Wow" Through Service
2. Embrace and Drive Change
3. Create Fun and a Little Weirdness
4. Be Adventurous, Creative, and Open-Minded
5. Pursue Growth and Learning
6. Build Open and Honest Relationships with Communication
7. Build a Positive Team and Family Spirit
8. Do More with Less
9. Be Passionate and Determined
10. Be Humble

50,000+ brands of shoes. The unconventional return policy remains in place, and the company continues caring about their employees, who get free lunches, have no-charge vending machines, a company library, a nap room, and free health care.

Secrets of Funding Your Business

The startup costs of a business can vary greatly depending on the type of business and the size at which you begin. A small business might check in at $5,000 to get off the ground. A larger company could cost anywhere from $50,000 to $500,000, or more, depending on the complexity of the site, the products being

▲

sold, and how many employees you will have handling fulfillment, customer service, and the various other aspects of the business.

Fund It Yourself!

If you are starting a small online e-business, you may have saved up enough money, beyond what you need to support yourself and/or your family, to get it off the ground on your own. This is of course the preferred method for many small-business owners because they are not paying back a bank loan or indebted to anyone. It is, however, also a financial risk, so the money needs to be earmarked specifically for such a venture.

In some cases you may have an asset that you can sell to get that startup cash in hand.

Start by making a list of all your potential startup costs from the development of the website through marketing, equipment costs, and so on.

A sample of some of your startup costs might include:

- New computer
- New scanner
- New printer
- Website design and hosting
- Software programs (Photoshop, Excel, QuickBooks for accounting, etc.)
- Business phone lines or new cell phone for business only
- Marketing
- Inventory (this can be minimized by ordering products as demand grows)
- Storage costs
- Business supplies (from labels to business cards, these are important)

Operating costs are those ongoing costs of the business that will be regular expenses. This will include phone bills, rent if you are renting an office space, hosting fees, etc. Anything that will be part of your ongoing business expenses is an operating cost.

You'll want to know from the beginning that you not only have money to start your business but to run it for at least six months to a year.

Entrepreneurs have used money from an inheritance, the sale of a summer home, downsizing to a smaller location once the kids have moved out, or even from selling a collection of old comic books to start their businesses. Assets can get you started.

Another avenue is to borrow from friends and family, but make sure to have a written agreement that says when you plan to pay them back and even with interest. Be realistic, but only choose people who:

a) Believe in you

b) Are sincere about their loan: no strings attached

c) Are not unlikely to interfere with your plans: silent partners

Banks and the SBA

> ## Beware!
> Too many people get into financial trouble borrowing against their home or their credit cards. Don't put your home on the line and stay aboveboard with your credit card payments. Remember, your credit rating is at stake and you do not want to have a bad rating when starting a business. You may want to get loans or a line of credit in the future to build your business.

Yes, you can also borrow from banks or get a small business loan from the SBA (www.sba.org).

Banks, however, are not very quick to back new business ventures unless you have entrepreneurial experience and collateral. The SBA, however, has been helping small-business owners for more than 60 years and has a section on their website all about loans. They are worth checking out.

If you are thinking about obtaining a loan from a bank, a credit union, or even through the SBA, several factors may come into play:

- The economic climate
- Your track record in business
- Your credit rating (very significant)
- Your business plan

Lending institutions want to know that you are a sound credit risk. They will also want to know exactly what your future plans are, beyond simply "opening an ecommerce business." This is where your business plan comes in handy. As for your business experience, that should be included in your business plan. If it is not, then make sure you highlight exactly what you have done before that makes you the ideal person to open such a business and run it successfully. A loan is often predicated on the person behind the business.

You will also need to put up collateral for the loan. Carefully consider assets that you can use for collateral. It's usually wise to start small. Many people have started web businesses for under $5,000 and run them successfully, showing profits in a short time (such as six months). By doing this, you can establish yourself and show lenders that you know what you are doing and can at least run such a business.

You can then ask for, and receive, a small loan or a commercial line of credit to upgrade and make improvements to your site. A loan, or a commercial line of credit, is often used for business improvements. Spell out the needs for the loan and illustrate the cost of the improvements you have in mind.

It's important to get your credit scores in order before seeking a loan. You'll need to start paying off any and all outstanding debts and get to a point where you can open a new credit card or take out a small loan and pay it back promptly, thus showing you are on solid financial ground.

Having your financial ducks all in a row is important when opening a new business, not only for lenders but for yourself. Starting a business when you are already in debt is ill advised.

If you are dissatisfied with your credit scores, work on improving them slowly by paying off your debts, which may mean working out deals with creditors. Never seek out places that can "magically" repair bad credit. Remember, anything that seems too good to be true is usually a major risk and you are very likely to find yourself in a worse situation than you were in before.

Smart Tip

Tip...

If you are thinking about borrowing money from a lender of any sort, contact at least one of the big three credit bureaus for your credit scores.

- *Equifax*: 1-800-685-1111, P.O. Box 740241, Atlanta, GA 30374; www.equifax.com
- *Experian*: 1-888-397-3742, P.O. Box 2002, Allen TX 75013, www.experian.com
- *TransUnion*: 1-800-888-4213, P.O. Box 2000, Chester, PA 19022; www.transunion.com

Do this once, since loan officers will also inquire and the more your credit ratings are checked, the more suspicious it may appear to lenders. Read your credit reports over very carefully, especially if your rating is not as good as you expected it to be. Credit bureaus make more mistakes than you would ever imagine. If there are errors, contact the credit bureau and make sure to have them corrected.

Show Them the Money

Always invest some of your own money into your business, even if you have to secretly borrow it from mom and pop. Lenders and outside investors look much more favorably on a business owner if he or she is standing alongside of them and taking the same risk. They figure that if you are willing to put your own money into this venture then you will stand behind it and take it much more seriously.

Venture Capitalists

You may also look for outside investors to help you launch and even maintain your new business. Venture capital is the term for the money you are seeking. A well-constructed business plan, as we will discuss shortly, and a good presentation are necessary to interest such investors. Since you, or you and your partner(s), will be running the show, the emphasis will be on what you have to offer in terms of experience, know-how, dedication, a feel for business, and your sales and marketing skills.

Big Winners

On paper, scoring VC funding looks simple. You write a business plan wherein you pay very close attention to the possible payday ahead (typically this is made vivid with charts that forecast revenue and profits). VCs do not want to hit singles. They swing for the bleachers, and to win funding, an idea has to have the clear potential to be a major winner.

Why do VCs want big winners? Simple. They're realists who know that only a few of the ventures they fund will succeed and one out of many will be a home run. But that one home run will generate so much cash, it will make up for the losses. VCs are very careful about what they choose to fund, meaning you need to know your business ideas and plans for success very well. If you can't answer all their questions about how your business will run, what makes it unique, who's on your management team, and how it will make money, then don't bother showing up for the meeting. In short, you must be very well prepared. This doesn't mean that they won't take a chance on a new company—they may even help you mold it into a better idea—but you should come in well prepared and very confident in your plan to make money. Venture capital companies are looking for a big payday and if you don't honestly believe in your e-business, they won't either.

Also think of the exit strategy. VCs don't invest to hold; they want a way to translate a business success into an economic success. Usually, that means the company gets bought by a bigger fish in the industry.

Once you have your plan in hand—with an exit strategy and a payday spelled out for you and your investors, you look for every way possible to get it (and yourself) in front of VCs. It isn't easy. So often internet entrepreneurs complain, "I have a great business plan, and nobody will fund it." Maybe the plan is great, maybe it isn't, but step one in proving you've got what it takes to prosper in the rugged internet economy is finding a way to get in front of VCs.

You've tried and can't seem to land VC money? Borrow whatever cash you can get from the legitimate investors, whether that's your parents or your neighbor's uncle's ex-wife. Get the business afloat and then maybe VCs will come calling with cash in their hands. Even better, once a business is

Smart Tip

Where to find venture capital firms? Check out the VC links on vFinance (vfinance. com) for leads to many VC firms.

Tip...

prospering, you can usually get much more favorable terms from VCs. The earlier they come in, the bigger piece of the company they want, which means second-stage VC financing may actually be more desirable.

Inside Information

Don't get discouraged about finding VC money. Guy Kawasaki was co-founder of Garage Technology Ventures and a news aggregation site called Alltop. Even though Kawasaki was interviewed nearly a decade ago, his comments are still quite relevant today.

Garage Technology Ventures, a venture capital investment bank for emerging technology companies, encourages submissions of business plans at its website (garage. com). Here, Guy Kawasaki, a managing director at the firm, and the author of *The Art of the Start* (Portfolio), eagerly tells how to win funding from Garage Technology Ventures. Kawasaki's trademark is irreverence—his wit is quick and pointed—but read between the lines in this Q&A, and you'll discover he's telling you what your chances are and how to make them better.

Entrepreneur: *What does an entrepreneur need to get venture funding?*

Guy Kawasaki: Circa 2005, the single most important factor was to show traction, that is, that someone is already paying you for your product. If not traction, then at least you need to show that someone is testing your product and will/might pay for the product soon.

Entrepreneur: *What's your ballpark estimate of the percentage of business plans that get funded?*

Kawasaki: We get about 2,000 to 2,500 plans per year and fund ten of them. We used to receive many more plans during the 1997 to 1999 time frame, but the quality is now much higher.

Entrepreneur: *A typical complaint is, "I know nobody. Where do I start looking?" What's your answer?*

Kawasaki: Raising capital today is very challenging. You can't leave any stone unturned. This means friends, fools, family, and potential customers . . . not to mention your own pocket. The days of raising a few million with a sketch on a napkin are gone—maybe not forever, but for a few years.

Entrepreneur: *What's the minimum (realistic) funding for launching a B2B site? A B2C site?*

Kawasaki: This is tough to answer because you can't glom all B2B- or B2C-type businesses together. You could start a company with $250,000 or $250 million. It all depends. Having said this, too much money is worse than too little [because people are usually less disciplined about the way they spend when funds are plentiful].

Entrepreneur: *What's the one thing an entrepreneur can do that's sure to turn you off?*

Kawasaki: Ask me to sign an NDA [nondisclosure agreement]. Actually, there's one more thing: Show up with a PowerPoint presentation containing 50 or so slides.

Entrepreneur: *What's the one thing an entrepreneur can do that's sure to catch your interest?*

Kawasaki: Tell us that in the last 12 months they did $1 million or more in business. What has Kawasaki told you? Develop a plan that emphasizes your strengths (the reasons to fund it), keep it short, don't ask for too much money, and never ask potential funders to sign an NDA. Why the last point? NDAs—which bind the signer not to reveal what you show or tell him about your plan—are unenforceable in many cases, and, just as bad, a busy investor probably has heard much the same idea from multiple sources already.

On the other hand, complaints that investors sometimes steal good ideas are epidemic. Are the beefs founded? Hard to say—but a Silicon Valley legend is that when Sabeer Bhatia shopped his idea for what became Hotmail, he lied to would-be funders in initial meetings, telling them about a totally different business idea. Only when they passed some kind of test for Bhatia did he lay out his real idea. Paranoid? Bhatia became a very rich man when Microsoft bought Hotmail—proof that, at least in his case, caution pays.

Do you need to be as cautious as Bhatia? Not likely. Most entrepreneurs who take that closed-mouth route will simply strike out with funders. A better route is to tell what you need to tell to spark interest and then keep offering more details as investor interest looks ever more genuine. Besides, if you treat people sincerely and honestly, more often than not, you'll get much the same in return. Sure, there are crooks in Silicon Valley—but most folks are decent,

> **Tip...**
>
> **Smart Tip**
> Monogamy isn't practiced by VCs.
> Rarely will a major VC firm act as sole funder. It seems strange, but it's a fact that a VC firm will often agree to fund if you can get another firm to fund you, too. Keep in mind: VCs like to minimize risk, and one way to do it is to share investments.

well-meaning, and well-intentioned. So play things straight, and usually you'll get the results you deserve.

Your Presentation

It's not only what is on paper but it is your presentation that needs to be polished. You want to be able to convey your passion for this endeavor and your commitment (remember, investing your own money is important) if you want to be taken seriously. You also need to be ready to answer all possible questions, politely and without hesitation. For example: How long do you think it will it be before you will see a profit? Answer the question and have the paperwork ready, as discussed earlier, with your one-, three-, and five-year projections.

The point is, for financial backing in any business, you need to figure out all of the particulars in advance and be ready to answer whatever questions are asked with confidence. Hint: Don't ramble. Short answers with good explanations or specific examples will suffice.

"For the GotChef catering business and food truck, this was key. I had known the head chef, Biagio, for quite some time. He runs the number-one Zagat's and number-one open-table-rated Italian restaurant in Connecticut. He runs an amazing restaurant and has a great reputation up here," notes Joe Rubin of FundingPost (FundingPost.com) who helped GotChef get funded. You might also check out some of the many events FundingPost has on their calendar to help entrepreneurs learn how to best present themselves to investors and to meet investors face to face.

Also, consider what you are giving this investor in exchange for his or her capital. Remember, it's not a donation, it's an investment, a risky investment, and investors want to know the upside for their bank account. How are they going to get their money back, and even a profit? Work with your accountant and /or a business advisor in advance and determine the best way to repay investors.

Smart Tip

Develop your elevator pitch. You should have a very concise pitch that defines your business idea briefly, providing the type of business, the costs, your background, and why this business can work. An "elevator" pitch, typically 30 seconds, is designed to be told to a captive investor in the time it takes to ride up in an elevator. Near the end of the 1988 movie *Working Girl,* Melanie Griffith actually gives her pitch to the major investors in an elevator and wins them over by presenting a very sound and logical business proposal in roughly 30 seconds. That's how it's done.

Your Business Plan

If you foresee yourself looking for outside funding, start by creating a business plan. It does not need to be elaborate, but it should follow the basic business plan structure. Here is what you should include:

- *A short executive summary of the overall business:* Even though this goes first, you might write it last after organizing and thinking everything else through.
- *A summary of ecommerce overall*
- *A summary of your industry* (food, fashion, etc.)
- *A review of your needs*: What will you be spending the money on?
- *How your business will operate*: Will it be ecommerce only or will it be in conjunction with your brick-and-mortar operation? How will it work? Walk the reader through the process of doing business.
- *Revenue streams*: How will you make money? Sales only? Sales and membership? Affiliate programs? Any revenue stream should be explained.
- *Competition*: Review some of the businesses out there doing what you do and explain what you can do better. Explain how you differ from the e-businesses in your industry.
- *Bio*: Briefly explain your background as it pertains to your new business. Also include the bios on your team members if you know who they will be. This is very important!
- *Financials*: Show profit and loss projections for the coming months and even three years. Hint: Be conservative in your estimates.

> **Beware!**
> Bring in VC money, and you could lose control of your business. That's just a reality. For every entrepreneur who stays on top, there are several entrepreneurs with ideas that are good enough to get funded who don't personally inspire confidence—and they get pushed aside.
> Discuss what the VC plans to do with your business: Don't be intimidated.

A business plan can help you see all the aspects of the business and serve as a personal guide. It can show investors that you literally mean business and can provide a snapshot of what it is your business will do and how it will make money. It is a document that essentially tells the story of what you plan to do and how you are going to use investors' money to achieve your goals. Hint: Be realistic, stick to the facts, and don't add a lot of hyperbole.

Why Financial Angels Fund Startups

Do you believe in angels? After reading this chapter, you just might. With a little luck and lots of persistence on your part, angels—of the flesh-and-blood variety—may fund your internet venture.

According to research conducted by Jeffrey E. Sohl, director of the Center for Venture Research at the University of New

Hampshire's Whittemore School of Business and Economics, there were approximately 50 formal business angel groups in the United States in 1997. By 2010 there were more than 150 formal and informal organizations located throughout leading technology and business regions in the United States and Canada. Collectively, these formal angel alliances represent only a portion of the angel market.

Where do you find angels? The Angel Capital Association (ACA, www.angelcapital association.org) has an online listing of angel groups that are members in good standing, as well as organizations affiliated with the ACA. You'll also find international angel groups from Gust.com if you click on Browse Ivestors & Startups. You could also visit FundingPost at www.fundingpost.com, where you can find events where investors can actually meet angels.

If you keep your eyes open, and do some networking, you also may find angels through personal connections because angels are often friends of friends or parents of friends.

Why do they invest? For many angels it's a thrill to get involved in a startup. Maybe they don't want to personally run one, but they are nonetheless excited about being on the periphery and offering advice in addition to capital. Of course, there is also the real possibility of hitting a major home run.

How does angel investing work? We found two angels who agreed to provide insight into what they do.

George McQuilkin is co-founder and a member of eCoast Angels Network (ecoastangels.com), a small group of angel investors in New Hampshire who offer funding on an individual basis to promising new companies as well as ongoing ventures. John May is managing partner of the New Vantage Group (newvantagegroup.com), a Washington, DC, company that manages next-generation early-stage venture funds for active angel investors. Their methods and approaches differ, but that's the norm: No two angels have exactly the same motivations. But if you understand who angels are and how to persuade them, you just might get one to put cash into your company.

George McQuilkin has been around the business block more than a few times. An MIT graduate, McQuilkin worked with IBM for 16 years, left to start a company called Spartacus Computers, and ran a few other companies, including RSA Security, which sold for more than $1.5 billion.

Entrepreneur: *How did you get into angel investing?*

George McQuilkin: I made some money on RSA Security, and I decided to use it to invest in some venture capital funds and, at the same time, I made some direct angel investments. I was at a limited partners meeting of a venture fund in the late 1990s when I realized that I seemed to be doing better on the investment I made directly, and I also took more satisfaction out of that. I had met influential people like Mort Goulder, an angel investor who had made well over 100 investments. He was the founder of the Breakfast Club, which in this part of the country is the oldest continually running angel investor group around. I thought it would be good to start a group like that because I wanted to increase the number of deals I looked at, have the ability to spread the risk, and have the ability to bring experience to bear. When I moved back to Portsmouth in 2000, I found four other like-minded individuals, and we started a group called the eCoast Angels.

Entrepreneur: *How does your group operate?*

McQuilkin: We started this angel group with an old-fashioned format: a group of people who come together for a common purpose. It's very Benjamin Franklin-y. We are neither a charity nor an economic development unit. We share advice and information, and we make up our own minds on each investment so there is no group fund. And we don't have a formal process, but that doesn't mean we don't have a process or we don't know what we're doing. It's just that we choose to make this decentralized so there's no administrative burden.

Entrepreneur: *What's the basic difference between an angel investor and a venture capitalist?*

McQuilkin: Motivation. Angels are investing their own money, and everyone has his or her own reasons for doing it. Mort Goulder said one of the key reasons he enjoyed being an angel investor is he liked to help the other guy. He said this technology and economic system had been really good to him, and he wants to give the other guy a chance to participate the same way. If you're a venture capitalist, you're actually investing somebody else's money and you have both the legal and the fiduciary responsibility to maximize their return. That doesn't mean you have to be unfair or unscrupulous, but it's harder to be an idealist with somebody else's money. An angel investor's motivation is to be part of the action, to be involved with new companies.

Most angels are entrepreneurs who started a successful business and they cashed out by selling the business or through an IPO. They don't just want to use their extra money; they want to be part of the excitement. A venture capitalist doesn't take the risks, doesn't meet the entrepreneur. If it's a tournament, you're jousting through surrogates. Some people like the hands-on feel, like the action, like being part of the technology. There is an arrogance among entrepreneurs, myself included, that causes them to want to start a business with one or two million dollars and go take on IBM or Google or Microsoft. It would be laughable if people hadn't been successful doing it, including Google and Microsoft. So there's the challenge, the opportunity, the matching of wits; that's a high. I think making money is lower down on the angel investor's list, though good angel investors on the whole tend to do better on returns on investment than do venture capitalists.

Entrepreneur: *How many plans does your group look at in a year?*

McQuilkin: We get in excess of 100 inquiries a year. I screen a lot of them myself or with someone else, and we look seriously at 20 to 25 a year. Of those, we'll probably invite 18 in to make a presentation. Sometimes we'll have a meeting without a formal presentation or sometimes I'll go to some other group's meeting. In other words, we'll meet with people without necessarily having them stand in front of the group. Of those submitted last year, we made 14 investments. Seven were new companies, and seven were follow-ups to previous investments. Not every member of the group invests every time. A typical angel in our group makes one to four investments a year.

Entrepreneur: *How much can an entrepreneur expect to get from you?*

McQuilkin: A very reasonable amount to ask for would be $500,000, though we could do $1 million or $2 million. We would then probably want to bring in other groups we are friendly with to share the risk. Getting an early-stage, fairly rapid investment of $300,000 to $500,000 is very realistic with our group.

Entrepreneur: *How can an entrepreneur find an angel?*

McQuilkin: They should talk to everyone they know, and they should use their own network. Angel groups tend to invest regionally. We have a broad experience in the group and good connections to companies, but we can't really use that for you unless you're an hour or two drive from here. Since we like to play an active role, we want to do that nearby. But if you're a serious entrepreneur and you pay attention to the business press and you can't find us, then you're not doing your job as an entrepreneur. You can also just approach us and say "I've heard of you." But again, you surely know somebody who knows us from the MIT Club, from the High Technology Council, the local high school, the community, lawyers, accountants, etc. An entrepreneur who is doing his job, which is to marshal resources in support of his vision, really ought to be able to find a better way to get to us than to just send us a generic cold email. The best email will say: "I met you at the meeting of the Technology Council and we talked about this and I know you might not remember me, but you had said you were interested in investments like this." Right away, I'm very receptive to that. The ones that say "to whom it may concern" are bad, very bad. If you're not willing to do a little bit of work to find us and get us information, I'm not willing to evaluate it.

Entrepreneur: *What can an entrepreneur do to get a yes, and what is sure to get a no?*

McQuilkin: The key is to explain why we want to invest in this business, not why your technology is a good idea. Typically entrepreneurs are in love with their business vision. That can be true if it's pizza sauce or extensive use of nanotechnology. So they'll get up, tell us all about their thing and run out of time, and never get around to telling us how much money they need and what they're going to do with it, and why this is good for us. They forget why they're talking to us. You'll also get turned down if you change the deal—that will get you almost thrown out. And finally, the entrepreneur has to have a realistic idea of what they're selling in terms of ownership and control. If you just say I want your money, but I'll run the business my own way and I don't need your advice or assistance, then I'm going to say then you don't need my money and you're not going to get it.

John May is not only the managing partner and co-founder of the New Vantage Group, but he has extensive experience as a venture fund manager, advisor, and angel. He has been a partner or consultant to five venture funds and is also managing general partner of Seraphim Capital, a London-based venture capital firm founded in 2006. The company specializes in providing capital and assistance to emerging growth companies through noninstitutional sources. May is also co-founder (in 2004) and current chairman of the Angel Capital Association, a North American professional alliance of angel groups. This fast-growing association brings together 103 angel group leaders around the country to share best practices, to network, and to help develop data about the field of angel investing. May has spoken extensively on angel and early-stage equity investing, is a Batten Fellow at the University of Virginia's Darden School of Business, and is the co-author of a book on angel investing, *Every Business Needs an Angel* (Crown Business).

Entrepreneur: *What's the difference between an angel and a venture capitalist?*

John May: The main difference is that angels consider psychic reward as one of their major criteria [in deciding what to invest in]. They get an emotional, or personal, benefit from it, as opposed to venture capitalists, who get more of a financial benefit from the transaction.

Entrepreneur: *What's the biggest mistake entrepreneurs make in approaching angels?*

May: Being fixated on their evaluation and not being flexible. An angel might be willing to have a negotiation about their role and their money, but if entrepreneurs assume that an angel is fixated on a high rate of return only, they will be shooting themselves in the foot.

Smart Tip

Tip...

Practice, practice, practice. Before you go into any meetings with VCs or angels, really hone your presentation on your business—this can prove a lot more crucial than your business plan in the funding decision. Why? Investors invest in people who inspire them. Go in with a pitch that wows listeners, and you may walk out with a big check.

Entrepreneur: *What's the one thing entrepreneurs can do to make their case stronger?*

May: Network through friends and trusted advisors. Also, if you are planning to be a high-growth company and you plan to raise outside money—which not every entrepreneur plans to do—it's probably a good idea to also have sophisticated counsel, accountants, and an advisory board.

Entrepreneur: *How many business plans come through your door monthly? How many do you think get funded by anybody?*

May: We generally look at about 50 to 100 plans per month. Most entrepreneurs submit through the web; most angel groups have application forms on their websites, and entrepreneurs either fill it out there or they send an executive summary attached to an email. This seems to be the dominant entry point for entrepreneurs. Out of 100 plans, 10 will most likely be presented to our group, and one or two of those may get funded. But keep in mind, there are far more angel transactions per year than venture capitalist transactions.

There are angel investors in all 50 states, and every major metropolitan area has an angel group, while venture capital is heavily concentrated in California and New England.

Entrepreneur: *What are angel investors looking for in startups?*

May: Today, they are looking for mature management rather than wide-eyed ideas.

Later On

Angels can help you later on, too! Most entrepreneurs need second or third rounds of funding once they get off the ground. Angel investments can also be perfect for businesses that are established beyond the startup phase, but are still early enough in the

> **Tip...**
>
> **Smart Tip**
>
> If you're based in the Washington, DC, or Seattle area, check out New Vantage Group (newvantagegroup.com), and see if there's anything there for you. Don't submit material too early—wait until it's polished. But once your business plan is solid, get a move on!

> **Beware!**
>
> Don't give it all away! You may find one or multiple investors ready to give you money for a piece of the action. While you may be excited about the funding, it is very important that you do not give everything away. You will be giving up a percentage of your profits, but keep a close eye on how much you are giving to your investors. Remember, you are in this to make money for yourself as well. Also, be careful not to give up control of your business. Guidance is fine, but do not let investors take over your company.

game that they need capital to develop a product or fund a marketing strategy. Angel investors may be very impressed once you've shown them that you have a business up and running and want to move on to the next phase. They can also serve as mentors, since most angels have a personal interest in the type of business in which they invest.

Echat with Corporate Toner's Kapil Juneja

Corporate Toners Inc.

Kapil Juneja, COO, CTO, and Co-founder
Location: Canoga Park, California
Year Started: 2002

Corporate Toners Inc., which was founded in 2002 by Kapil Juneja and Mike Costache, prides itself on providing the highest-quality inkjet cartridges, refill kits, remanufactured cartridges, and toner

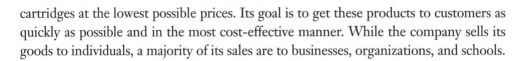

cartridges at the lowest possible prices. Its goal is to get these products to customers as quickly as possible and in the most cost-effective manner. While the company sells its goods to individuals, a majority of its sales are to businesses, organizations, and schools.

Entrepreneur: *What's been your biggest surprise at Corporate Toners?*

Kapil Juneja: We were astonished when we found ourselves struggling to get the banks to provide us with additional credit-card processing capacity every third month as our company grew 100 percent month-on-month during the first year. We were a startup company with a short track record, run by two fresh college graduates. It was a big challenge to convince the banks that we were a legitimate business with real growth. It was like doing everything right in starting a business just to find out that you can't collect money from the banks. Finally, the banks issued a bigger credit line, and since then we created a multimillion-dollar company.

A booming business should be a cause for celebration, but at Corporate Toners, it was something of a mixed blessing. As sales increased sharply—from 150 orders per day in August 2004 to 300 per day by January 2005, we found that an old infrastructure was making it hard to manage new business. Customer records were incomplete, customer inquiries were not attended to on time, and business information was scattered across different databases. It was a less-than-ideal way [to run and grow a business].

With sales information stored on so many systems and so many login passwords to remember, it was hard to find customers' data when customers called us. We quickly adopted an all-in-one ecommerce CRM [customer relations management system], and back-end technology platform provided by a San Mateo, California-based company, NetSuite Inc. They offered everything we needed from the ability to have all data in one central location to the ability to set up customized transactions for each of our sites so we could integrate all the processes in an online platform available to all our employees at different locations.

Entrepreneur: *Did you approach investors?*

Juneja: We sure did. We went to various seminars and events organized by the likes of the Los Angeles Venture Association (LAVA); The Indus Entrepreneurs (TiE), a Washington, DC-based nonprofit global network of entrepreneurs and professionals, established to foster entrepreneurship and nurture entrepreneurs; and the Larta Institute, a Los Angeles-based nonprofit group that connects technology startups with funding. And we networked with alumni from our school, Pepperdine University.

We actually met an interested investor at LAVA's annual Investment Capital Conference in early 2002, and the fact that he was an alumnus of Pepperdine and had a large accounting firm and the gray hair we needed made us think we found our ideal investor.

We talked to various [other] investors, but in 2002, nobody cared to finance a B2B startup with no proprietary technology and no real competitive advantage. Every door we opened was shut with a nice, "Come back with something more tangible, 'cause I like you guys, and I see your burning desire to be entrepreneurs." But we knew that we had something going for us: We were experts in getting on the top five results in search engines through search engine optimization. This traffic cost us nothing since we understood how the search engines worked and reverse-engineered the process to beat their rules.

We were about to make a huge mistake by giving 33 percent of the company's equity for $35,000 in cash and office space for the first year in our investor/incubator's firm [the accounting company mentioned earlier]. Luckily for us, the investor kept prolonging the negotiations, knowing that we were two young guys out of college pressured for money. We decided to stop all negotiations since we realized that it was a really bad deal for us. That was probably the best decision we've made to date.

Entrepreneur: *How is building a B2B site different from building a B2C site?*

Juneja: It's a completely different mentality when servicing a $20,000 repeat order from a B2B customer than a $53 one-time order from John Doe with no loyalty to your product or service. During the early phases of running an e-business, we realized that—and our research concluded the same—businesses are the biggest consumers of printer supply products. They remain loyal as long as you consistently provide them with good products and excellent service.

So we built a professional-looking B2B website while providing 100 percent quality products, money-back guarantees, and good customer service. We wanted the website to be easy to navigate, quick to load, and have quality content to keep the trust and loyalty of our corporate customers. In the online B2B marketplace, you compete with the companies that might be 10 to 1,000 times larger than your company. The disadvantage of being a smaller company compared with the big sharks is overcome by employing the right back-end management and sales tools. We learned it the hard way when we lost a couple of our big corporate customers as we were not able to service them accurately on time.

[That's when we integrated] NetSuite, which gave us better organization of our sales data and more information on our customers, which boosts customer service and leads to customer retention and repeat business. NetSuite offers us the tools to provide a world-class service to our B2B customers.

Beware!
Juneja was smart: He had a bad feeling about an investor who was stringing the company along, so he decided to stop all negotiations. The moral of the story? When it comes to money, go with your gut.

▲

Entrepreneur: *Is there a potentially bigger payout in B2B? Why?*

Juneja: B2B has a different cash flow model where customers want competitive pricing with payment terms compared with B2C credit card transactions, where the bank provides the money in three to five days from the transaction date. Selling to well-established businesses requires that you provide them with a high level of customer service (pre- and post-sale). Price is not always the key, but service is. An individual one-time buyer is much more price-sensitive compared with a corporate client, who may

> ⚠️ **Beware!**
> In a struggling U.S. economy, there are an increasing number of both businesses and consumers who support American businesses and frown upon companies taking jobs away from American workers by outsourcing them to other countries. You need to consider the potential of losing some customers and the possible backlash if you go this route.

remain your customer for life as long as you consistently provide them with good products and service. Higher sales volume, repeat business, and high retention rate are some of the major advantages when you deal with corporate clients. In the long run, B2B definitely is a bigger payout. As long as you keep your business customers happy, they will continue to give their business to you.

Entrepreneur: *What advantage do you have over the many competitors in your space?*

Juneja: We specialize in marketing our website online on various search engines where we are able to get high ranking on thousands of keywords related to our products. Of course, customer service, quality products, and competitive prices all matter, but our margins are bigger than our competitors because we have a very low cost of customer acquisition.

Technology is one of the key advantages that we have over our competitors. Using NetSuite's technology with our websites, we have an all-in-one system to manage all our business processes compared with our competitors, who may use a virtual armada of stand-alone software packages. We not only save our time and customers' time, we are able to provide a superb customer service, which is a key when dealing with corporate customers.

Since our systems and websites are based online, we also enjoy the advantages of running our inbound customer service and outbound telemarketing call center from New Delhi, India. The lower cost of running the operation in India combined with highly skilled English-speaking employees enables us to provide excellent service to our customers on time.

Finally, we have better coordination between our warehouse and our sales office in Los Angeles and our back-end customer service and support.

Cheap Tricks with Redwagons.com's Tony Roeder

RedWagons.com

Tony Roeder, President and Founder
Location: River Forest, Illinois
Year Started: 1998

Talk about a niche market! This is the most preeminent kid's

wagon lover's website of them all (or of the few out there).

Sure they have scooters and some bikes, but this is *the* place to find that red wagon for your kids, or that you secretly want to pull around when nobody's looking.

Tony Roeder is the type of entrepreneur you want to be—with a smart observation and a lot of hard work, he's built a sustainable web business. In 1998, with virtually no experience, capital, or programming skills, he launched RedWagons.com, a site that sells a full line of Radio Flyer wagons, accessories, and other products. The company, which initially enjoyed rapid growth by being a niche business, rode the ups and downs of the "early internet era." Fifteen years later, although not a household name, RedWagons.com shares a once-empty niche with Amazon.com, ToysRUs.com, Target.com, Walmart.com, and a whole other host of toy startups. RedWagons.com continues on, constantly changing and innovating to stay competitive in the face of stiff and powerful competition.

How did Roeder, a former handyman, get the idea to launch the site?

In 1998, he was on a customer's porch assembling a Radio Flyer wagon when he was struck by the look and feel of the wagon. He had lots of memories of Radio Flyer products growing up and started thinking about what a great company Radio Flyer was. Says Roeder, "Radio Flyer has been a part of my earliest childhood memories, from the Radio Flyer wagon we had careening down our suburban driveway, to the old rusty wagon I pulled my children around in at the time I was sitting on that porch."

He was also looking for another line of work and wondered about etailing, since he worked regularly with a hardware store that had started selling Weber grills online. Roeder realized there was a lot of opportunity in this arena.

Then, by chance, he ran into a person who worked for Radio Flyer and had a casual conversation with the employee about putting a wagon together for one of his customers. When he learned that Radio Flyer was not selling its products online—despite its online presence—he jumped at the chance to do just that, despite the fact that he had no internet experience at the time.

Here, Roeder offers his insights into starting a successful dotcom company.

Entrepreneur: *How did you start your website?*

Tony Roeder: I first hired a web designer for $4,000 who worked for Radio Flyer's informational website, but he had never done an ecommerce site before and basically could not get the site up in a reasonable [amount of time]. I had to fire him. I then contacted Yahoo! and built my site on the Yahoo! Store [now called Yahoo! Merchant Solutions] system. Their costs were pay as you go, and back then, it was about $200 or $300 per month, which was less than what the designer was going to charge me for monthly maintenance.

Yahoo! made it possible for me to be my own web designer and store builder virtually overnight. The site went live in November 1998, just in time for the holiday season.

Entrepreneur: *How do you handle fulfillment?*

Roeder: Fulfillment is an ever-evolving process, but the key is that we make an effort to get products shipped out as soon as possible.

Entrepreneur: *What are the secrets to your success?*

Roeder: The combination of the Yahoo! exposure, good search engine placement, and good links put us on the map.

Technology has also been very important to our company. Most of our challenges have been met by judiciously applying technology to our processes.

Entrepreneur: *What are your plans for the future? Your goals and objectives?*

Roeder: In general, our objective is to maintain profitability and to be innovative. Our birth, growth, and explosion were due to having a vision and openness for change in my life; being at the right place at the right time; and the willingness to take risks. Those particular opportunities may not exist today, but there are always new ones. You have to be able to identify them and take the necessary actions to get the business rolling. We try to stay current with what is new and what is changing in the industry and adjust appropriately. We are also constantly refining our processes, our marketing, and our communication—and we try to always be aware of our competition so we can continue to grow as a company.

Smart Tip

Tip...

An opportunity to start a successful business can happen when you least expect it. For Tony Roeder, a chance meeting with someone from Radio Flyer, the red wagon company, was the catalyst that prompted him to start his company, RedWagons.com. Always keep an open mind; you never know where or when a chance to start a business will pop up.

Cashing in on Affiliate Programs

Want to generate cash, now, from your website? Even sites that aren't ecommerce-enabled—meaning they retail nothing—can put money in your pocket through the many affiliate programs found on the web. Affiliate marketing is used by many websites and by bloggers to generate "passive income."

From Amazon to OfficeMax, leading online retailers are eager to pay you for driving sales their way. How? By putting their link, which can be a banner or even text, on your site. Numerous coupon sites today are also now offering affiliate programs where all you need to do is link to their site and you can post their coupons.

For every click-through that results in a sale, you will earn a commission, anywhere from 1 to 25 percent for multichannel retailers or 30 to 50 percent in the software sector. In some cases, you can get commissions on all sales that take place up to 10 days after you send someone to a site. For example, if a customer visits your site and clicks on the leading online company's banner ad and doesn't buy anything right away but purchases something a few days later, you still get credit for the sale.

In some cases, you are compensated even if the visitor doesn't buy anything, just for having driven traffic to the merchant's site. This is not as popular as the former examples, however. The affiliate's reward varies from merchant to merchant and program to program, depending on the terms of the merchant's offer.

In the Beginning

Amazingly it was two decades ago, in 1994, that Amazon launched an affiliate program as a marketing strategy, making it among the earliest online companies to utilize this approach. It is now estimated that Amazon has over a million affiliates worldwide.

It All Clicks

Supposedly, the idea for affiliate programs—where big merchants enlist small sites as a de facto sales force—got its start when a woman talking with Amazon.com founder Jeff Bezos at a cocktail party in 1996 asked how she might sell books about divorce on her website. Bezos noodled the idea, and a light bulb went on. He realized the opportunities for both to benefit were great, and the upshot was the launch of Amazon's affiliate program, one of the industry's most successful.

What's the appeal of affiliate programs? "The [main] appeal lies in the fact that affiliate marketing is primarily tied to performance," says Wayne Porter, co-founder of ReveNews.com, which focuses on internet-related industries such as online marketing, affiliate marketing, retail (ecommerce) and more. "Marketers are not paying for relationships or placements that aren't productive. It is not without risk, nor is it always the most cost-effective in the long term, but dollar for dollar, it is usually a good investment."

How big is affiliate marketing? Although it's not as big a part of their overall sales and marketing program as paid search or email, affiliate marketing is an effective strategy to build broader brand awareness and drive motivated buyers to business-to-consumer ecommerce sites, say web retailers participating in *Internet Retailer* surveys.

Many web retailers have already made a multiyear investment in affiliate marketing and count on a network of several thousand affiliates to drive visitor traffic, according to the magazine's survey. But most have pared back their programs because of unqualified traffic and fear of litigation. The trend has steered away from automatic approval where anybody could become a partner. Now retailers are scrutinizing partner candidates.

Google AdSense Makes Sense

Since 2003, one of the most significant changes in affiliate marketing has been the emergence of Google's AdSense. Today, AdSense (www.google.com/adsense) lets you utilize display ads on your website that are suited to your audience's interests, and earn revenue from valid clicks or impressions. You can also use mobile web pages so people can click from anywhere. AdSense is staying ahead of the curve when it comes to new ways to utilize your site to make money.

There are many pluses to using AdSense. For example, proponents say AdSense is simple and free to join, you don't have to use different codes for various affiliate programs, and you can concentrate on providing good content because Google does the work of finding the best ads for your pages from more than 600,000 AdWords advertisers.

The payment you receive per click depends on how much advertisers are paying per click to advertise using Google's AdWords service. "Small affiliates now have a more acceptable way to monetize their web real estate for internet content, including RSS feeds, podcasts, and video," says Porter.

A key reason for the success of AdSense is its revenue model: It offered a cost-per-click model vs. a cost-per-action or cost-per-sale model. In other words, for affiliates to get paid, visitors to a site "just had to send a qualified click instead of having to complete a transaction," explains Porter. "One of the reasons for the success of the cost-per-click model is it shifted the risk away from the affiliate, making it simpler. Now Google has added cost-per-action, traditional affiliate style, into the mix."

▲

Solid Links

AdSense aside, is it difficult to create an affiliate link? The job is simple, and you'll have it done within a minute or three. It works like this: You select the logo or link you want to show on your site. Most etailers offer many choices in their affiliate programs, so you can get exactly the look you want. Click the logo you like, and the etailer will automatically generate code that does two things: links to the etailer and includes your affiliate ID so you can earn commissions. Then you copy that code and paste it into the proper location on your site.

Doing all this is grunt work, not rocket science, and within a few minutes the link should look spiffy. Want to see this procedure in action? Head to Amazon's excellent resources for affiliates at affiliate-program.amazon.com.

No matter how spiffy your affiliate links appear and how heavy your traffic is, you won't necessarily see big profits resulting from affiliate programs. To make money, you have to follow the rules.

- *Rule Number 1.* Don't make affiliate links your sole content. The advice seems obvious, but the web still includes sites that are simply cluttered with pages that consist of nothing but banners from affiliates. Nobody is apt to buy anything from these sites. That's why a basic element in setting up a thriving affiliation deal is to strictly limit the number of programs you join. You don't want a blizzard of banners on your site.

- *Rule Number 2.* "Do contextual placement; it's important," advises ReveNews. com's Porter. Rarely should there be more than a single affiliate link on any page—and if you explain why you are endorsing this merchant and merchandise, you may just get visitors to check it out. A saloon owner, for instance, might recommend a cocktail recipe book; a website design firm might endorse a web hosting service. An exception to this rule might be a comparison shopping service.

- *Rule Number 3.* Seek feedback from your site visitors. Do they find the links to affiliates useful? Distracting? Annoying? Pay attention to what they tell you—and if they're not clicking through to your affiliate merchants,

Smart Tip

Tip...

Once you've pasted in an affiliate code, always preview the revised page in all relevant browsers before going live. Often the placement isn't where you'd thought it would be (centering a logo can be downright tricky—just use trial and error), and sometimes the link is dead (usually because a tiny bit of code got cut off during copying and pasting).

that, too, tells you something. Put up different banners, try another merchant mix or placement of the real estate, or take them down altogether.

Pros and Cons of Affiliate Marketing

As is always the case when it comes to making money, there are upsides and downsides and affiliate marketing certainly has both.

 Beware!
Never forget that a bad shopping experience at an affiliate site will tarnish your reputation, too. Choose affiliates cautiously, monitor them (check into their sites), and carefully heed any feedback you get from your visitors. Better still, shop at your affiliated merchants yourself and swiftly eliminate any that don't measure up. You simply can't afford links to bad affiliates.

The Positives

- Affiliate programs are easy to find and typically very easy to set up. This means you have a low-cost means of making some additional revenue.

- Typically they are cost free. You are helping the merchant make additional sales, as well as market their business, so you should not have to pay.

- You can tie in appropriate products for your demographic audience. For example, they can buy your cookware and then link to Amazon and buy a cookbook, from which you get a commission.

- It's an additional revenue stream for your business.

The Negatives

- If you are affiliated with Amazon or another major merchant, you are one of many affiliates, which will make it difficult to generate much money.

- Affiliate contracts often have a lot of fine print, which means there are often many stipulations before you collect your money. You may also find membership fees or other fees that you have to pay. Steer clear of any such fee-based programs.

- If you connect with a less than reputable merchant you will be jeopardizing your own reputation.

- Links may not always work or the merchant may suddenly change the program.

▲

Guard Your Affiliate ID

With its high payoff potential, affiliate marketing has become a target for scammers and devious individuals wanting to earn from other people's hard work. Therefore, it's important that you know whom you are dealing with. There are also hijackers who feed on affiliate sites, often by simply changing the end of the site address, which is the affiliate ID, and replacing it with their own. You need to make sure you have as much online protection as possible for your site and your links. What you can do, as a simple means of thwarting hijackers, is use a Javascript redirect page. By doing this you can hide the link on the page and it will redirect to your affiliate page. They can still change the redirect link, but many folks who are looking to quickly make a change to their link won't bother. However, to stop more determined hijackers, you'll want to use URL encryption and read up on (or consult with an expert in) hijack preventions. In the end, it's hard to shut them down, but the harder you make it for someone to get to your affiliate ID the safer you are.

- Selling for someone else can detract from making your own sales. You don't want to lose visitors to another site or divert their attention from what you are selling.

Another way of connecting with other merchants is through a partnership. Typically this is hard to find when you are first starting out since you have little traffic to entice someone to partner with your site. But once you have built up your site through marketing, and if you have a complementary product or service, you may make a direct partnership whereby you sell one another's products and/or make a commission for doing so.

Making a direct partnership means you will be transparent to one another. This way you can work together on the offers that you make on each other's sites. You can also hone your ads to fit your partner's sites and vice versa.

When affiliate programs work, they work, but when they don't, no website owner should hesitate to take down the links and call it a noble but failed experiment. Check out affiliate programs, but don't be shy about pulling the plug if you're not seeing meaningful returns.

Teaming Up with Big Brick-and-Mortar Companies

Forming alliances with major corporations has become a common strategy for dotcom companies seeking to carve out a niche for themselves in an ever more brutally competitive marketplace. Why? Nowadays branding is crucial—it takes a name and a sizable chunk of consumer mind share to win eyeballs, and getting there is an expensive proposition.

While many small companies are able to use clever social media marketing to gain brand awareness, teaming up with a bigger, established, business in some manner can also be a benefit. Sometimes the bigger fish even pays top dollar for the smaller one in an acquisition.

Aligning with a big partner lets you instantly get multiple pluses: cash, deep management expertise, and—when it benefits you—a name you can use to help open doors. Those are very real, very substantial benefits, and that's why partnering takes place (in the best possible sense of the word) among dotcoms.

A good example of a dotcom company partnering successfully with a big brick-and-mortar company is The Knot Inc. (TheKnot.com). This New York-based life-stage media company offers products and services for couples in the five-year span from proposal to pregnancy. Before the network expanded to this five-year period, The Knot got its start in weddings and formed a strategic alliance with The May Department Stores Co. in St. Louis.

In 2002, the two companies launched a strategic marketing alliance linking TheKnot.com to the wedding-gift registry sites of May's department stores. With a $5 million investment, May purchased a 19.5 percent interest in The Knot and was given a place on The Knot's board of directors. Since the May Company became part of the Federated Department Store's retail empire, operating as Macy's, the partnership has grown. Through their joint venture, The Knot and Macy's launched their own Lifestyle Registry, a unique registry tool located on TheKnot.com, designed to help couples jump-start the overwhelming process of crafting the perfect wedding registry.

The Knot has formed other partnerships as well. In November 2004, The Knot and Michael C. Fina, a New York City specialty retailer of fine home goods and jewelry, signed an agreement making Michael C. Fina the exclusive provider of china, crystal, and silver to The Knot's Gift Registry. In addition, in April 2005, the Target Club Wedd gift registry announced that it formed a partnership with The Knot. Under the agreement, Target Club Wedd was The Knot's premier registry provider and was featured prominently in The Knot's Gift Registry Center.

The partnerships with Michael C. Fina and Target have since expired and been replaced, largely due to the monumental acquisition of WeddingChannel.com—the leading wedding registry resource—by The Knot in 2006.

In addition, WeddingChannel.com, which provides everything from wedding hairstyles to honeymoons, has partnered with various other leading retailers in the United States, forming the largest aggregated registry service on the internet. WeddingChannel has a patent on registry aggregation and currently has more than 2.2 million registries searchable for prospective gift givers in its registry finder.

This is just one example of how one site can have a number of successful alliances.

Risky Business

As good as some of the news is about the partnerships that are proliferating throughout the dotcom world, there's also a dark side. For example, big companies often put up their money but are unprepared to offer anything more. Another trouble spot is pointed out by INSEAD's Philip Anderson: "Almost by definition, you're taking the larger brand where it hasn't been before. That's a recipe for conflict." Chew on that, because it's at the paradoxical core of small-big alliances. The big company wants the little partner for its creativity, its innovation, and its ability to plunge into terrain previously unexplored by the big fellow. But once the deal is done, the risk aversion that is at the heart of virtually all mega-corporations kicks in, and suddenly the partner is counseling caution and slow forward motion.

Another problem is that today it is more difficult for young technology companies to find willing deep-pocketed partners, says Christopher O'Leary, a vice president with The Concours Group, a management consulting, research, and education firm in Kingwood, Texas. He points to several reasons for this, including the increasing scarcity of capital, the equivocal success of past alliances, and simply the fact that there are more Cinderellas looking for a ticket to the ball.

Another worry is that a big company may acquire effective control of a little company, meaning that although a straightforward acquisition hasn't been done, by taking command of key functions such as accounting, or by assuming multiple board seats, the big company has simply grabbed control. As a result, you absolutely need a third party to assist you in creating a fair deal.

Ken Burke, founder and CEO of Petaluma, California–based MarketLive, an ecommerce tool developer that in 1998 brought in print manufacturer R.R. Donnelly as a sizable partner, seconds that recommendation. It took eight months to negotiate the deal—which, according to Burke, left him still controlling the vast majority of the company's ownership. "Donnelly has no real decision-making power," he says. But, he says, a key for him was hiring good lawyers. "They found many things in the deal we had to get revised or deleted. You don't want to negotiate this sort of thing alone."

> ## Smart Tip
> Tip...
>
> Don't use just any lawyer to consult with when a tech marriage looms. Find one in a tech center—Silicon Valley; San Francisco; New York City; Austin, Texas—with prior experience in doing deals, and be prepared to pay fees that start upward of $500 per hour. Look at that money as an investment in your future, because that's exactly what it is.

Don't pop the cork to celebrate a business alliance too soon—60 percent of alliances fall apart within three and a half years, says Larraine Segil, author of *FastAlliances: Power Your E-Business* (John Wiley & Sons) and *Partnering: The New Face of Leadership* (Amacom). Just why do these marriages unravel? Incompatible corporate cultures were cited by a majority of the executives Segil surveyed. Seventy-three percent pointed to incompatible management cultures, 63 percent referred to incompatible management personalities, and 55 percent said that different business priorities contributed to the falling out. A majority of the companies surveyed felt that all three factors contributed, but some felt that one or two contributed more than others.

That's why Segil tells small companies to ask themselves: If this marriage ends in divorce, do I have the resources to recover?

Beware!

Are you concerned about simply being acquired—and losing all effective control? Before making any partnership deal, do research that tells you how many small companies the big company that's courting you has swallowed up in the past few years. If the number is high, that's not necessarily an indication that you need to back away from the deal. But it does mean you need to be aware of the possible outcomes. Do your homework and see how many of the companies that were purchased have remained autonomous and how many have taken on the brand and business model of the larger company.

If you don't, get moving on developing a separation strategy. Maybe it will never be deployed, but with more than half of corporate marriages ending in quickie divorces, prudence dictates concocting an exit strategy before entering into a partnership agreement.

There are other things companies can do to help the alliance succeed. "In order for partnerships to work, it is important that the courtship be more deliberate and involve deeper investigation than may have been required in the past," says The Concours Group's O'Leary. He explains that enterprise strategies and operating models should be compared for compatibility and consistency.

In general, "a dedication of resources to alliances and the adoption of best practices are crucial to successful alliances," says Bill Lundberg, founding president and executive director of the Association of Strategic Alliance Professionals Inc. (ASAP) in Wellesley, Massachusetts.

What are some of these best practices? "Alliances formed must be driven from the business development objectives that the company has," says Lundberg.

Which companies would be preferred partners? Lundberg says asking where the value is migrating in the market, what resources you need to deliver that are valuable to the customer, which of those resources you have, and which you need to bring in from the outside will give you the profile of preferred partners.

Then, Lundberg says, "You have to make sure that the alliance is built around a compelling value proposition, both for each of the alliance partners and for the customer. If it is not compelling and doesn't add substantial value, it's not worth doing."

Lundberg says you also need a clear operations plan for the alliance, clear metrics to measure the value being created, clear commitments of resources to drive performance of the alliance, clear commitment by senior management of each partner, and champions driving the daily performance of the alliance.

> **Beware!**
>
> Toysmart, the now-defunct online toy store, thought it had a primo deal when Disney acquired it in 1999 for an undisclosed amount. Those hopes turned to dust in mid-2000, when Disney simply unplugged Toysmart, shutting down the site to stop its losses. Big companies may have deep pockets, but they may also have shallow patience—and that's a real pitfall. The cruel fact is, just as they have the resources to quickly make substantial investments in a little dotcom, they can also—without a shudder or any hesitation—afford to write off all that money and walk away.

For more information about these best practices and other information about strategic alliances, visit ASAP's website at strategic-alliances.org.

Forging Ahead

Know that it won't be easy to create a partnership with a big company—no matter how good your dotcom is. How tough will it be? Here's a true story that ends with success, but the going was tough along the way.

Picture this: You have a great idea for a dotcom. You'll sell gift certificates that can be redeemed at many major retailers, and you'll make a little bit on every transaction. Sounds terrific, except there's a problem: How do you talk retailers into letting you sell their gift certificates?

Jonas Lee, former CEO of GiftCertificates.com, knows—and he also knows how hard it was to do the persuading. Currently, the company has hundreds of major retailers, but, "We knocked on many doors before we signed the first deals," he says. Why? Startups are potentially pathways to wealth, but they may also be fly-by-night

▲

Getting Hitched

Want to pursue alliances? Make up a list of potential partners, and make very sure that you see the deal from their perspective as well as yours. Then put yourself in front of those potential partners' faces. Talk to them at trade shows, for instance, and take every step that comes to mind that will increase their awareness of you. But let them make the first move.

In every instance of successful partnerships I've heard about, the big company made the initial suggestion. Maybe there's no jinx involved in taking a direct approach, but maybe there is. So wait to be wooed.

concerns. Major established businesses don't want to risk tarnishing their brand by partnering with a startup that goes bust.

Eventually Lee got his initial commitments from a couple of name-brand shops—Barnes & Noble and The Sharper Image. "It took me two or three months of persistent calling and explaining," he says. "You may have a good idea, but you have to also convince people you are a good businessperson, and that takes time." The broader point: Partnerships can be wonderful, but persuading partners to ally with you is about as hard as building a winning website in the first place.

Echat with eBags.com's Peter Cobb

eBags.com

Peter Cobb, Co-founder, Senior Vice President of Marketing and Merchandising
Location: Greenwood Village, Colorado
Year Started: 1998

Eliot and Peter Cobb, Frank Steed, Andy Young, and Jon Nordmark

all joined forces in spring 1998 to build a major store for shoes and accessories out of bytes, not bricks, and boy, have they pulled it off. Currently, eBags remains the self-proclaimed world's largest online retailer of bags and accessories. They carry a wide range of premium and popular brands, including Samsonite, JanSport, The North Face, and Eagle Creek. From backpacks and carry-ons to computer cases and handbags, they offer a lot of choices.

The company also launched eBags in Europe and has seen strong sales in the United Kingdom. Eliot, Frank, and Andy are no longer involved in the business, but Peter and Jon are as active as ever.

To start the company in early 1998, each of the five founders—who collectively had more than 60 years of bag and retail experience in companies like Samsonite USA, American Tourister, and The Wherehouse—came up with a significant amount of cash and worked without pay for eight months. Then eBags raised $8 million from angel investors, friends, and family. The company then decided it wanted to get venture capital funding, too, so to make room for the capital infusion, eBags cut its angel funding by 50 percent (to $4 million) and sent checks back to all of its angels. In 1999, financial relief came from VC firm Benchmark Capital. Other investors have followed, allowing eBags to continually invest in people and technology.

A key to the company's success? It does not overspend. For example, executives don't have golden parachutes or big bonuses. And, after 9/11, all employees, including the executives, took a 10 percent pay cut without complaint. This kind of frugal approach is one reason eBags.com is still around when so many other dotcoms aren't.

Another success secret? eBags maintains little or no inventory of its own. Instead, it relies on manufacturers to drop-ship products directly to customers.

In fact, the majority of the brands eBags sells are drop-shipped, including High Sierra Sport Co., Samsonite, and Kipling. The practice has turned eBags into a luggage category killer, offering a selection of more than 33,000 items that dwarfs the several hundred products carried by the average specialty baggage store. Company executives believe their lack of inventory is one of the primary reasons eBags has survived.

Here, Peter Cobb discusses some other secrets to eBags' success.

Entrepreneur: *What made you decide to launch eBags.com?*

Peter Cobb: In May 1998, we saw what was going on with people starting companies selling books and music online and there was a product we knew and loved: bags. We knew [they] would be a great fit for the internet. We knew from our research that many people were buying bags through catalogs, so people didn't need to feel and touch the product to make a purchase decision. They were comfortable buying bags from Orvis, L.L. Bean, Lands' End, and Eddie Bauer catalogs. Bags and accessories weren't like clothes or shoes, where people really needed to see the color, the size, and the materials. Also, people don't really get excited about going to the mall Saturday afternoon to pick out some luggage or a backpack for their son. So with three, four, or five photographs nicely done for a product, you can really get the point across.

Another key reason we started was because the retail bag market was very fragmented. If you wanted luggage, you'd probably go to a travel goods specialty store. If you wanted a ladies' handbag, you'd probably go to a department store. And if you were looking for backpacks, you'd go to a sporting goods store. There was no "Bags R Us." Because of this fragmentation, we knew there'd be a great opportunity. And there happened to be nice margins on the product—markups [average] 50 percent.

The other important thing is that in the brick-and-mortar retail world, when inventory comes in, it's there for 180 days. If somebody buys a bag, the store orders another one. What's more, these stores are limited to about 250 products because of physical space.

> **Tip...**
>
> ### Smart Tip
>
> Is there a niche out there that you are familiar with that doesn't have a central website? Is there a niche that could be covered in a better manner? This is where you can capitalize. It's hard to find anything that isn't sold on the internet, but by offering more products, unique products, customer service, a great return policy, special sales, discounts, or free shipping, you can become the big fish in a small pond, or niche market for that matter. Competition on the internet is fierce, especially with huge players like Amazon. That's why you need to be the best in your niche market.

Because we do business on the internet, however, we can offer more than 33,000 products, and when we take an order, we pass it on to Samsonite, for example, and Samsonite ships it to the customer. We get the sale and then, 30 to 90 days later, we pay the brand.

Entrepreneur: *How long did it take to go from idea to funding to launch?*
Cobb: Idea to funding was about eight months; idea to launch was ten months.

Entrepreneur: *What's been the biggest surprise you've had in building eBags?*
Cobb: There have been a few of them. The biggest surprise is how we've been able to gain such fantastic momentum. We've shipped 7 million bags.

Another one probably has been watching the flame-out of all the etailers that took in many times more money than we did and somehow spent it all. It's been a huge surprise to see companies that I thought were pretty solid companies fail—like Planet RX, Garden.com, and MotherNature.com, sites I shopped on and had great shopping experiences with. What you don't know, however, is what is going on behind

▲

the scenes. These companies were spending tens of millions of dollars on inventory in their warehouses, which we didn't have to do. They were also spending money on TV advertising, which we never really did. We have a saying at eBags: "Too much money makes you stupid." We just kept seeing that over and over again. We didn't raise nearly as much money as these guys did, and we always understood that the money we were dealing with was our money—money we put into the company with some investors' help. Every decision we made was, "This is our money; how should we spend it?" as opposed to, "Boy, we've got $80 million in the bank, so who cares if we spend $1 million on Super Bowl ads?"

Another surprise has been how much internet retailing has taken hold with a large percentage of the population. I think it has mainstreamed. The growth of broadband has [also] made online shopping faster and more enjoyable. I think that says good things for the future of internet retailing for those who are doing it right.

Entrepreneur: *What's been your biggest challenge?*
Cobb: I think the biggest challenge is managing your cash properly while continuing to grow.

Entrepreneur: *How many VCs did you meet with before you got a funding commitment?*
Cobb: We met with well over 100 VC firms.

Entrepreneur: *What's your strategy in coming out ahead of competitors?*
Cobb: Our competition is really brick-and-mortar stores. Online shopping isn't for everybody. Some people want to feel and touch and taste and smell before they buy a product, and that's OK. But a large majority of shoppers value convenience and selection, and that's why online shopping is experiencing explosive growth. Bags and accessories is a $40 billion market. Our strategy is just to continue to offer the ultimate shopping experience on eBags.com.

Cheap Tricks with Blinds.com's Jay Steinfeld

Blinds.com

**Jay Steinfeld, CEO and Founder
Location: Houston, Texas
Year Started: 1996**

Who likes buying window coverings? Probably nobody, a fact that Jay Steinfeld—founder and CEO of Blinds.com—has turned into a thriving web-based business that was started with just $3,000 and has been profitable from Day One. Steinfeld tells his story here.

Entrepreneur: *Where did you get the idea for the site? When did the site go live?*

Jay Steinfeld: My wife and I owned a full-service brick-and-mortar window coverings store [in Houston]. We owned the store for about 14 years, so we knew the window coverings business inside and out. But we wanted to expand into a different niche—the price-sensitive, do-it-yourself market. In June 1996, we launched our first website, and then in March 2001, we went full time online. With the internet, I have a website working 24 hours a day. I'm able to do so much more volume online than what I could have done in a 1,000-square-foot store. Sales have increased every year since then and now we're the largest online seller of blinds in the world. Why? Because people are becoming more comfortable with the internet, and even in a bad economy, people are trying to get good deals, and they naturally associate the internet with a good deal. We also make the whole process simple and allow people to buy confidently.

We wanted to make it easy, too, a no-brainer. So we called our first site NoBrainerBlinds.com. That name occurred to me in about two minutes. As soon as I said it, I knew it would work. It made sense, it's descriptive of our mission, and people get it. We later launched our flagship site, Blinds.com, based on everything we learned from our NoBrainerBlinds.com site—and its sales have soared. The site has more products, better help, is faster, and has better navigational experiences than the NoBrainerBlinds.com site.

Entrepreneur: *Have you sought outside funding?*

Steinfeld: We did get some financing from some local angel investors in February 2001, and it enabled us to buy our then-biggest competitor, Blindswholesale.com. This was a fantastic acquisition, and it let us have access to the technology we needed to expand our business. This acquisition tripled the size of our business, and we've grown tenfold since then.

There are some blinds factories and many investors that have made offers to buy us, so who knows; maybe one day we'll sell. This is my baby, so it would be hard to sell. On the other hand, I suppose everything is for sale.

Entrepreneur: *How do you attract visitors to your site?*

Steinfeld: We use all the guerrilla tactics—newsgroups, link building, and search engine optimization. We have about 12,000 sites linking to us. We also encourage our existing customers to tell their friends by providing them with an experience that exceeds their expectations. These days, 45 percent of our volume is either repeat customers or referrals. We also do paid advertising, such as keyword buys. For Blinds.

com, we also intend to advertise on radio and TV, because our name is so easy to remember.

Entrepreneur: *What's your look-to-buy ratio?*

Steinfeld: About 5 to 10 percent.

Entrepreneur: *How big is the average purchase?*

Steinfeld: When we were just NoBrainerBlinds.com, the average order size was about $460, but now it's about $350 because we added lower-priced products for those customers who just want a no-frills, quality blind at the lowest price possible. We attracted many more customers, but we attracted customers who buy at lower levels. That's fine, because they are so happy to tell all their friends about what a great deal they got with Blinds.com. That yields a lot more sales. That $350 is still over two times the industry average, which is $150.

Entrepreneur: *For the consumer, what's the advantage of buying online?*

Steinfeld: They save a bunch of money, and they can read up on the options/products at their own pace—no pressure. They can also read thousands of actual reviews written by consumers so they can tell which products others like, to help them make an informed decision. We have created our own private-label product line, accounting for more than two-thirds of our products sold. Those products are custom-made by the well-known manufacturers, but without their labels—and all have lifetime warranties. Plus, all our products have a money-back satisfaction guarantee.

Entrepreneur: *What challenge do you face in making this site grow?*

Steinfeld: Our challenge right now is to make sure that our success doesn't cause us to implode. We now have to start looking at the company in a different way. We have to start thinking of systems, procedures, control, and—God forbid—coming up with an organizational chart. We will have to write memos now and then and have meetings. We're going to have to get organized. Hiring the right people and getting them trained into the best positions to help us grow smart will be the key.

In April 2008, we launched yet another site, Blinds.ca, which we believe will be the Canadian equivalent of Blinds.com. Today, Blinds.ca is the number one online seller of blinds in Canada.

Website Traffic Builders

Here's the bad news: the World Wide Web is nearing 1 billion active websites. Wow! That's a lot of websites out there competing for attention. You've done your best to build a great site that users will want to visit again and again, but the tough reality is that no matter how great your site is, chances are slim that a customer will randomly happen on to your site. It's imperative that you use a variety of strategies to get your website noticed by the nearly 2.5 billion people who now surf the web. They make up over a third of the planet's population.

Traditional marketing campaigns don't necessarily produce results for websites, warns Mark DiMassimo, CEO of DiMassimo Brand Advertising, an agency that has handled many dotcom clients. "The only offline medium that works is TV," says DiMassimo. "In fact, the complaint of many dotcoms is that they can't find other forms of offline media to compete with TV. That's a scary place to be because you don't want to be overly dependent on any one advertising medium."

Baiting Your Hook

Winning visitors becomes a matter of creative, persistent marketing. The good news is that it's still the little things that will bring plenty of traffic your way.

There are fundamental steps that too many businesses neglect. For instance? You should always put your URL and a reason to visit your website on all printed matter, including your business cards. You should also mention what people will get when they visit the site, such as a newsletter or a list of "Top 10 Tips" or some types of content that will pique their interest. That substantially increases visitors, and eventually visitors become customers and/or subscribers.

An email signature is also an especially powerful and absolutely free tool. Create a signature with a link to your website in it and have it automatically attached to every one of your outgoing emails. It takes only a few seconds to create an email signature, and it may bring in visitors to your site every day.

Another low-cost traffic builder is online discussion groups and chats. Where appropriate, give out your URL. Look for places in which you can join in discussions on topics that relate to what you sell, but don't be a salesman. You wouldn't walk into a party and start selling to everyone you meet. They would probably roll their eyes at your ill-timed sales pitch and walk away.

Beware!
A strong bias against overt advertising remains on internet forums. As a new member of a forum group, be sure to read the posting rules before extolling the virtues of your offering or even including a hyperlink in your posting signature. Without first building a positive reputation as a human (and not a "spam-bot"), you are likely to receive hostile responses from anti-ad folks and may become permanently banned from a group before they even get to know you or your company.

> ## Snazzy Signatures
>
> **P**retty much every email program offers the ability to include a signature that goes out with every email. Think of a signature—"sig" in tech-speak—as a teaser, a fast ad for your website. How do you create a signature? In Microsoft Outlook Express, for example, go to "Tools/Options/Signatures." Some advice: Shorter is better than longer with signatures. Rarely should you use more than six short lines, and three or four are better.
>
> What to include? If your website sells foreign language tapes, for instance, you might use this sig:
>
> John Smith
>
> President, TapesRUs.com
>
> "Learn Languages by Tape"
>
> Tapesrus.com
>
> Once you've set it up, that signature will appear on every email you send out (unless you override the default). If you send out 20 emails in a day, that's 20 repetitions of a fast ad message. It's one of the net's best marketing bargains.

The same social etiquette is true when you talk in online groups, be it on the social media, such as LinkedIn groups, or any other interest groups. Be knowledgeable, show your expertise, provide helpful solutions, and point out great articles on the topic. Eventually, people will read your profile or ask how you know so much and then you can mention that you work in the industry. Make people want to come to you, visit your site, and buy. That's what inbound marketing is all about. You put yourself out there and people come to you, rather than the old-school advertising approach of chasing down customers and hitting them over the head with your advertising messages.

A good place to find groups is at Google Groups (http://groups.google.com), which archives discussion lists. Getting active in these groups spreads the word about you and your site. You'll get traffic coming to you.

As mentioned earlier, LinkedIn has plenty of groups in which to talk and display your expertise, but not sell.

Similar advice can be given for social networking sites like Facebook, Twitter, and Google+. You'll want to create a profile for your business, get active in the groups that cater to your web audience, and befriend other like-minded businesses and people. Like any community-oriented activity online, you don't want to cross the line into spam. Only "friend" people when it makes sense. And keep your profiles updated. If you'll be participating in real-world events with your business, put that in your "events" section on your Facebook page, for example. If you've updated a section of your site or added a new product or service, broadcast that on your Twitter feed to instantly alert your audience. Facebook, Twitter, Google+, Pinterest and other social media platforms are ideal ways to draw traffic to your website with links and content that tie into your site.

The Most Bang for Your Buck

Another big-time traffic builder for any website that retails is posting items for sale on the major auction and marketplace sites, such as eBay, Yahoo!, and Amazon. Those sites let you identify yourself to viewers, and a few dollars spent on highlighting your items on those sites may just bring in lots of traffic from surfers seeking more information. Many small etailers tell me their entire advertising budget consists of less than $100 monthly spent on eBay, but they nonetheless are seeing traffic counts above 500 daily, with most of those viewers coming via eBay. My advice: Put up a few items for bid or for sale on each of the leading auction and marketplace sites and then track the traffic. Even if you sell those specific goods at no profit, the traffic increase your site may experience could well justify your efforts by leading to additional, or future, sales.

The New World of Online Advertising

Say goodbye to banner ads and hello to robust ad platforms like Facebook Ads or Google AdWords, which can provide effective marketing and results at a low cost by using intelligent, finely tuned targeting. For example, a baby blanket ad on Facebook can be targeted to only be shown to new parents (based on Facebook's information about its users). Or, a plumber can set a Google AdWords campaign to only display ads alongside plumbing-related searches by users within a certain service area. This cuts costs and increases marketing efficiency by reducing the money spent on advertising to unlikely customers on the internet at large.

If you have a real-world component to your business, be sure to try out Craigslist (craigslist.org). Most ads on Craigslist are free, except for those in a handful of popular categories in prominent markets, like brokered apartment listings in New York City. It takes just a few minutes to post an ad, so it's worth your time to see if anyone bites. With over 50 billion page views each month, 700 local sites in the United States and abroad, and more than 60 million monthly users in the U.S., you know people will see your ad—and hopefully answer it.

For my money, classified ads, at least the freebies, represent one of the very top ways to generate no-cost traffic. And classified ads are becoming a major online advertising category, outpacing all predictions for growth.

Should you buy ads on other websites? That depends on your budget and the type of results you're seeking. The key is to stay away from companies that offer to put your ad on thousands of websites for

very little money. Instead, work with an ad network that will help you build long-lasting, profitable relationships with your target audience. For example, check out BannerSpace (bannerspace.com). There you can choose to advertise on premium sites: high-traffic destinations, portals, and directories with well-known brands. Or, you can save money with channel advertising by placing your banners on sites that have specific content related to your offer. Is that money well spent? If you have a quality banner ad and a large number of exposures on premium sites, you may see a traffic jump. However, banner ads, as noted earlier, have lost significant power to GoogleAds and other pay-per-click ads that are honed to where you want them to appear.

There are also ad networks that specifically target bloggers, which may be worthwhile if you have a very narrowly targeted niche—say kayaks or knitting supplies—and want to focus on places where such hobbyists gather.

With any ad campaign you purchase, closely monitor results. Renew only the deals that are generating traffic to your site, and know that net advertisers have a big plus over advertisers in offline media, such as magazines, because on the net it is very easy to track—via your log files (see Chapter 33)—which ads are producing which results. That takes the guesswork out of decisions to renew media buys.

What's a fair payback? If small businesses goof, it's in wildly overestimating the results they can anticipate from a media purchase.

When it comes to offline advertising, expert opinion is mixed. Some pros advocate big investments in traditional media, while others tell you to fish where the fish are, and that means advertising online to promote an online store. I split the difference here, and my advice is to incorporate your URL prominently into all offline advertising,

Never overlook a chance to plug your website—but don't launch an offline campaign for an online-only property. Sure, many of the big guys, such as Priceline (priceline.com), Go Daddy (godaddy.com), and Overstock (overstock.com) extensively advertise on TV, but these are big businesses with tons of money to spend. Go where you know you'll find surfers—and that means hunting online.

A Direct Approach

For many businesses, good old email may be the surest and certainly the cheapest tool for building traffic. And it gets results: Customized email can generate response rates upward of 6 percent—sometimes as high as 30 percent, but that kind of response is rare even for an in-house list. Plus, people are quick to delete anything that sounds like an email ad, and that is if their spam filter doesn't stop it first. You have a better chance with press releases about your business, but there too, many people will hit delete before reading what you have to say.

News Flash

A good way to get folks to opt in to your email list, which, of course, they will have the option of opting out of, is to offer a free monthly email newsletter.

About what? Content is wide open, but effective newsletters usually mix news about trends in your field with tips and updates on sales or special pricing. Whatever you do, keep it short. How short? About 500 words is probably the maximum length. Create interesting lists, give them tidbits, factoids, trivia, or anything they can digest quickly. People do not even want to bother scrolling down, so give them as much as you can in the preview screen with a little more below the line. The sides and corners are for promoting your products and services.

You can also put more promotional material below the content for those who are curious enough to keep on scrolling and reading, but those will be the exception to the rule. Try different formats but keep your email newsletters interesting. Have great catchy headlines and something inviting and titillating in the subject line. Also make the "from" line the name of your business. If you simply put your name or the name of your newsletter's editor, people will hit "delete" since they won't know it's from your business.

> **Tip...**
>
> **Smart Tip**
> Always give email recipients an easy way to opt out of future mailings—and whenever anybody asks to be removed from your list, honor that request immediately.

Socializing for Fun and Profit

If you want to draw attention to your website, go where online crowds converge: Twitter, Facebook, and LinkedIn. Whether you're marketing to other businesses or to consumers, social networks must be in your marketing mix. Start by creating a free profile, but be careful—your profile shouldn't be a blatant advertisement. It should be about your business, or yourself, in a friendly manner that lets people know what you and/or your business are doing. Most social media sites are not about trying to sell but about establishing relationships. Let people know what makes you and/or your business interesting so they will want to connect with you.

Which social networking site should you use? Whichever one best suits your audience and is easiest for you to maintain consistently. For example, while your thoughtful comments and posts about working with the latest tax codes may be profound, they may receive a better response on professionally oriented LinkedIn than on socially oriented Facebook or newsblast-oriented Twitter.

Take some time to review the demographics of the different social media platforms and see which one(s) match your business demographics most closely. Then adhere to the style of the site. For example, Pinterest is very visual, so you'll want to use your best visuals to show off your products.

Another key: Include hyperlinks so that interested readers can, with a single click, go directly to your site and find out more about a topic of interest. And, if you provide great content, add "forward to a friend" so that they can spread the word about your business. Always think viral with online marketing. Whether you are emailing a newsletter or using Facebook or Twitter, you want to encourage others to spread the word, since word-of-mouth marketing is the best possible means of no-cost marketing. It is also how you use the power of social media to grow your following.

How often should you mail? Often enough to build a relationship with your readers, but not so frequently you become a pest.

Daily updates are a big mistake, and weekly ones are probably ill-advised, too. The reason: Recipients will ask to be deleted from the list or, worse, they'll simply delete each of your emails, unread, as soon as they come in.

Special Delivery

A solution to these common mailing hassles is to use a mailing service. Three good choices? Salesforce (salesforce.com), Constant Contact (constantcontact.com), and Mail Chimp (mailchimp.com). These services maintain mailing lists and, on your schedule, send out the mailings you provide.

A lot of the grunt work involved in mailings is handled by these services, including handling your opt-outs in a timely fashion and helping you measure your email newsletter results, which leaves you free to focus on the fun part: your message. Keep it simple, keep it sharp, and always use email to drive traffic to your site. Don't make the big mistake of trying to cram your website's entire message into every email. Nobody has the patience for that. Email should stick to "headline news," with the full story residing on your website.

Is your list succeeding? There's no reason to guess at the answer. Just track site traffic for a few days before a mailing and a few days afterward. Effective email ought to produce a sharp upward spike in visitors. How big a spike? That answer hinges on your usual traffic, the size of your list and your personal goals. A good target, though, is a 6 percent response rate.

If you don't see an increase in traffic, take a hard look at what you're mailing. Is it succinct? Focused? Does it encourage readers to click through for more information? If not, odds are you need to hone your message to encourage recipients to click through.

Another possible reason for less-than-desirable results: Your mailing list is bad. Send a vegan mailing to a list of self-proclaimed steak lovers, and you're knocking on the wrong door.

The best way to build a targeted mailing list is to make it simple for site visitors to sign up to receive it. Ask customers each time they complete a transaction on your site if they'd like to receive a newsletter.

Smart Tip

Tip...

Don't want to take on the task of producing a regular email newsletter? There are many freelance writers who can handle a newsletter for a small fee. No, it's not a lot of writing and it seems simple, but a lot rides on having the right few words that appeal to your prospective customers. That's why good advertising copywriters make a lot of money. Even if they only write a few simple words (like "You Deserve a Break Today") they can change the course of a business. You need not pay very high rates, but, as mentioned earlier, do not leave the future of your business in the hands of your nephew, a college kid who likes to write, if he doesn't know what will appeal to your customers. Again, your business is on the line. Make sure you give the writer plenty of direction—it still has to be your newsletter.

Best Bets

How can email help you be a more effective marketer? In a report titled "Actionable Insights Into Email Marketing," the Direct Marketing Association (DMA) offers some practical advice for marketers on how to be more successful at reaching current and potential customers or donors through focused email messages. "The email marketing channel offers fantastic opportunities for reaching customers efficiently," says Sue Geramian, the DMA's senior vice president for interactive and emerging media. "However, legitimate marketers must continue to monitor the evolving delivery landscape, especially emerging technologies that are helping to distinguish legitimate email communications from fraudulent efforts."

These best practices are intended to improve the likelihood of permission-based email being delivered to the inbox and read by the intended recipient. The recommendations suggest that email marketers:

○ Encourage customers and prospects to add the marketer's legitimate sending address to their personal "approved list/address book" and provide upfront instructions on how to do so in registration pages. Benefits vary by mailbox provider but may include special icon designation, full image content/link rendering, and no lost emails in the spam folder. Being an "approved" sender yields higher response rates and generates fewer complaints and blocking issues.

○ Carefully consider the content and presentation of marketing messages, as recipients are increasingly labeling any email communication that's not relevant or looks suspicious as spam. In addition, marketers are encouraged to create messages that strike a balance between images.

○ Follow established protocols such as authentication and white-listing criteria to ensure that email messages "pass muster" with mailbox providers. A growing number of ISPs use spam-filtering software to eliminate junk mail. This technology uses algorithms to determine whether incoming messages qualify as junk email and filters them out before they get to an end user's inbox. In addition, marketers should register for all mailbox-provider feedback loops. In general, marketers should aim to keep complaint rates (total complaints divided by total delivered email) below 0.1 percent to avoid temporary or long-term blocks.

▲

Leave the "yes" box unchecked, though, so you're not "accidentally" opting in those who don't want to receive it. People do not like to be tricked and companies who do so usually lose customers quickly. Include an easy-to-find newsletter sign-up box or link prominently throughout your site. You may even want to offer a special coupon or free download for those who sign up.

Stick It to Me

"Sticky" is the dream that keeps website builders going. When your site is sticky, visitors hang around, and that means they're reading and buying—and the time a surfer sticks to your site translates into greater brand awareness for you. Whether you're in a mall or your site is stand-alone, sticky is the Holy Grail, but making your site sticky doesn't have to be that elusive. The key is to offer information—that is, content—that will interest your visitors.

So what do the winning sites have in common? Good, engaging content. In both cases, people actually play on the site—and the sites are easy to navigate. The following are concrete building blocks for making any site stickier:

- *Fast loading time*. Surfers are impatient. Force them to watch a stagnant screen as dense images or fancy Java applets load, and they will be out of there before your cool bells and whistles ever come into sight. It's tempting to use these gizmos—you might think they'd increase your visitor stays because just watching them load eats up minutes—but in most cases, forget it. When you force surfers to wait until meaningful stuff happens, they won't. They will simply leave—

often in a huff—and that means they won't be bookmarking your site for future visits.

- *Good copy.* "The web is still about text, words," says Motley Fool (fool.com) co-founder David Gardner, and he's spot on. Are you a criminal lawyer? Put up a list of the "Ten Dumbest Mistakes Defendants Make." An accountant could do likewise with "Tax Return Blunders." An electrician could put up a list of dangerous goofs made by do-it-yourselfers. Think snappy and useful, and try to provide info readers cannot easily find at thousands of other websites. Monitor other sites to see what they are posting.

Beware!

While encouraging more frequent shopping with a loyalty program for existing customers is a smart strategy, promoting loyalty on the web does pose some challenges. For example, establishing loyalty online tends to be difficult, given the nature of the web environment and its one-click access to competitors. So what should an online merchant do? You need to make sure you do not require the user to jump through hoops to participate, and provide a simple reward structure and clear value for information given.

- *Loyalty programs.* Another way to get targeted customers coming back for more is by using online incentive marketing, such as setting up loyalty programs on your site. Why? You always want returning customers. Remember, there's a documented business principle that says 80 percent of your business will come from return customers. It's also

Big Data

Services like Salesforce and Google Analytics harness the power of complex databases to allow etailers to capture more information about their customers than ever before. This data can be used for A/B testing (does Subject Line A yield more visitors than Subject Line B?), targeted loyalty and engagement programs (offer a special coupon on a customer's third visit), and even product research and development (what other products did this visitor view before making a purchase?). This data can also be integrated with offline buying habits through the use of unique customer barcodes on fliers and postcards. The most successful companies are those who best know, understand, and serve their customers.

cheaper and easier to maintain customers than to constantly be searching for new ones.

There are numerous such programs out there. You could do something as simple as offering customers the ability to earn gifts—like T-shirts emblazoned with your logo— if they buy enough merchandise on your site. Or you could go with the most popular option, known as a frequent-buyer or points program. This choice gives customers the opportunity to receive discounts or points toward the purchase of merchandise by buying products on your site. The more your customers spend—which can also mean the more times they come back to your site—the bigger the discounts or the more points they receive.

Echat with GiftTree's Craig Bowen

GiftTree.com

Craig Bowen, CEO and Co-founder
Location: Vancouver, Washington
Year Started: 1997

Sometimes etailers find taking a step backward technologically—into the world of print catalogs—is a big step forward for their business. Craig Bowen, CEO and co-founder (with his wife, Esther

Diez) of GiftTree (gifttree.com), is a successful etailer who found that mail order was the best growth option for his business.

In business since 1997, GiftTree is a premier gift services provider. Its clients include many large multinational and U.S. corporations as well as individuals. Its products include handcrafted gift baskets, as well as new-baby gifts, balloon bouquets, thank-you gifts, get-well gifts, wedding gifts, and business gifts.

In 2003, the online merchant decided to add a catalog to its etailing business. Why? Because catalogs keep etailers "top of mind" with customers and ultimately encourage those customers to come back for more, Bowen says. The company now makes its catalog a key part of its marketing plan. Here's a closer look at Bowen's mail order experience.

Entrepreneur: *Tell me about your company. Where and when was the company founded?*

Craig Bowen: Our company was started in 1997 by myself and my wife in our studio apartment in Key West, Florida. My wife is from Spain, and our dream was to build an internet company, sell it, and move back to Spain (where we met). We're still working on the "move back to Spain" part.

Entrepreneur: *Why did you decide to start the company?*

Bowen: We felt the internet was the perfect medium for busy people to buy and send gifts. I really liked the idea of jumping into the internet revolution to see how we'd do running our own business.

Entrepreneur: *When did you decide to add a mail order or catalog component to your company?*

Bowen: Our first catalog went out in 2003. It was sent to a small group of very specific clients during the holiday season, and it worked very well: We saw a lift in sales. We were encouraged by its success and began to grow our catalog distribution. We sent another during the holiday season in 2004 and then sent two out in 2005—one in the fall and one around holiday time. We expanded our distribution to five catalogs in 2007. Today GiftTree sends an annual catalog out only to those requesting it.

Entrepreneur: *How did you go about launching the catalog? How expensive was it?*

Bowen: GiftTree decided to create and design its catalog in-house. Employees took photographs of GiftTree's products in the company's own photo studio. We hired a printer to print the catalogs and then mailed the catalogs through the U.S. Postal Service.

Since the catalog was launched in tandem with other fliers—and since GiftTree used in-house employees for the work—it's hard for me to give an answer as to how much the whole project cost. However, taking on this kind of project is definitely not cheap. It can cost at least $100,000 once you factor in the costs of hiring an agency to produce it, printing, mailing, and perhaps buying or renting a prospect list. Basically, it is as expensive as you'd like it to be. Also, we have exceptional technological capability for a company our size, so most of these things are costing us far less than other companies our size.

Entrepreneur: *In general, was adding a mail order component to your company difficult to do?*

Bowen: It's time consuming, and mistakes and missteps can be costly. There is a lot of knowledge available on the subject, and time

> **Beware!**
> While Craig Bowen has had success with his catalog, keep in mind that a nice-looking catalog that works is usually a very expensive proposition. And once you're in it, you're in it for the long haul. So before you decide to launch a catalog, make sure you have exhausted all the other ways to promote your products—such as pay-per-click advertising and email marketing.

spent on research will make things easier, or at least reduce some anxieties you might feel when creating your first catalog. For those who can afford it, a website and a catalog make the perfect marriage. There's a reason people do catalogs: They work. If you make a very beautiful catalog, and it's got what consumers want, they are far more likely to order from you than if you didn't send them something.

Entrepreneur: *What types of challenges did you face?*

Bowen: Making our product "appear" more like a catalog product. There is a difference between web and print. Catalogs are not interactive, and that was new for us. Print is also very unforgiving; once you make a decision, you can't undo it with a few keystrokes.

Entrepreneur: *Has the catalog side of your business helped the growth of your company?*

Bowen: Yes, and we expect it to add more as we move forward.

Entrepreneur: *How successful is your company?*

Bowen: I think we are very successful. We're still a bit of a diamond in the rough, but we've done most of the hard work already.

Entrepreneur: *What are your secrets to success?*

Bowen: Never give up. Never surrender.

Secrets of Search Engines

Search engines are a crucial part of the online experience for internet users. Led by Google, search engines find the data you are seeking and provide you with a listing of sources that meet your needs.

But the listings do not necessarily put the most popular results, or necessarily the ones that best meet your needs, on

▲

What Is Search Engine Optimization?

According to *Collins World English Dictionary*, it is defined as "the process of adjusting the content, structure, etc., of a website so that it will be displayed prominently by a search engine."

the top of the list. Search engines have their own ever-changing criteria that determine how to rank websites. And, those who know all about the workings of search engine optimization (SEO) can determine the best manner in which to "work the system" to get higher rankings. In fact, there are well-paid SEO experts, entire companies and even courses devoted to helping websites achieve higher rankings on search engines.

Improving Your Ranking

You can review each search engine's criteria on each search engine's site. Typically you'll find what you need under tools or by searching for SEO guidelines on the site. You will note similarities between what the search engines look for. It's not in your best interest to try to please every search engine. You want to be on Google, Bing, and Yahoo!, which are the biggest players. After that, you're on your own. You can go to Google.com/addurl and enter your site's URL under Webmaster Tools. Once you register you should take some time to read about how Google's SEO tools work. You'll find helpful articles at the Help Center by typing in SEO.

Every search engine will provide you with information on how to register and tips on generating more visitors. Be forewarned, you shouldn't pay for website registration or SEO tips. There's a misconception out there that SEO has to cost an arm and a leg. And while it's true that the very best SEO services will cost you (mainly because it costs the SEO company to provide it!), there are plenty of free SEO optimization techniques you can apply to your blog or corporate website. You can:

- Shore up your on-page SEO
- Analyze your competition with free SEO tools
- Research keywords with the Google Keyword Tool
- Contact other bloggers for guest blogging opportunities
- Write excellent content for articles or your blog that will attract links and visitors

- Update content often

While search engines are great for marketing, getting your site listed where consumers are sure to see it isn't always easy. With billions of pages on the web, how do you win a high ranking in search engine results? The inside scoop is that many engines use algorithms—mathematical formulas—to rank sites. Not only do they all use different algorithms, but they don't reveal them, and, worse still, they change frequently. Should you just shrug your shoulders and give up? You can't. Experts agree that search engines have to figure largely in any website's marketing plan because they are where users hunt for the information they want.

Getting Listed

Just about every search engine provides tools for easy submission of new sites. Just look for the "Add URL" or "Submit Your Site" button, and then follow the directions (ordinarily no more complex than typing in the address and hitting "Send").

There are hundreds of search engines to choose from. For-hire site registration services typically say they submit to more than 100 engines. But, other than having them charge you to do a ridiculous amount of submissions, there's no point to being on an index no one uses, which is why e-business owners should focus only on a handful of high-traffic engines.

Below are the ten most popular search engines as of August 2013, as listed on eBizMBA Rank with the estimated number of unique monthly visitors.

1. Google: 900,000,000
2. Bing: 165,000,000
3. Yahoo!: 160,000,000
4. Ask: 125,000,000
5. AOL Search: 33,000,000
6. MyWebSearch: 19,000,000
7. Blekko: 9,000,000
8. Lycos: 4,300,000
9. Dogpile: 2,900,000
10. WebCrawler: 2,700,000

Clearly Google is the place to be, totaling more unique monthly visitors than the following nine sites combined. But people have their favorites, and it's to your advantage to work with a few of the others.

Engine Trouble

One hitch in the listing process: Don't expect immediate results. It can take a month or so for the major crawlers to index your pages. Engines list new sites in their own time frames, and because they're constantly hit with a tsunami of new web pages, queues of "to be added" sites have grown.

Rank and File

Getting listed is the easy part. Getting a high position in the search engines is another story, but that's also where the money gets made. It does little good to be the 212th business plan writer in Yahoo!'s search listings. Who will wade through 21 screens to find you? Nobody is likely to read that many pages of information. Most searchers only look at perhaps three pages or 30 results from a given search. In rare cases someone may be persistent and look at as many as 50 or 100 if the query is proving elusive. Patience runs only so deep, and a surfer's attention span isn't infinite.

Can you do some of this yourself? You bet. The best way to score high in search engines is to have good, solid content, especially with regard to the terms that you want to be found for. Experts say it is also important to continually add new content to your site.

Homespun SEO

Without getting very technical, you can do a lot of things to improve your search ranking. Here are a few examples:

1. *Make a list of all the keywords and key phrases* that would drive people to your site. Try to think beyond the obvious ones.

2. *Write great, original content.* You want people to spend time on your website. If your content is not interesting, original, and timely, they may leave. If people stick around it will help your search ranking. Also, websites should have at least 500 words to get noticed.

3. *Focus on having keywords or phrases in your title tag.* The HTML title tag for your site will appear in the title bar of the web browser and in your favorites, or bookmarks. It is also used by search engines, so have your keywords in there as well as (generically) in your copy.

Bounce Rate

Bounce rate is all about how quickly people "bounce" away from your site. It is calculated as the percentage of site visitors who only make it to one of your website's pages before navigating away. Clearly, you want people to stay longer so you can:

○ Make a sale

○ Get a higher search engine ranking

○ Build a relationship with a potential customer

Since search engines record how much time people spend on your website before bouncing, you want to make sure the site is well-organized and easy to navigate so people don't get frustrated looking for what interests them and leave. One of the main reasons people leave websites is because of poor or slow navigation. Continue seeking out ways to make navigation as smooth as possible.

4. *Have a keyword in your domain name.* If you're a tailor, work *tailor* into your domain name; if you own an online shoe store, work *shoes* or *shoe store* into your domain name. This helps search engines (and visitors) find you.

5. *Don't overdo it.* Keywords and key phrases are very important, BUT the latest in technology can catch on if you're just loading up on keywords. Many so-called SEO "gurus" hire people to write articles (for next to no money) based solely around packing in keywords; occasionally it works, but often they are left with a dreadful article that even the search engines do not want to read.

6. *Get links!* Look for various businesses with which you can exchange links. Seek out links that have something to do with your business but are obviously not competitors. Links just for the sake of building up links can be a red flag to the search engines, crawlers (or spiders). Also, be careful whom you link with since your reputation is on the line.

7. *Add a sitemap.* This is a plus for visitors navigating your site and for search engine optimization. You can do this through XML or plain old HTML.

8. *Don't use DHTML.* Tuck content away in PDF files or use Flash. It's more difficult for the search engines to navigate with DHTML.

9. *Social media links.* Search engines are now looking at your links to Facebook, Twitter, etc. Now is the time to utilize social media platforms and link to the ones you like best.

10. *Review the search engine criteria often.* In the world of technology everything changes quickly, so keep up on the latest rules so you can adjust your site to remain high in the search engine rankings.

> **Smart Tip** Tip...
>
> Think about the title of your page. It is not technically considered meta data, but rather HTML. However, it's also used in the same way as meta information. It's the text that shows up in the top bar of your browser when you visit a site. When someone bookmarks your site, it's also the text that pops up as the link in the bookmarks folder. And when your site shows up in a search engine, it's going to be the text that is hyperlinked to your site.

There are plenty of other tips found online and new suggestions appearing often. But before you can optimize, you need to make sure you have the content and keywords all ready for your site. Most significantly, you need to read the guidelines on each search engine carefully.

Five more points to keep in mind:

1. *SEO is a slow process.* This is one of the more simple SEO tips to understand, although one of the most frustrating. You have to prove yourself for Google to reward you with a top-ten ranking.

2. *SEO is always tough for beginners.* It can be a rough first few weeks and months for beginners who want to learn SEO. There's a lot of new terminology to memorize, lots of outdated information, and the competition is fierce and getting more intense every day. But here's the good news: Every SEO expert today was a beginner at some point in the past, and they reached guru status by a constant focus on improving their SEO game. No one is born with SEO knowledge; it doesn't "come naturally" to anyone since SEO itself was invented years after each of us was born.

3. *SEO comes before web design.* Web design is inherently sexy. SEO...not so much. And although we're the first to admit that web design is extremely important, it's a good idea to take care of your SEO basics before you work on your web design. Your web designer should either be versed in SEO or have a professional SEO at his or her side with whom to work.

This simple SEO tip will save you hours of headaches later down the line, as it's an absolute pain to go back and have to change your core web design to make it search-engine friendly. Plan your keywords and phrases ahead of time as well as possible sites with which to link.

4. *Read the top online SEO forums.* This is probably the simplest SEO tip on this list. It doesn't take any special software or expert knowledge. All you have to do is read.

There are plenty of knowledgeable people who are more than happy to help you succeed in your SEO efforts. They provide an absolute goldmine of free information just by searching for SEO tips and tricks. If you're paying attention, you'll be able to recognize the experts from the novices. Once you do, pay extra attention to each of their posts, as they've been through it all and back.

5. *Don't give up.* I can't count the number of times I've seen beautiful websites go to waste because their owners just gave up on the SEO game. Too much work, too much time, too much money, so they say.

> **Smart Tip**
>
> *Tip...*
>
> You should know a little about search engine marketing (SEM). An umbrella term, SEM includes things like SEO, paid listings, and other search engine-related activities that could increase exposure and traffic to your website. SEO refers to techniques that use the content on your site to help it appear higher in a list of search engine results. SEO is important because most people find sites through search engines. The higher a web page "ranks," the more searchers will visit that site. BUT, you want to consider all that you can do to improve your overall SEM.

Directory Assistance

There's another way to get your site in front of users' eyes: directories at Yahoo! or the Open Directory Project (ODP) (dmoz.org).

Should you submit your site to these types of directories? By all means. When you submit your site to these indexes, keep in mind that the tricks used to maximize search engine placement will not work with these human-edited directories. What's especially important about getting listed here? Good, relevant content and design are the secrets with the human-edited directories.

How do you get listed in a human-edited directory? You can go to the sites and—as with search engines—look for an "Add URL" or "Submit Your Site" tab. Then cross your fingers, and you just may show up in that directory. "Getting listed in these directories provides important links that may help you rank better with crawlers," says Search Engine Land's author and contributor Danny Sullivan. You can go to web-directories.ws/ or webdirectorylists.net for free and paid directories.

Paid Placement

What are paid placement and paid inclusion programs? Paid placement—also known as sponsored search or pay-per-click—offers the ability to place your site in the top results of search engines for the terms you are interested in within a day or less. Basically, every major search engine accepts paid listings, and they are usually marked as "Sponsored Links."

In the Google AdWords program, Google sells paid listings that appear above and to the side of its regular results, as well as on its partner sites. Since it may take time for a new site to appear within Google, "these advertising opportunities offer a fast way to get listed with the service," says Sullivan.

In the Google AdWords program, the cost of your campaigns really depends on you. The question is: How much are you willing to pay and how well do you know your audience? It all boils down to knowing your own goals and letting Google know what they are.

There is a nominal, one-time activation fee for Google AdWords. After that, you pay only for clicks on your keyword-targeted AdWords ads, or for impressions on your site-targeted AdWords ads. You can control your costs by telling Google how much you are willing to pay per click (CPC, cost per click) or per impression (CPM, cost per thousand) and by setting a daily budget for spending.

For example, a new advertiser can activate his or her AdWords account and then choose a maximum cost-per-click.

Daily budgets start as low as 1 cent up to whatever limit the advertiser is comfortable spending. Site-targeted ads, which let AdWords advertisers choose individual sites in the Google content network where they'd like their ads to appear, require a maximum CPM price of 25 cents.

While there are myriad choices out there and the concepts may seem confusing, many small businesses swear by paid search programs.

Planning your budget will include several factors. If, for example, you are looking for a national audience, you need to be prepared to spend more. Also, if you are in a highly competitive market, you'll need to pay more to move your ad up higher in a long list of competitors. If you have niche market and are looking primarily for customers from a certain region of the country, then you will pay less, since you have less competition and are reaching out to a smaller segment of the audience. You can tailor such pay-per-click (PPC) advertising to meet your needs. Google, or any site offering PPC advertising, wants you as a steady customer, so they are not trying to get you to pay a fortune for ads that are meaningless.

You can also try a few different ads to see which one draws the most attention and generates the most results. Remember, it's not how many clicks you get, but how many

follow through to conversion. Your conversion rates are how many people followed through to purchase a product or service, sign up for a membership, or do whatever it is you want people to do on your site. Therefore, if you have 200 clicks and only one sale, you are not seeing the same results as having 100 clicks and making three sales. Conversion rate is very important to track when running an ad campaign.

It is also very important that you follow your analytics carefully to determine whether you are reaching your target market. A misleading word in an ad might get you hundreds of clicks from people who are not at all interested in your offerings, thus wasting your money. eBay, for example, stopped using Google AdWords because they felt it simply didn't work for them. The problem was that eBay was using all sorts of ridiculous words to grab attention, such as "Baby." Since you cannot "buy a baby," the ad, like many that they used, was misleading and a waste of money to have people click on it. Using any word to get attention will, as eBay found out, be very costly and unproductive.

Google Analytics will let you know how much traffic is going to your site from your keywords and phrases so you can adjust accordingly. Most sites offering PPC also provide detailed analytics.

Test your ads before posting. This concept goes way back in the history of advertising as a must. For ages, ad men and women have run their ads past potential audiences to make sure they are clear (not misunderstood) and catch the reader's attention.

As long as you plan your campaigns carefully, budget properly, and read the fine print, they can really help you improve your reach.

Each search engine also provides its own PPC system. You'll want to learn as much as you can about how it works before you get started. Like Google, with their learning center, you can find out exactly how each PPC system is set up and what you need to know.

It's to your advantage not to jump the gun when trying to determine if the PPC campaign works. You should give it 60 to 90 days to get off the ground before you start acting on the results you see.

You also want to drive traffic to pages that pertain to your ad. If your ad is very broad based and you are introducing them to your business for the first time, you may send them to your homepage. But if your ad features something you are selling, you will want to drive them to a landing page featuring that product or service. Whenever you are directing people to your website, focus in on where you want them to land; it doesn't have to be the homepage. You might even set up a special landing page for a particular offer.

Spider Webs

User submissions aren't the only—or even the main—way search engines compile their indexes. A popular tool used by the engines in scoping out the lay of the web are spiders—also called crawlers—which meander from site to site, following links and reporting findings back to the search engine.

These documents are discovered and crawled because other web pages contain links directing to these documents.

Has your website been spidered? Check your log file (see Chapter 33 for more on logs), and you'll easily see a spider's trail. A sure tip-off that a spider has come is when the log file reveals a request for the "robots.txt" file—a file that tells a visiting spider what parts of a website are off-limits.

As part of its crawling effort, the crawler takes robots.txt standards into account to ensure it doesn't crawl and index content from pages whose content someone doesn't want included in the search. If a page is disallowed to be crawled the spider will not read or use the contents of that page. The URL of a protected page may be included. Links and reference text from other public web pages provide identifiable information about a URL and may be indexed as part of web search coverage.

Do you need a robots.txt file? Some say no. Why? Because if you have nothing that's meant to be strictly private stored on your website—and you shouldn't, because if a file is on the web, it's in the public domain—there's no need to tell a spider "hands off." What's more, a downside to having a robots.txt file is that a spider may miss key pages. If this happens, resubmit those pages to the search engine. Maybe the engine already knows them; maybe it doesn't. Either way, resubmitting is always a good policy.

Are You Ready?

There was a TV commercial a few years ago that showed several people sitting around a computer on which they were watching the launch of their site. They were all quite excited to see the first orders coming in. However, within seconds they were besieged by sales and couldn't handle the volume. In real life this does not happen quite so quickly, but in time, even a short time, you will get responses to your ads, or from any type of marketing you do. Remember, by moving your listing up higher through SEO, more people are seeing your business and many of them may respond.

The question, as stated above, is: Are you ready?

Before you can grow a business, you need to be sure that you have everything in place to handle the possible upsurge. After all, getting ten times more inquiries on your site is only worthwhile if you can close some of those sales.

What this means is that you need to make sure your server can handle the additional traffic, your shopping cart and payment system are ready and can also handle increased volume, you have someone (or a few people) at the ready to handle customer service, and that you have the shipping materials you need (or anything else necessary) to conduct business.

Before advertising or optimizing, make sure you can handle the increased traffic and additional customers. The folks on the TV commercial were not at all prepared.

Echat with Drugstore.com's Dawn Lepore

Drugstore.com

**Dawn Lepore, President,
CEO, and Chairman of the Board
Location: Bellevue, Washington
Year Started: 1998**

Since its inception in 1998, Drugstore.com has been a leading

retail force on the web—and it is continuing to be popular, thanks to its recently appointed president, CEO and chairman of the board, Dawn Lepore.

After a 21-year career at discount brokerage Charles Schwab, Lepore—who had risen to vice chairman of technology, operations, and administration, and was responsible for moving Schwab onto the internet in 1995—moved with her family in October 2004 from the San Francisco Bay Area to Bellevue, Washington, to run Drugstore.com. Listen up as Lepore explains what prompted her to head up Drugstore.com and what she believed it would take to succeed in the online drugstore space.

Entrepreneur: *Why did you join Drugstore.com?*

Dawn Lepore: I love retail businesses, and I am a firm believer that the internet is at the beginning of its evolution. I believe in what Drugstore.com is offering, which can make a difference in customers' lives. Also, the company is not a technology company, but technology plays a huge role [in its success], and that was attractive to me. I met so many happy customers and really loved the passion of the employees—so the combination of that, along with the investors and the board members, all made it a great opportunity from my perspective.

Entrepreneur: *Can you elaborate on how Drugstore.com has helped people?*

Lepore: There are two pieces to this. One is that you can't pick up a newspaper today without hearing about affordable prescriptions for Americans, and of course we all know that many people are going outside of the country and buying things from pharmacies that may be less regulated, and there might be some kind of risk associated with that. We, however, are a fully licensed U.S. pharmacy; our prices are up to 70 percent lower for generics and up to 30 percent lower for brand-name drugs when compared with traditional brick-and-mortar pharmacies. We have less overhead because we are not operating a lot of drugstores—we just operate through our website.

Another way Drugstore.com benefits our customers is our breadth of product. We offer more than 30,000 over-the-counter (OTC) products in addition to our pharmacy. We focus on men and women, but our demographic happens to be predominantly female. I have very young children, so I know what it's like when it's 10 o'clock at night before you really have time to think about doing the errands you need to do for your family or for yourself. I've heard from so many women who sit down at 10 o'clock at night, log on to the site and get diapers for their children, shampoo, their favorite face cream, and their husband's favorite products all at one sitting. They just love the convenience, they love the service, and they love the breadth of our offering.

Entrepreneur: *Who is your major competition?*

Lepore: Competition is a lot about people's habits, such as stopping at the drugstore on their way home from work. We have to continually remind them to come online. It takes time to change customer behavior, but I think we are at the beginning of the trend of people moving these types of purchases online and that we will be the beneficiary of that.

Besides the brick-and-mortar stores, we also compete with some niche players in different categories, such as Sephora [a makeup company] and the sites that sell online vitamins. But what our customers tell us they love about us is that they can get Maybelline mascara, Philosophy face cream, and vitamins all in one place.

Entrepreneur: *Hasn't the online drugstore space taken off more slowly than many expected?*
Lepore: I do think this category was a little bit slower to adapt online, and I think that it had to do with the fact that it takes a while to change customer behavior. There are so many brick-and-mortar stores out there,

> ## Smart Tip
>
> How do you persuade wary consumers to buy? For Drugstore.com, the answer is information—and that's an area where the net can excel. For example, Drugstore.com's website has customer reviews. Here, people can write reviews about products they use and post them on the site. The site also offers FAQs on prescription drugs. Sites can include articles, blogs and other content. This is something you won't get in brick-and-mortar stores. And keep in mind that on the web, an etailer can offer this kind of information at very little cost, while gaining a leg up on traditional retailers.

but the problem is, people don't like the customer experience in a brick-and-mortar store, and they can't find all the products they want. [And] sometimes people run out of their shampoo or deodorant or toothpaste. And what we need to do is train people to order a few days before they are going to run out.

Entrepreneur: *How will you beat competitors?*
Lepore: It's the breadth of product, our prices—which are very, very competitive—our offers, and our free shipping if you spend at least $35 on nonprescription products from Drugstore.com or Beauty.com™. Our convenience, service, and customer experience [will also help us beat the competition]. We make it very easy for our customers to order and reorder. For example, we will send you "your list," and you just click on what you want. All these things add to our competitive advantage.

Entrepreneur: *Where will your profits come from—prescription drugs or other merchandise?*
Lepore: Our OTC category—which includes prestige beauty products in our Beauty.com web store—is our fastest-growing and highest-margin category. That's where most of our profitability comes from. The prescription part of our business is important, but it is not the growth engine for the company. Certainly our customers appreciate the fact that we carry prescriptions.

Entrepreneur: *Critics say online drugstores sell drugs to kids—is this a worry?*

Lepore: We absolutely have to have a valid prescription. We verify the prescription with doctors—so there is no way that you can get a drug that you don't have a valid prescription for. We take lots of information, and we do insurance claims, etc. And then, from a quality perspective, we check, double-check, and triple-check those prescriptions going out of our distribution center. We are very, very confident in the quality and the legality of our prescription business.

Entrepreneur: *In your opinion, what will ecommerce look like in a few years?*

Lepore: I definitely think ecommerce's growth will continue, and there are certain categories where that growth will accelerate.

> **Tip...**
>
> ### Smart Tip
> Closely scan your product sales reports—and don't be thrown for a loop if there are a few surprises in the mix. Audiences you never expected can find you on the web. However, when you see unanticipated sales trends, react fast. That's a key competitive edge for ecommerce over other kinds of retailing. Being online, you can quickly adjust your product mix to meet customer needs and redo pages to point to what customers are looking for. Remember, your web pages can serve as your window display except you don't have to open up early and change the mannequins. You can post new items up anytime you like.

Cheap Tricks with eHolster.com's Scott Quarterman

eHolster.com

Scott Quarterman, Owner and Co-founder
Location: Norcross, Georgia
Year Started: 2000

Who hasn't lost their phone, tablet, or even their Kindle? There's never any place to comfortably tuck them, and that is why they are so easy to leave behind in restaurants, airplane seats, and such. But

▲

that also meant a big business opportunity for Scott Quarterman, co-founder of eHolster.com, where the products are shoulder holsters and wallet cases for your mobile devices. eHolster cases are unique because they are modular by design and can be worn on a shoulder harness one day and then easily moved to your belt or across your chest another day. Most items are in the $20 to $50 range depending on the type of case and the material.

The web is ideal for launching an innovative product because there aren't dozens of other sites all selling essentially the same product. You can find a broad audience online and don't have to fight to get your product on big-box retail shelves. On the other hand, it takes work, time, money, and even luck to build public awareness that these new products exist. As Quarterman learned, it can be done, but it's not enough to simply come up with a clever product idea.

Here, Quarterman tells how he designed the holster product, arranged for its manufacture, and built his website, all on a thin budget.

Entrepreneur: *What were your startup costs?*

Scott Quarterman: Total costs amounted to roughly $25,000 to develop the eHolster product, create the electronic storefront, and complete the trademark searches, the LLC, etc. We earned those startup costs back within the first three months of opening our online "doors." The business has been profitable ever since.

Entrepreneur: *How long did it take to build the site?*

Quarterman: First, we needed to fully design the product, which took about nine months. Then it was on to the website, which took another six months.

Entrepreneur: *What are you doing now to bring in new site visitors?*

Quarterman: We still have the eHolster branding label on all our harnesses, which helps get the brand out there. However, the bulk of our traffic and sales comes from word-of-mouth advertising from our long list of very satisfied customers. Many of our new customers are referred to us from friends who have owned our products and have been very happy with them. We also purchase keywords on Google and Yahoo! to help drive customers to the site. Our website is optimized for the search engines and ranks very high (usually in the top three spots) in Google's organic listings for keywords like "cellphone holster" and "tablet holster." This helps drive a good percentage of the traffic to our website.

Accepting Credit Cards and PayPal

The number-one question on the minds of most new online entrepreneurs is whether or not they will be able to accept credit cards and how it works.

Thanks to the growth of ecommerce sites over the past ten years, credit card accounts are now very easy to set up on your site.

The common methods of accepting credit card payments is either by using your own merchant account or by utilizing a payment gateway account, also known as a third party merchant.

Taking Credit

An internet merchant account gives you the ability to process credit cards, and can be obtained through a bank. It is viewed by the bank as a line of credit that is extended to you. You must apply for this, just like you would any loan.

A good place to start your search for a merchant account is your own bank. Most issue credit cards, and if you have a long-term relationship with the institution, that's a big plus. What if your bank says no? Try a few other local banks and even offer to move all your accounts there or at least set up a business account. You just may be rewarded with merchant status.

You can also log onto Google or Yahoo! and search for credit card processing. You'll find dozens of outfits, large and small, that are on the prowl for startups seeking merchant accounts.

You will also probably need a payment gateway account, which is an online credit card processor or transaction handler that is capable of hooking into credit card accounts belonging to the online shopper and your internet merchant account. The payment gateway handles verification and transfer requests. It interacts with the card issuer's bank to authorize the credit card in real time when a purchase is made on a website.

The leading providers of payment gateway accounts targeting smaller merchants include:

- PayPal, paypal.com
- Authorize.Net, authorize.net
- Cybersource, cybersource.com
- Verisign, verisign.com

If you don't have a merchant account, these providers can help you set one up and offer a payment gateway in one convenient package.

Credit cards aren't processed cheaply, at least not for a startup. A typical fee schedule

> **Beware!**
> Plenty of shady outfits are bent on getting rich by offering bogus merchant accounts to gullible online beginners. Before shelling out any cash, make sure you're setting up an account that will handle industry-standard cards (such as MasterCard and Visa, not "Big Bob's Lollapalooza Credit Card" or some specialty card). It's a good idea to stop at the Better Business Bureau (bbbonline.com) before inking any costly deal with an unknown vendor.

Do Some Shopping Cart Shopping

Chances are, if you have used a host builder, you already have a shopping cart. But you may want to switch to one in the near future with more flexibility.

There are numerous shopping cart software programs out there. Compare and contrast. Many will give you a free trial, so use that time to see what you do and do not like. The cart should be easy to navigate and fast. You'll also want a program that can be customized to meet your needs and one that will be able to manage the potential growth of your business.

Shopping carts are very important to your ecommerce success as they are the final destination your customer sees when they are ready to purchase something from your business. Therefore, the cart needs to handle the ordering, shipping, and payment processes flawlessly. You'll also want an inventory update prior to the start of the actual payment process, letting potential buyers know when you are out of a product beforehand, not after they have entered all of their data.

Software to consider includes: Cubecart at cubecart.com, PrestaShop at prestashop.com, and Shop Factory at Shopfactory.com.

---

for a small-volume account (fewer than 1,000 transactions monthly) would include monthly processing fees ranging from $10 to $100, plus transaction fees of about 3 to 5 percent per transaction. Some providers also charge startup fees, but shop around—in many cases the startup fee will be waived if you ask.

Small-Business Pal

Founded in 1998, PayPal enables any individual or business with an email address to securely, easily, and quickly send and receive payments online. PayPal's service builds on the existing financial infrastructure of bank accounts and credit cards, and uses advanced proprietary fraud-prevention systems to create a safe, global, real-time payment solution.

PayPal has quickly become a global leader in online payment solutions. There are two major PayPal offerings for merchants.

PayPal Website Payments Standard

This is an easy, quick way to start accepting credit cards online. A simple integration into your shopping cart allows your customers to pay securely and easily. (PayPal seamlessly integrates with hundreds of compatible carts or custom-built storefronts.) If you don't have a shopping cart, the free PayPal Shopping Cart can be set up quickly and easily as well.

After setting up the system on your website—which takes just a few minutes—you will be able to accept all major credit cards, debit cards, and bank transfers. Website Payments Standard is secure, and you don't need a separate merchant account or gateway. Your customers don't need a PayPal account. Transaction fees are low.

PayPal Website Payments Pro

This all-in-one solution gives you features comparable to merchant accounts and gateways, through a single provider and at a lower cost. There is a $30 monthly fee, but no setup fee. Transaction fees are listed on the PayPal website under PayPal Website Payments Pro.

With this service, customers paying by credit card stay on your website for the entire transaction; PayPal is invisible. Website Payments Pro is already integrated into many popular shopping carts, or it can be easily added to a custom-built shopping cart.

PayPal Website Payments Pro includes a Virtual Terminal, which allows you to process payments for phone, fax, and mail orders. The secure solution offers comprehensive online reports to help you measure sales easily, and allows PayPal account holders to check out quickly with saved information.

Secure Horizons

The one must-have for online credit card processing is secure, encrypted connections. You've seen this many times yourself. Go to virtually any major etailer, commence a purchase, and you are put into a "secure server" environment, where transaction data is scrambled to provide a measure of safety against hackers. Truth is, worries about credit card theft from nonsecure sites are generally unfounded—the odds of a hacker grabbing an unencrypted credit card number from a nonsecure website are pretty slender—but buyers by now expect a site to be secure, and that means you need to provide security.

Is this a technical hassle for you? It shouldn't be. Whatever vendor sells you your credit card processing services should also, as part of the package, provide a secure transaction environment. If they don't, look elsewhere.

It may sound daunting to arrange for online credit card processing, a secure server, etc., but nowadays, you can have all this in place in a matter of minutes—especially

You'd Better Shop Around

My hunt for online credit card processing services revealed wide variations in fees and pricing menus. Startup fees ranged from free to more than $500, with monthly fees ranging from free to more than $100. Volume is a key factor—sites anticipating fewer than 1,000 transactions monthly can often arrange low-cost credit card deals—but a lot of this seems to be Wild West pricing.

Should you go with the lowest price? Not necessarily. My advice is to go with companies you trust. If there's a premium involved, pay it if you can. Always do business with your local bank, if it will accept you as a customer, even if the rate schedules are higher than those charged by online credit card processing specialists. There have been many, many crooked operators, and caution in this realm can pay off big time.

if you use a hosted ecommerce solution. Sign up with Yahoo! Merchant Solutions, for instance, and it's simple to tack on an application for credit card processing through Chase Paymentech or PayPal Website Payments Pro. Yahoo! then charges a transaction fee for all sales by its merchants, and the fee varies depending on the level of Merchant Solutions package you choose (Starter, Standard, Professional). It also varies by payment method used, such as credit card, PayPal, etc.

The Yahoo! Merchant Solutions program has deals for new startups with no setup fees and low monthly fees for the first several months.

Check out smallbusiness.yahoo.com/ecommerce for their offers.

So, Which Is Better?

Both merchant and third party accounts (aka gateway accounts) have their advantages and disadvantages.

The primary advantages of having a merchant account include:

- *Ease of transaction*
- *Protection.* Banks are protected by the FDIC and merchant accounts typically come with fraud protection.

- *You maintain control* since the transaction is directly between the customer and your merchant account. There is no intermediary handling the money or getting the customer's information.
- *Typically you'll receive payments faster* than if you use a third party payment service.
- *Your business name is on the transaction statement.*

Disadvantages of a merchant account include:

- *Cost.* Collecting credit and debit cards comes with a price tag for entrepreneurs.
- *You must handle disputes.* If you have your own merchant account, you will be responsible for disputes, chargebacks, and any compliance, fraud, or security issues that may arise.
- *Hidden fees.* You can get hit with them, so it's advisable to read your contract very, very carefully.

Advantages of a third party merchant account:

- You don't need to get approved for merchant services by a bank. If you have low credit scores or no credit you can sidestep the approval process.
- You have a company on your side when disputes arise. They can play middleman and work on behalf of your business. They can also do a lot for you to free you up to focus on your business.
- PayPal, if you choose to use it, is very well known and a trusted service for transactions.

Shop Around Again!

When deciding among the many merchant services providers or payment gateways, you need to consider the setup costs (if there are any) as well as what percentages they are taking from transactions. Then you'll want to compare transaction fees. You also want to know how long it will take you to collect your money. In addition, you'll have to be sure that the merchant services provider has all the internet-based features, such as virtual terminals or mobile readers. It's also advisable to check out the company's approval rating at different websites showing comparisons and general satisfaction or dissatisfaction with merchant services or payment gateways.

Disadvantages of third-party merchants:

- *Potentially higher fees.*
- *Their name is on the transaction* and possibly links to their sites or those of other businesses.
- *Reputation.* Not all third party merchants are PayPal, and while many have excellent reputations, others are known for working primarily with adult websites. Still others have been cited for fraud. You need to choose carefully.

Echat with Newegg.com's Bernard Luthi

Newegg.com

**Bernard Luthi, Vice President of Merchandising
Location: City of Industry, California
Year Started: 2001**

Have you ever heard of Newegg.com? If you're interested in hardware or software products, you probably have.

▲

Founded in 2001, Newegg.com is an online ecommerce company that has created a powerful channel for manufacturers of computer hardware and software, consumer electronics, and communications products to reach do-it-yourselfers, hard-core gamers, students, small-to-midsize businesses, IT professionals, and resellers.

At Newegg.com, consumers can find the latest technology parts and products, along with product information, pictures, how-tos, customer product reviews, and opportunities to interact with other members of the technology and game enthusiast community.

Newegg.com topped the $2.5 billion mark in revenue in 2010 for the first time and has maintained similar sales numbers since, while employing some 2,500 people.

To get an inside look at Newegg.com, we chatted with Bernard Luthi, vice president of merchandising.

Entrepreneur: *Tell me about Newegg. When was it started? Why?*

Bernard Luthi: Newegg.com was founded on January 1, 2001, by our CEO and chairman, Fred Chang, a Taiwanese immigrant. The predecessor to Newegg was ABS Computer Technologies Inc., a systems integrator that made build-to-order PCs. ABS was founded by Fred in 1990 and specialized in high-end gaming PCs. During the late '90s, we started to recognize an emerging market in the DIY space. Since ABS had many customers from years past, many of them began to inquire if ABS could help them with upgrade parts for their existing systems. The answer was no, since ABS could only sell a complete system. This is how we recognized this emerging market of tech-savvy customers who were not afraid to crack open the case and upgrade or build their systems themselves.

Entrepreneur: *What were your startup costs?*

Luthi: Newegg was founded with only $100,000, and grew to be just about a $1 billion revenue company within four years.

Entrepreneur: *What types of marketing do you do?*

Luthi: At Newegg, we believe our best advertisers are our customers. We owe our success primarily to word-of-mouth and customer loyalty. We also use print, online banners, search engine marketing, as well as billboards, radio, and TV advertising.

Entrepreneur: *What was your goal when starting? Have you achieved that goal?*

Luthi: Our goal was to provide the best online shopping experience. To accomplish this, we needed to go above and beyond customers' expectations, thus establishing Newegg's three pillars of excellence, each of which helps ensure unsurpassed customer satisfaction.

First, we strived to offer the best value to the customer, combining selection and competitive pricing. Anybody can make a website and sell products; however, we differentiated ourselves by becoming the most efficient solution between supply and demand. Today Newegg provides not only a myriad of tech products, but also an abundance of relevant information and product reviews. By doing this, we not only better serve the customer, but also help our vendors reach and educate consumers on their products. The result is a stronger partnership between Newegg and vendors, which leads to better support and pricing for the customer. Since IT was our background and expertise, we have one of the deepest selections of cutting-edge technology components with the best prices.

Our second pillar is state-of-the-art logistics. In early 2001, our sales orders were climbing quickly. The executive vice president at the time, Ken Lam, commissioned the design and implementation of a state-of-the-art logistics center. I remember before Newegg was hatched, I would order from the internet and if the item was in stock, it would take several days to process the order. If it was not in stock, it sometimes took weeks to ship. Then it was another week or more for the item to arrive at my doorstep. You would be lucky to receive your order within two weeks.

To change that, Newegg set out to establish a new standard in online order processing: Ship same day and deliver next day. We created a custom logistics system that today allows us to ship over 98 percent of approved orders within one business day. Whether a customer buys a single item, like a video card, or 30 different items to build a system from scratch, we can pick, pack, and load for shipping within two to four hours with over 99 percent accuracy. This speed and precision of delivery without any extra premium was key to helping grow Newegg in the early days.

Our last, but not least, pillar is our commitment to excellent customer service. Back in 1999 to 2000, online companies were notorious for having poor customer service. In the absence of an opportunity to build a relationship with the customer through face-to-face interaction, we sought other ways to earn the customers' trust and respect. We established a customer-centric business model aiming to become the most loved and trusted company on the web. Having reached the number-one customer satisfaction rating in our industry, fastest logistics, and best selection/pricing value have been the keys to our success. I would say we are happy with our accomplishments toward the goals set forth at the time the company was established, but never satisfied. We continue to seek new ways to ensure the best online shopping experience.

Entrepreneur: *What advice do you have for entrepreneurs thinking about starting an online company today?*

Luthi: Never forget that business success begins and ends with satisfying customers. Find out what the customer wants and provide it. The online world is extremely competitive and fast-changing. Therefore, it is crucial that you understand your customers and bring added value to them. There's very little margin for error in a retail environment where a competitor is a mouse click away—that is why Newegg has, since Day One, tried to treat every customer as our only customer.

Entrepreneur: *What are some best practices in online retailing in your opinion?*

Luthi: Being customer-centric is a must. The beauty of the internet is that many aspects can be tracked and boiled down to a science. Best practices include having a good analytics tool to help generate the metrics and reports you need to make good business decisions.

Entrepreneur: *Who do you perceive as your biggest competitors today?*

Luthi: I would say our biggest competitors today would be players like Best Buy, Circuit City, Dell, Tiger Direct, and a host of other smaller online companies.

While NewEgg.com remains a highly successful online location for all sorts of electronics and communications devices, there have been some bumps along the way. For example, in 2010 Newegg.com was cited for selling 300 counterfeit Intel Core i7-920 CPUs. At first, Newegg responded by stating these were just demo units, but soon they realized the claim was true. Apparently one of Newegg's suppliers had indeed provided them with the counterfeit CPUs. After severing their relationship with the supplier, Newegg then offered anyone who received a counterfeit Intel CPU a replacement. The company recognized the crisis and reacted, thus showing their customers that they would respond under pressure and make good on their promise to provide excellent customer service.

Cheap Tricks with Bowling Connection.com's Gary Forrester

BowlingConnection.com

Gary Forrester, Owner
Location: Sahuarita, Arizona
Year Started: 1999

Turned on by pink retro bowling shirts? How about bowling jackets and T-shirts? If bowling is your passion, you want to know about BowlingConnection, where pretty much everything a bowler craves is on sale.

Site owner Gary Forrester has implemented many changes over the course of his business, some because of technology and others because of the products he was carrying. After starting BowlingConnection.com for "just about zero" using an e-business solution, he quickly launched two more sites: Southwest-gifts.com and USATiles.com. In 2001, he combined BowlingConnection.com with another one of his sites, RockinRetro.com, and renamed it Creative Productions (cpstore.com). A year later, he combined his tile site and Southwestern gift site into TeissedreDesigns.com.

He had several reasons for making those changes: He moved to a new, faster server that could handle more products, and he found that some of his products crossed over to multiple sites.

By 2005, however, he made BowlingConnection independent from CPstore again. "The bowling shirts that we sold on the BowlingConnection website from the start of our business in 1999 were only those of the '50s retro style," says Forrester. "The costumes that we sold on the Creative Productions website were also only from the '50s. So basically, everything we were selling was from the 1950s era. [In 2005,] we decided to add modern-style bowling shirts and costumes from other eras. We didn't want to overload one website with too many categories or products. We gave this a lot of thought before separating the websites because we knew that it was going to take time, and it was going to cost money. Besides using our own shopping experiences, we talked to friends and customers about theirs. What our unofficial research showed was that people enjoy shopping on a website that isn't cluttered. Hence, the separation occurred."

Entrepreneur: *What were your startup costs?*

Gary Forrester: My startup costs were almost zero. I already owned the computer, and US West Sitematic made it so easy to build the website, I didn't have to employ any outside sources at all. One of my original websites cost $49.95 per month, and the other two sites are $79.95 per month because the catalogs are bigger. I look at that cost as my "rent" payment. Where can you have a store that is open to the world 24 hours a day, and you don't even have to pay employees to take care of your customers? You actually make money while you sleep.

Entrepreneur: *What is your monthly revenue?*

Forrester: The monthly revenue has leveled off, but we are still very comfortable. My partner, Connie (who is also my wife), and I have had many opportunities to take our business to the next level, but we decided that we like it the way it is. We don't want

Way to Grow

J. Peterman built a hugely successful business starting from one item—a duster-type raincoat that he happened to discover in the West. It was a cool coat, different, and he began running little ads selling it. Orders came in, and he expanded. Yes, he eventually filed for bankruptcy, but that doesn't mean there wasn't a good business in that duster, or in Forrester's retro bowling shirts. Think about it: It cost Peterman big bucks to buy even little ads in places like *The New York Times*. A website's cost is mere pennies by comparison. What cool products can you build a site around? Think unusual, easy to ship, and good profit margins.

to rent office or warehouse space. Instead, we bought a four-and-a-half-acre ranch with a nice home, and we built a detached 400-square-foot office, a stockroom, and an additional 250-square-foot building for more stock.

Entrepreneur: *What has been the biggest surprise?*

Forrester: The first [1999] Christmas season was our biggest surprise. I expected business to pick up a little more than usual. I didn't expect it to get crazy. We worked day, night, and weekends to fill the orders. It was a challenge, but we did it—all our customers received their orders by Christmas.

Entrepreneur: *Has your business continued to stay seasonal, like that first year?*

Forrester: Overall, our bowling shirt sales have continued to increase each year. Not only have we added new shirts to our online catalog, but our custom screen-printing and embroidery services continue to grow. So now, our busy season starts in the middle of August because people are buying bowling shirts for their winter leagues, which usually start on Labor Day.

Entrepreneur: *How do you promote the site?*

Forrester: There is a helpful site called selfpromotion.com that makes it easy to list your site with all the search engines. When we started, we promoted our BowlingConnection website by passing out fliers at bowling tournaments. We promoted our other three websites by opening a temporary gift store in Las Vegas. We passed out a lot of fliers and business cards to tourists from all over the world.

We no longer pass out fliers and business cards, and we don't promote our website [by posting auctions] on eBay anymore. In fact, eBay no longer allows you to promote your own website. Because of that, very seldom do we put anything up for auction on eBay. Now, the only form of paid advertising that we use is the PPC search engines—Yahoo! and Google—and we find this is our best way to advertise. The cost is reasonable, and we have complete control over how we advertise each individual product. Of course, we do get repeat business, and word-of-mouth is still the cheapest form of advertising. We have sold to Bon Jovi, Campbell's Soup, Merrill Lynch, PricewaterhouseCoopers, Disneyland, and many more.

Entrepreneur: *How do you handle online purchasing?*

Forrester: Our website is still very secure, and customers can feel confident when they order from us. We do not sell, trade, or give away any information about any of our customers whatsoever. Due to changes in our product line and because our customers have "must have" dates, 25 percent of the orders are made by phone. If they need their order by a certain date because of a company event, they feel more confident talking to a real person instead of just sending the order through the website. We don't mind at all when our customers call on the phone. Imagine sitting in your home office talking on the telephone to Bon Jovi's marketing manager.

We are going into our eighth year in business, and we are still enjoying it tremendously. We are really in our element. The busy season, August to December, can get a little rough sometimes, though, working some long hours just to keep up. Connie and I were working late one night catching up on getting the orders processed. It was about 3 A.M. I was at the shipping table packing orders, and she was at the computer typing up invoices. I happened to look over where she was sitting and she had fallen asleep at the keyboard. I spoke a little louder than normal to get her attention, and I said, "Hey, honey, do you want to go to Jamaica this year?" She looked up, finished the invoices, and we jammed out some more orders.

Tapping International Markets

One of the lures of the web is that once your site is up, you are open for business around the world 24 hours a day. But don't be too quick to take the hype at face value: It can also be a drawback, especially the international part. For some, you may not see very many, or any, international orders. For other entrepreneurs, however, international sales make up a significant portion of their business.

There are excellent reasons for many online entrepreneurs to aggressively pursue global business, but before you let yourself get dazzled by the upside, chew on the negatives. Then, once you have seen that international business can present unique hassles, you can decide if you still want to seek business from abroad.

Foreign Affairs

Here's the root of the problem with selling internationally: Whenever you ship abroad, you enter into a complicated maze of the other country's laws. Let's assume you're in the United States. You know Uncle Sam's laws, and you know that one neat thing about doing business in the United States is that barriers against interstate commerce are few. For a Nevada business owner, shipping to California is no more complicated than putting the gizmo in a box and dropping it off at the post office. With some exceptions, few etailers collect sales tax on interstate sales.

Sell abroad, however, and it's a quick step into a maze of complexities, including customs, for instance. Generally, it's up to the buyer (not you) to pay any customs owed, but make sure your buyers know that additional charges, imposed by their home countries and payable directly to them, are their responsibility to pay.

Some countries also charge a national sales tax, or a value-added tax (ranging from 15 to 25 percent on many items in European countries). Again, as a small foreign retailer, you can pretty safely not worry about collecting these monies, but your buyers may (and probably will) be asked to pay, and they need to understand this is not a charge on your end.

Mailing costs, too, escalate for foreign shipments. Airmail is the best way to go for just about any package, and that gets pricey. A one-pound first-class shipment to Europe costs more than $10, for instance. Insurance, too, is a must for most shipments abroad, mainly because the more miles a package travels, the more chance of damage or loss. To get insurance for international mail, you must step up from first-class mail to priority mail. The insurance is free, but the cost of mailing doubles, adding to the charges you've got to pass on to the customer. Add up the many fees—customs, value-added taxes, postage, getting insurance—and what might

> **Beware!**
> It's tempting: If you declare that an item is an unsolicited gift, the recipient often will not have to pay any customs charges. The amount that can be exempted varies from country to country; usually, it's $50 to $100. But don't make that declaration even if a buyer requests it (and savvy ones frequently will). They are asking you to break the law and it's not worth jeopardizing your business over one sale.

initially seem a bargain price to a buyer can easily be nudged into the stratosphere.

Getting authorization on foreign credit cards can also be time-consuming. Although many major U.S. cards are well-entrenched abroad (especially American Express and Diner's Club), and validating them for a foreign cardholder is frequently not difficult, as a rule, this process is fraught with risks for the merchant, so be careful.

You will also need to familiarize yourself with currency rates and make sure you can collect your money in U.S. Dollars (assuming you are based in the United States). You may want to check out Dynamic Converter's website (dynamicconverter. com) or search for other conversion software so you are prepared to accept currency from abroad. You will also want to look at the exchange rate and the economy overseas. In a shaky world economy, you'll have to look very carefully at the bottom line, making sure you will be able to make a profit from international sales.

> ### Dollar Stretcher
>
> Want a no-cost translation of your site? Offer a link to PROMT-Online (translation2.paralink.com), a free online translation service. Before putting this up, however, ask friends—or pay an expert—to take a look at the translation. These types of services usually offer excellent work, but you don't want your site's translation to be the embarrassing exception. Google has a slick (and free) translation tool, too. Google Translate (google. com/translate_t) works by typing in your web page's URL and clicking on the desired language. The page instantly pops up with all the text translated.

All Aboard

If you're still not discouraged, do one more reality check to make sure international sales make sense for you. Is what you are selling readily available outside your country? Will what you sell ship reasonably easily and at a favorable price? Even with the costs of shipping factored in, will buying from you rather than from domestic sellers be a benefit to your customers? If you pass these tests, you are ready to get down to business.

Step one in getting more global business is to make your site as friendly as possible to foreign customers. Does this mean you need to offer the site in multiple languages? For very large companies, yes. (American Express, for instance, has more than 70 worldwide sites accessible at americanexpress.com, and many of them are written in different languages.) But the costs of doing a good translation are steep and, worse, whenever you modify pages—which ought to be regularly—you'll need to get the new material translated, too.

Small sites can usually get away with using English only and still be able to prosper abroad. Consider this: Search for homes for sale on Greek islands, and you'll find as many sites in English as in Greek. Why English? Because it's an international language. A merchant in Athens will probably know English because it lets him talk with French, German, Dutch, Turkish, and Italian customers. An English-only website will find fluent readers in many nations. (But keep the English on your site as simple and as traditional as possible. The latest slang may not have made its way to English speakers in Istanbul or Tokyo.)

Still, it's important to recognize that more than 65 percent of web users speak a language other than English. Providing the means of translating your English content to another language will go a long way toward building good customer relationships with people outside the United States. Your multilingual website becomes more accessible and popular if users can translate your website content into their native language.

One way to make this possible is to provide one of the free web-based language translation tools offered by AltaVista Babelfish (http://translator-bg.com/content/view/15/28/lang,en/, or Google Translate (google.com/translate_t). Both work similarly. For Babelfish, all you have to do is cut and paste some simple code, and web audiences who speak Chinese (traditional and simplified), Dutch, English, French, German, Greek, Italian, Japanese, Korean, Portuguese, Russian, or Spanish will be able to translate websites into their native language with one click.

At the very least, you should make your site friendlier to customers abroad by creating a page—clearly marked—filled with tips especially for them plus photos and simple pictures for directions. If you have the budget, get this one page translated into various key languages. A local college student might do a one-page translation for around $20. In the meantime, routinely scan your log files in a hunt for any patterns of international activity. If you notice that, say, Norway is producing a stream of visitors and no orders, that may prompt you to search for ways to coax Norwegians into buying. Try including a daily special for this demographic group and include some industry news that relates to Norway. Therefore, if you are in the fashion industry, have an article on your site about Norway's latest fashion trends.

Smart Tip

Tip...

When is a foreign customer not a foreign customer? When he or she wants you to ship to a U.S. address (perhaps an Edinburgh father sending a birthday gift to his daughter at a Boston college) or when the customer is an American in the military or diplomatic corps (shipping to their address is no different from mailing to a domestic one). Don't judge an email address by its domain. The address may end in "it" (Italy) or "de" (Germany), but it can still be a U.S. order.

Clues about international visitors will also help you select places to advertise your site. While an ad campaign on Yahoo! may be beyond your budget, it's entirely realistic to explore, say, ads on Yahoo! Sweden. If you notice an increase in visitors (or buyers!) from a specific country, explore the cost of mounting a marketing campaign that explicitly targets them.

At the end of the day, whether or not you reap substantial foreign orders is up to you. If you want them, they can be grabbed, because the promise of the web is true in the sense that it wipes out time zones, borders, and other barriers to commerce. That doesn't mean these transactions are easy—they can be challenging, as you've seen— but for the etailer determined to sell globally, there is no better tool than the web.

Tips for International Business

1. *Check all legal issues.* You never know what you can and cannot transport legally these days. Before even venturing into international waters, make sure whatever you are selling can be transported into various countries without paying extra fees or landing in jail.

2. *Let international business find you.* Unless you have a very specific product that you know will work well in certain countries (or one country), it's hard to go after an international market. Most international commerce for small businesses is the result of inquiries from abroad.

3. *Hire a customer service rep that is bilingual, at least in English and Spanish.* You might also show your customer service reps how to use translation sites.

4. *Make sure at the end of the process you will still come out ahead.* Once you factor in the shipping and insurance factors, you'll need to know that you are still making a profit. With that in mind, you are better focusing on international B2B rather than sell-

Smart Tip

Tip...

If you can align yourself with a vendor or have someone you are comfortable working with in a foreign land, you may be able to set up an easy means of fulfillment whereby you send in bulk to your associate and he or she handles the local sales. This way if you sell 40 pairs of dress shoes to a specific region in France during a short time period, you can ship them to your rep or vendor all at one time. Bulk shipping is easier, plus the customer now has someone to reach out to (in their own country) if there is a problem. You can also have this person serve as your sales rep taking store orders and being a point of contact.

ing to individual customers unless you are selling products with a decent price tag and a high markup. If you sell handbags for $500 that cost you only $250, you'll likely come out ahead on an individual customer purchase. But selling $30 shirts is probably not worthwhile unless you are selling 100 of them to a store or an overseas vendor.

Echat with ProFlowers' Jared Polis

ProFlowers

Jared Polis, Founder
Location: San Diego
Year Started: 1998

When Jared Polis launched ProFlowers (proflowers.com) in 1998,

his vision for the venture was to provide customers with a fast, easy, reliable way to send the freshest-quality cut flowers and plants—shipped directly from growers—at a competitive price to and from anywhere in the world.

Over the years, the company has undergone a number of changes. In 2003, ProFlowers was renamed Provide Commerce Inc., reflecting the company's broader mission to be the leading ecommerce marketplace for the delivery of perishable products direct from supplier to customer. That same year, Provide launched two new websites: Uptown Prime (UptownPrime.com) for premium meat and Cherry Moon Farms (CherryMoonFarms.com) for fruit and gift baskets. Secret Spoon (SecretSpoon.com), a high-end sweets ecommerce site, was launched in 2005. Provide Commerce was purchased in 2006 by Liberty Media Corp. for $477 million in cash and is now a wholly owned subsidiary.

ProFlowers, however, is still around, focusing on its core mission. Valentine's Day 2008 marked ten years of "growth" for ProFlowers. History tells the tale of ProFlowers' success: On February 14, 1998, ProFlowers delivered its first 500 bouquets of roses shipped direct from a single farm in California. For Valentine's Day 2008, the company served more than 1 million customers with 185 different varieties of fresh-cut flowers shipped from eight different countries around the world.

Entrepreneur: *Why did you decide to focus on flowers on the internet?*

Jared Polis: I had been involved in several internet businesses before [Polis founded, funded, and/or ran several high-tech startups, including BlueMountain.com, American Information Systems Inc., Onesage.com, Dan's Chocolates, Lucidity Inc., and FrogMagic Inc.], and what excites me the most is introducing new efficiencies into the economy. The way that flowers were sent to people was obsolete. Most retail floral companies buy their flowers through wholesalers and distributors, so the companies not only incur overhead along the way, but by the time they were delivered, they were much older flowers. So I saw the opportunity to use new technology to disintermediate the supply chain to get better flowers at better prices. ProFlowers ships direct from suppliers to the end consumer.

ProFlowers has also developed a technology that allows us to electronically interact with the customer, shipper, and supplier within minutes after a customer places an order. Without any human intervention, the system automatically transmits a shipping label, packing slip, and customer-generated gift message to the supplier. Through our automated link to FedEx's and UPS' shipping and billing data, email notifications are sent to customers when orders are confirmed, shipped, and delivered. The system is entirely automated, expediting the order and delivery process and allowing us to deliver superior customer service in a cost-effective manner.

Entrepreneur: *Do you ever have problems with your growers where they're not able to provide what your customers want?*

Polis: Actually, that's another competitive advantage of our business model. We can guarantee what each bouquet consists of. The legacy model used by companies such as FTD.com and 1-800-Flowers relies on whatever a local florist has in inventory. For example, they can say that they have a spring bouquet, but they cannot say that it has three mums, two tulips and one red rose in it, for example, because it depends on what the local florist has. We can tell our customers exactly what each bouquet consists of because we get the flowers from the source, and we design the bouquets ourselves so we know what goes in them.

Entrepreneur: *How did you fund the company?*

Polis: In a variety of ways. We bootstrapped it for a while, and then I sold one of my companies—American Information Systems—and I put some of that money back into ProFlowers. We also raised the minimum amount of money that we thought we could to build the company. We didn't raise significant outside capital. Among our many investors, there were some venture capital firms that offered small amounts, but I'm not a big fan of venture capital, so we tried to avoid venture capital wherever possible.

Entrepreneur: *Tell me about your marketing techniques.*

Polis: Flowers are a very marketing-intense category, so we do a variety of marketing. The key metric we look at is cost of customer acquisition. So we look at the cost of acquiring a customer across different channels like radio, TV, print, online, etc. With any [advertising or marketing] deal where we can acquire customers at the right price, we will take it.

Entrepreneur: *How do you ensure good customer service, which is essential with gift items like flowers?*

Polis: Maintaining the quality of product is a key part of our long-term success. Every week, we survey hundreds of recipients so we can quickly identify which bouquets—and which growers—are delivering the best value to our customers. And because our flowers come directly to the consumer from the fields, we deliver the freshest flowers possible. We also give our customers a seven-day freshness guarantee. And that means your flowers are guaranteed to last seven days, or you receive a replacement bouquet or full refund.

Cheap Tricks with Fridgedoor's Chris Gwynn

Fridgedoor Inc.

Chris Gwynn, President and Founder
Location: Quincy, Massachusetts
Year Started: 1997

Fridgedoor Inc. (Fridgedoor.com) has one primary goal: to be the single largest stop for all things magnetic.

The company, founded in May 1997 and located outside Boston, is a retailer of novelty magnets for consumers, custom magnets for businesses, and magnetic supplies for consumers and businesses. The items are purchased at wholesale from more than 100 suppliers around the world. The company stocks close to 3,500 items for immediate shipment. Visit fridgedoor.com and you're greeted by lists of dozens and dozens of magnets—everything from Superman magnets to increasingly popular magnets for cars. Products include humorous magnets sets, such as the popular Cat Butts set, custom-imprinted business-card-size magnets, attractive magnetic bulletin boards, and sheets of magnet material.

Fridgedoor was founded and is operated by Chris Gwynn, whose online experience dates from early 1994 and encompasses marketing and ecommerce positions with Ziff-Davis' ZDNet, the AT&T Business Network, and Industry.net, and as a B2B internet commerce analyst for the Yankee Group. Gwynn started Fridgedoor as a part-time endeavor in May 1997 while employed as the product marketing manager for Industry. net. Revenue had reached a point by the end of 1999 that Gwynn felt comfortable enough about the company's future to quit his day job.

Entrepreneur: *What were your startup costs?*

Chris Gwynn: The startup costs came to approximately $20,000. The most significant expenses were inventory and a software program to handle all back-end order processing, credit card payments, and inventory management functions. Smaller expenses, such as hosting fees, domain name registration, telephones, etc., collectively get expensive.

Entrepreneur: *Is this do-it-yourself, or did you hire a programmer?*

Gwynn: I created the site myself using a template-based store builder and hosting solution designed for nontechnical users like myself. I wanted to avoid a situation where I was beholden to a programmer to make changes and maintain the site. Creating a basic site took less than a day. The time-consuming part is determining the products you want to offer, and creating product images and descriptive copy. Creating the site is the easy part.

Entrepreneur: *Where did you get the idea for the site?*

Gwynn: I had always wanted to start my own businesses and thought the web

Dollar Stretcher

Do you make something unique or special? Put up a website, submit the URL to all the main search engines, and see if traffic comes in. Chris Gwynn suggests building traffic on the cheap. His is not the kind of site that's likely to become a gazillion-dollar business, but it's a site that can easily generate a nice, steady cash flow, month in and month out.

was a unique opportunity for someone with a limited budget. I also felt I had an understanding of how people buy online that I developed by working in marketing for an online service and later at web-based companies. I looked for a "low touch" product that was easily displayed online, easy to ship, and relatively hard to find, all in a fragmented market. I hit on magnets, which I personally like, and decided to give it a try. Luckily, it worked.

Entrepreneur: *How do you attract visitors?*

Gwynn: We rely heavily on search engines, word-of-mouth, and press [coverage]. Since we've been around for a while, we're extensively indexed by the search engines. Our market is very fragmented, making it difficult to profitably attract customers through traditional print advertising. Creating positive word-of-mouth by handling customers properly is our best advertisement.

Knowing Your Customers

Know thy customer. If there's a first commandment of business, that's it. Run a brick-and-mortar store, and knowing customers is easy. Talk to them, size up their clothing, note if they have kids in tow, check out their car when they head to the parking lot, and in a matter of seconds, a traditional storefront owner knows a lot about who's stopping in. But the question for companies doing business on the web is, "How do we know customers when all they amount to is a cybervisitor?"

This is a key issue because knowing your visitors can help you more precisely target your website. Suddenly notice a flood of visitors from, say, Japan, and that could lead to a decision to edit certain sections of a website to make them friendlier for those users. See that you're a hit on a particular college campus or in a government agency, and you can post a special deal just for those people. Observe that you're getting a lot of traffic from Puerto Rico, and that's a clear signal to market there. Not making an effort to get to know your customers makes as much sense as golfing in the dark.

Knowing your customers, or your demographic audience, can help you in many ways. It can help you hone your:

- Sales approach
- Advertising and marketing campaigns
- Social media marketing strategies
- Actual products or services
- Price points

Web Analytics

This is the measurement, collection, analysis, and reporting of internet data for purposes of understanding and optimizing web usage. Not only can you use such analytic tools to see how many people are visiting your site, but you can see the times at which people visited, from where, how long they stayed, which pages they viewed, and whether or not they made a purchase. Analytic tools can measure all behaviors that take place on your website to give you an idea of your peak sales time of the day (week, month), the age group shopping at your site, and how long people stick around before bouncing elsewhere. Web analytics let you do as much or as little business and market research as you deem necessary to get a better feel for your target

Beware!
There are tons of possible analytics available. It's very easy to get caught up looking at statistics and analyzing a myriad of details, but don't be overwhelmed by the numbers. Consider what matters most to you and your business. For example, a service-oriented website, such as a lawn care company in Kentucky, may not necessarily need to know how much traffic they are receiving from Zimbabwe, or even Nebraska. Look for the statistics you need and act accordingly.

market. All businesses have a target market. Some comprise a very broad market and others a narrow niche market, so you need to determine yours.

The most popular site web analytics service today is Google Analytics (google.com/analytics), a free service that measures the effectiveness of websites and online marketing campaigns. Google Analytics allows users of its AdWords service to see exactly how visitors interact with their website and how their advertising campaigns are faring. The hosted service is available in English and 25 other languages.

Website owners can see exactly where visitors come from, which links on the site are getting the most traffic, which pages visitors are viewing, how long people stay on the site, which products on merchant sites are being sold, and where people give up in multistep checkout processes.

Marketers can also use the service to track banner, email, nonpaid, and paid search advertising campaigns from other ad service providers. That service is free even if companies do not advertise with AdWords, as long as their users do not view more than five million web pages in a given month.

Which should you use? The Google offering sounds promising, but you can also try the free version of SiteMeter or look around for other analytic tools. There are many such tools on the market, some of which hone in on specific information. Crazy Egg, for example, offers heat maps that provide a simple, visual representation showing you where users click and what they do when they get there.

Among the top choices among traffic-analysis tools and services are:

- *WebTrends*. One of the original analytic tools, from 1993, WebTrends includes story versions of the data to make for easy reading.

- *Coremetrics*. One of the highest rated analytic products, Coremetrics includes numbers, features, and first-rate customer service.

- *Omniture*. Including video monitoring and easy-to-create reports, Omniture is good enough for companies such as Ford, GM, HP, Microsoft, Napster, Pepsi, CBS, CNN, and the Gap, so why not your business?

- *Clicky*. Offering numerous features, Clicky is very simple to install and includes real-time data so you know immediately what's happening on your website today.

When you are looking for a web analytics solution, you'll want to consider how easy it is to install, how much it will cost (some

> **Dollar Stretcher**
> Find plenty more free analysis tools and hit counters at TheFreeSite.com, a page devoted to linking with just about every tool around (thefreesite.com).

are free until you hit a certain number of visitors), how easy it is to customize the dashboard to focus on the metrics you need, what data collection options are available, which features are included (and there are so many possibilities), and how much you can learn about your visitors.

Getting to Know You

Did you know? All web servers generate access *log files* which contain all of the requests made to the server. You can import and analyze your web server logs, which provide a step toward knowing your customer, but more can be done. Here, the big guys can clue you in on strategies you can use.

Smart Tip

Tip...

A must in website customer service is to include a phone number on your website. Different folks like different channels. Some thrive on email, but others still need the reassurance of a human voice before placing a large order. I've done it myself. On the L.L. Bean website (llbean. com), I found furniture I liked—but rather than click the "Buy" button, I called the 800 number, and the friendly voice that answered the phone helped win a big order. The web changes many, many things—but it won't soon eliminate the need to pick up the phone.

Don't wait: Do a survey right now. Keep it short, and offer a tangible reward. You don't have Amazon's many millions of people to survey, so randomly choose 10 or 100 customers. Then—and this is crucial—read every answer that comes in. Trust me: Jeff Bezos isn't doing this surveying to fill slow days. The CEO of Amazon honestly wants to know what's on his customers' minds, and, for sure, every response is logged. Odds are, Bezos—a notoriously hands-on boss—personally puts in time eyeballing survey

Crowd Sourcing

You can benefit from crowd sourcing, whereby you ask questions of your customers to gather feedback. This is very popular on the social media platforms but can certainly be effective on your own site as well. Often business owners will ask what style, color, or product design their Facebook friends, Twitter followers, or online visitors like best. They can then use the responses to guide their manufacturing, purchasing, or their sales or marketing strategies, depending on the type of business.

data because he knows what every CEO needs to know: If you want to find out ways to run your business better, look at it as customers do.

Creating a survey is easy with tools like SurveyMonkey (SurveyMonkey.com). In a matter of minutes, you can customize and publish a survey, then view the results graphically and in real time. There's a free basic version of SurveyMonkey, but you can also opt for the Select Version, Gold Version, or Platinum Version, ranging from $17 to $65 per month and offering much more than the basics.

Going to the Polls

Online polls can be tailored to serve many ends, and you'll find many variations. For example, check out Sparklit (SparkLit.com) or Pollwizard (PollWizard.com), which offers free polling.

These tools may cost you next to nothing, but, used intelligently, they can be powerful. How good will the data you collect be? As good as the polls you create and as good as the tools you use for analyzing your responses.

Sometimes polls are a means of drawing traffic, so they can be fun and your readers will enjoy completing them, at least when they're short (never go over 10 questions in a poll—five or fewer questions is ideal). But the real payoffs come when you carefully construct polls to target highly specific concerns. Do customers like your website's speed? Your product selection? Pricing? Ask them, and watch out—they'll love telling you their answers. Big corporations pay megabucks to marketing wizards to examine customers and their motivations, but the truth is, you can get most of the payoffs free of charge, just by using the polling tools that are readily at hand.

It's also imperative in business to read and respond to as many customer emails, and comments on your website, as possible. These are great windows to customers and their motivations. Strangely, many small businesses, when asked, will mumble and admit that they don't read emails often and certainly don't respond to them. Sadly, there is no faster way to make yourself obsolete than to stay aloof from customers Sure, for every customer who has good things to say about you, nine customers will write with complaints, but read them, absorb them, and be aware of any trends in the responses. If one person complains about your packaging materials, big deal. However, if ten people complain in one week and you only sent out 12 orders

> **Smart Tip** *Tip...*
>
> Want to wow your customers? Respond to all email the same day—and offer answers that are truly responsive to what the customers are writing about. One sure way for a small business to excel is with a personal touch, and email gives you a powerful weapon. Use it.

that week, you have a problem—and the great thing is that now you also have the opportunity to fix it.

Stay in touch with your social media fans and followers as well. They not only have things to say, but can also say it to a large audience. So, respond promptly and try to alleviate any problems before they circulate virally across the social media.

Private Eyes

Now that you're excited about gathering information on your customers, know this: It all has to be done gently, respectfully, and cautiously. The web is a powerful tool for gathering information, and while that's useful as a business owner, it makes privacy a very big concern for consumers. Web snooping is a touchy topic—and sensitivities are increasing as more users realize exactly how detailed a trail they leave behind when visiting websites.

But there is a remedy—one that will let you gather the information you need while also reassuring visitors. It's simple: Develop a privacy policy. If you don't, this lack just may cost you big bucks.

Why? Because by not winning trust—and by not safeguarding visitor privacy—you just may be inadvertently pushing would-be customers toward the exits before the cash registers ring.

Be Careful

One of the first things you must do when launching a website that will gather any type of data from visitors (including credit cards numbers) is to have a privacy and data use policy in place. Both should be written based on the existing ones you see on major websites AND with the guidance of an attorney. Don't skimp on legal fees now to find yourself in hot water later. Make sure all terms and conditions are easy for visitors to find on your site.

You also need to understand that metrics and analytics are now able to provide a wealth of data. Therefore, you can learn a lot about people visiting your site. But—and this is important—what you do with that data needs to be spelled out very carefully.

One of the most criticized media sites regarding users' privacy concerns had been Facebook. The mega-site faced a backlash late in 2007 after launching a service that allowed users to share their activity on outside partner sites with their Facebook network. The company was quickly criticized for sharing too much information with these partner sites and for making the service an automatic "opt-in," therefore requiring users to take steps not to participate. Fast forward several years and Facebook, with millions of people sharing all sorts of information of their own volition, now has a lengthy, detailed Data Use Policy divided into multiple parts. This is an attempt to make it easier to understand how Facebook will and will not use member information.

They make it clear from the start that they can record and access ALL information that appears on their site, BUT they cannot share all of it with others, including advertisers. They can also access some information from other websites that are connected through clicking a "like" button. This means that Facebook can actually gather a wealth of information about someone even if he or she does not go on the site at all and doesn't even have an account. This is done through third parties. However, the site also makes it all clear (if you read it carefully) in their Data Use policy what they can and cannot do with this additional data.

The point here is that you can gather a lot of data, but users must know about it. You can share data (not advised), but again, users need to know about it. Basically, if you are transparent and tell people exactly what you are up to, you can protect yourself in the murky waters of data collection and sharing.

Hint: Ask people to share, but don't pry. Once you seek too much information people start to worry about their privacy.

Confidence Boosters

As a rule, mainstream websites openly explain their privacy policy. At the Entrepreneur.com site, for instance, at the bottom of every page is a link that says "Privacy Policy." Click it, and you are delivered to a clear, concise statement of what information is collected from visitors, what's done with it, and if it's made available to other companies. (The answer in this case is no, unless you otherwise agree.) Another trend: privacy promises made by third parties, such as TRUSTe (truste.com). Program mechanics vary a bit, but the essence is that a business site meets certain basic privacy requirements, pays a fee, and then gets to display a button on the website touting that it fulfills the program's requirements. Some users grumble that these programs don't truly guarantee privacy as much as they promise—disclosure of what happens to information surfers reveal—but pretty much everybody agrees that such programs are a step in the right direction.

Why do websites want information in the first place? Mainly because it's a marketer's dream. In an era when "knowing thy customer" is seen as a path to riches, it's hard to resist collecting vast stores of customer data that tumble into your lap when you create a website.

▲

Can the Spam

The ability to reach millions of people instantly has proved too seductive for some unscrupulous and shortsighted people. These are the advertisers who spread spam on the internet.

Spam is the internet term for unsolicited email (email you didn't ask for). Think of it as junk mail—only it's sent via email instead of the USPS. In practice, spam is utterly undifferentiated advertising that's sent to millions of people daily, offering instant riches, lucrative investment opportunities, and other suckers-only come-ons.

The problem was so prevalent that the Controlling the Assault of Non-Solicited Pornography and Marketing Act (or CAN-SPAM Act) was passed into law and went into effect in 2004. The law requires commercial email messages to be labeled and to include opt-out instructions as well as the sender's physical address. It also prohibits the use of deceptive subject lines and false headers.

Fortunately the multitude of spam has finally dissipated. This, however, doesn't mean that inboxes still do not have a host of unwanted emails from websites where they may have once inadvertently signed up.

So follow the law, don't spam. Also, minimize your emails, even the ones they've signed up for. Giving you an email address doesn't mean you can or should abuse it. Fifty emails a week will not ingratiate you to customers.

That's so tempting that some sites dramatically up the ante by overtly collecting more detailed and personal information from visitors. Usually that occurs in tandem with an offer the visitor accepts. This is common, and experienced web surfers have come to expect a trade-off of personal information for freebies. But the savviest surfers long ago stopped giving out accurate information. Many maintain a separate email box just for use in connection with freebies and simply lie when filling out the forms.

Another dose of bad news is that, in some cases, information collected in "cookies" has been transmitted to third-party sites which can strike fear in just about everybody. A cookie is a bit of information about you that's written to your hard drive while visiting a website that will let that website identify you as a repeat visitor in the future. This is how some sites greet a visitor with "Welcome Back, Fragonard" (or whatever the person's name is) when they return. Cookies, their architects argue, save users time and make the surfing process more efficient. Who could complain? Well, cookies by themselves don't pose a serious security threat. People just need to understand what information is being stored in them and how it's being used. For example, users should not allow financial information to be stored in a cookie. Likewise, users should not allow a site to use a cookie to log them in automatically if the site contains sensitive personal or financial information (like online banking), because it could be accessed by anyone with access to their computer, like a co-worker or a hacker.

> **Beware!**
> There are tons of possible analytics available. It's very easy to get caught up looking at statistics and analyzing a myriad of details, but don't be overwhelmed by the numbers. Consider what matters most to you and your business. For example, a service-oriented website, such as a lawn care company in Kentucky, may not necessarily need to know how much traffic they are receiving from Zimbabwe, or even Nebraska. Look for the statistics you need and act accordingly.

A last potential privacy breach can occur wherever someone goes on the net since they leave a trail.

Very good hackers can hide their trails, but 99.9 percent of us leave tracks that are easy to follow. That is no big deal to most of us. But it means that your feeling of anonymity on the net is a false one: Your movements can be cataloged and associated with you.

Added up, the situation is this: Experienced surfers do their best to mock the system, while comparative newcomers—fearing privacy violations, avoid making purchases to protect their identities. This is not good for you, and it's not good for web users, either, because it is limiting their use of the medium.

The reality is that once people start visiting websites, using social media, or make online purchases, they are putting their data out there. It can lead to any number of consequences, good or bad.

Your job is to establish trust with your customers and do everything in your power to maintain and safeguard their information by being extra careful not to be the source of information going anywhere that a customer would not want it to go. Use firewalls and encryption, and take all safety precautions against hackers. Be smart and protect the data of your visitors, your fans, and your customers.

To sum up, you should post a link to your privacy policy in a prominent place on your site. In that policy, be clear, simple, and direct. A good strategy is to say: "We do not sell or disseminate in any manner any information that we collect about you to anybody."

▲

On the Block

Not getting the response you thought you would from an emarketing campaign? The problem may be with the major email service providers and ISPs that block email via their spam filters. According to MailChimp.com, expect 10 to 20 percent of your emails to just get lost in cyberspace, mostly due to overzealous spam filters. AOL, Gmail, and Hotmail are notorious for over-filtering incoming email. What do these filters look for? Use of large or colored fonts and ALL CAPS; use of words such as "free," "special," or "click here"; language in a subject line that says something like "urgent assistance needed"; and incorrect or old date stamps.

The popular spam filter Spam Assassin seeks out emails that:

❍ Talk a lot about money

❍ Describe some sort of breakthrough

❍ Look like a mortgage pitch

❍ Contain an "urgent" matter

❍ Offer a money-back guarantee

❍ Use the phrase: Why Pay More?

Check your own ISP, too. Some ISPs will also block based on volume. If they see an IP address that's blasting a bunch of email messages, they may block it or shut it down to investigate or simply block any outgoing email that's being sent to more than 200 people. The message won't get to anyone on the list, and you might not find out for days.

Customer Service for Success

"Be our guest, be our guest, put our service to the test." These Disney lyrics from *Beauty and the Beast* hold so true in business, especially today when bad or unsatisfactory service can be shared all over the internet.

Online business owners may have once believed that their anonymity would render all customer service a thing of the

▲

past because, after all, the entire sales and service process would be neatly (and oh-so-inexpensively) automated. Ha! If there's a mantra for ecommerce players, it's this: Customers may be virtual, but their dollars are real.

Nowadays, consumers expect a high level of service from online retailers. How can you use customer service as a competitive advantage? Just follow the leaders:

- *Anticipate questions.* Many etailers anticipate questions and then answer them in their FAQs. This may save you and your customers time. However, with the complexity of the internet and the possible products and/or services offered, FAQs very often do not answer the myriad of possible questions. Therefore, customers will email or even call your customer service reps with questions that are not answered in your FAQs. This is where your customer service department can shine, or cost you business. The old adage "the customer is always right" still prevails, if you want to hold onto your customers, and you do. With that in mind:

  1. The 80-20 rule says 80 percent of your business comes from repeat customers and 20 percent from new customers.
  2. An unhappy customer can spread the word like wildfire thanks to online reviews, social media, and, of course, word-of-mouth
  3. Happy customers tell their friends, who tell their friends, and so on.

  You therefore need to be prepared to answer all of the commonly asked questions and then go the extra mile to answer the tough ones to the satisfaction of your customer(s).

- *Stay in touch.* Many companies will follow up with anyone who has contacted customer service to see if they were satisfied with the way in which their questions were answered and whether or not the problem was solved. If all went well, that's a plus for your customer service team. If the problem was not solved, the conversation should continue.

- *Turn feedback into action.* The more feedback you receive from customers, the more overlap you will see. If many customers are complaining about the navigation of the site, you will then be able to evaluate the problem and make a change. The more you ask for feedback and follow up with those who contact customer service, the more changes you will be able to make.

- *Respond quickly.* The web is an instant medium, except when it comes to getting responses from many businesses, which seem to route incoming email into a folder labeled "Ignore Forever." Smart ecommerce entrepreneurs know better. Through email, texting, or even a phone call, you should never go more than 24 hours without responding to a customer service request. Many businesses have customer service reps working 24/7. However, for a smaller business, make sure that your customer service hours are readily found on your website.

Smart companies are always raising the bar, with responses within an hour emerging as the new goal of many. What's right for you? With a smaller staff (and probably no overnight staff), you might find a 24-hour standard to be enough of a challenge. But monitor customers. If they demand faster response, somehow you have to find a way to meet their needs.

- *Hold their hands and be consumer-friendly.* While you may have expertise in your area of business, not everyone coming to your site understands your ecommerce solutions or what to look for when purchasing a wireless IP surveillance camera with angle controls. You may need to walk them through the process.

  Even shoppers seeking simple nontechnical products may not know exactly where to find what they need on the site or how to make a transaction. Your customer service reps, or you (if you are a small operation), need to have patience and be able to walk people through whatever it is they do not understand. From allergies to zodiac signs, people will have their reasons why they do and do not want to purchase something, and they will ask for more information.

  Also remember to talk in a language they understand, not "techie talk" or "business speak."

- *Use cut and paste.* Canned responses—cut-and-pasted scripts—are used by all the leading sites, which track questions, hunt for the most asked, and produce templates for their representatives. You can do likewise. As you answer customer questions, file away your responses. Odds are, you will be asked the same question within the week, and it's a great labor saver to have an answer ready, but don't become a slave to canned responses. People catch on quickly and want a real person, or an unscripted person, with whom to converse. Let your customers know that you are there if the canned response didn't do the trick. Companies with the most successful customer service, such as Zappos, do not use scripts.

- *Stay sensitive.* It's easy to seem cold and unresponsive in the formality of the written word. Read and reread your responses before they go out. You want to appear (and should actually be) interested in the customer's issues and eager to find solutions.

> ### Smart Tip
> Tip...
>
> You'll dazzle your customers when you send instant responses. Maybe that's not a realistic goal for you to set, but if you happen to be online when an email comes in, try answering it right then—and know you're really impressing the customer who gets an instant and personalized response.

- *Have the right attitude.* Successful entrepreneurs say that the only way to do online service right is to have the right attitude, really believe the customer is king, and make sure that every one of their customer service reps knows it. Many fail on this score, but when you've made customer service your top and continuing priority,

success is within reach. Don't get seduced by the notion that the websites with the best technology will inevitably win. Usable, reliable technology is a must, but where the real ecommerce battlefield will be is in service. That's the irony about ecommerce: At the end, what prevails online is what prevails offline — and that's consistent, respectful, considerate service.

Aim Higher

Perhaps some great customer service stories will help you set the bar at a high level.

When an 89-year-old World War II veteran got snowed in with very little food in the house, his daughter started calling around to see if any grocery store was able to deliver. She got one store that didn't actually do deliveries, but agreed to do it for the elderly veteran who was also on a low-sodium diet. The store was Trader Joe's, and not only did they make an exception to their delivery rule that snowy night, but they gave the young woman's grandfather several days' worth of food on the house.

Another very simple customer service story, that other entrepreneurs can certainly duplicate, comes from Panera Bread. A young woman called during the holiday season to see if they had their holiday bread available. Unfortunately, they had sold out. While the customer was ready to simply look for similar bread elsewhere, the customer service rep offered to drive to one of their other locations that had the bread the customer really wanted, pick it up, and bring it back for her. Thanks to his efforts, the customer was able to pick up the bread less than an hour later. She was also able to spread the news that Panera went the extra mile (literally) for their customers.

One of the many reasons why Amazon is so incredibly successful is their customer service. Not too long ago a mom and dad ordered a PlayStation from Amazon in advance of Christmas for their young son. The PlayStation was delivered on time, but a neighbor had signed for it and left it on their front porch, where it was stolen. As one might expect, the parents were quite upset that their son would be disappointed at Christmas. While the neighbor was probably to blame and the delivery service might have been a second choice at which to point a finger, Amazon was not really at fault. Yet, dad called up Amazon to tell the story in hopes that maybe they could do something, anything to help him buy a new one on such short notice. Not only did Amazon come through, sending a PlayStation that arrived before Christmas, but they didn't charge the couple for the shipping.

And then there's Zappos with several stories, including one from a woman who was returning her husband's boots in conjunction with the company's 365-day return policy. She mentioned that she was

> ## Smart Tip
>
> Take a tactic used by the slick catalog companies, and when you haven't heard from a customer in a while, drop him or her an email: "Have we disappointed you in any way? We would really value your feedback." Maybe the customer is indeed irked with you; maybe not. Either way, this email will remind the customer that you are a site that cares.

returning the boots because he had been killed in a motorcycle accident. Zappos accepted the return and also sent her flowers. In another story, a woman returned six pair of shoes that she had bought for her mother who was recovering from medical treatments that she had recently had done on her feet. Zappos sent flowers and later a VIP membership for both her and her mother so that when her mother was once again able to buy new shoes they would have free shipping on all their orders. Another Zappos story comes from a customer service rep who, determined to remedy a situation, broke the record for the longest customer service phone call. She stayed on the phone with the customer for eight hours in order to remedy the situation. Now, that's dedication!

Echat with ICanHas Cheezburger.com's Ben Huh

I Can Has Cheezburger?

Eric Nakagawa and Kari Unebesami, Founders
Location: Seattle, Washington
Year Started: 2007

The web is not only about etailing. It's about meeting the needs of the public, one of which is to add a little humor to life. With that in mind, a Hawaiian blogger named Eric Nakagawa teamed with his friend

Kari Unebesami to present visual humor featuring "LOLcats," which may be better described as cats in photos with classic captions designed to be shared across the internet. The site began with a cat known as Happycat asking, "I can has cheezburger?"

Clearly, funny LOLcats worked on the internet. Within four months of Happycat's sincere request for a cheezburger, the site was garnering tremendous attention and generating some 1.5 million hits per day.

From such an auspicious start, the site grew to include some 25 additional sites, generating content primarily from reader contributions. Ben Huh, founder of Pet Holdings Inc., wasted no time and bought ICanHasCheezBurger.com in the fall of the site's first year. He has been the CEO ever since. There have also been a series of books developed in conjunction with the site.

Entrepreneur: *You have a degree in journalism from Northwestern University—what made you stray from that career path?*

Ben Huh: I wanted to be a journalist all my life. But then I found out how much it paid. And it was 1999, and they were handing out signing bonuses to college kids to go work at dotcoms. So I sold out. Absolutely.

Entrepreneur: *Did you pick up much about being an entrepreneur while working for tech startups?*

Huh: Well, I can't say I learned anything related to the content I handle now. That part probably came more from me just liking things on the internet and goofing around, which I guess is not how people usually consider starting a startup. But I learned how to keep costs low and make sure that whatever commitment you make to employees, you keep—fundamental rules that I think people overlook. No matter how strange or ridiculous a business looks, those fundamentals still need to be there.

Entrepreneur: *If you were talking to someone who hasn't seen any of your sites, what would you tell him that Pet Holdings does?*

Huh: Pet Holdings basically makes people happy for five minutes every day. That's really all we want to do. It's a simple-sounding goal, but to be consistently funny day in and day out for five minutes (which is the average attention span of a blog reader) is actually very difficult to do.

Entrepreneur: *Is there a strategy in how you choose which sites to buy?*

Huh: We're interested in stuff that has longevity and has the ability to gain new audiences. So it can't be too specific. So even though ICanHasCheezburger is relatively old in the world of internet memes, we don't know if it will die down. It seems to me that if the content is good enough, it will survive and grow.

But we're just having fun [*laughs*]. It's not very entrepreneur-y or business-y, but we've always been very much counterculture when it comes to marketing.

Entrepreneur: *You don't have a business plan.*

Huh: No, not exactly. We have a good time and we think if we enjoy something, other people will, too. It's counterintuitive, but we don't actually plan anything beyond 30 days. We tell ourselves we're here to be flexible and to be nimble, and not necessarily to stick to a master plan.

Entrepreneur: *So advertisers "get" this?*

Huh: I think more and more people are getting it. What's more surprising is that smaller companies have gotten it. We have a ton of small- and midsize businesses [SMBs] that come back and advertise month after month. We are just now starting to see more pickup from bigger businesses. They're just slower to move because they have that corporate mentality.

Entrepreneur: *In some ways, it sounds almost too good to be true. You saw something you liked on the internet, and then you bought it, and it became this huge phenomenon. Was it really that easy?*

Huh: Uh, yes. I don't know how else to put it [*laughs*]. We bought something, and then that month it sort of skyrocketed, and we got another website and the month we bought it, it started skyrocketing, and so on and so forth. Luck had a lot to do with it.

Entrepreneur: *That's nice. Most people probably don't have such a good time while they're making money.*

Huh: That's kind of the ridiculous part about this whole business, where I think no one else knows what the hell is going on. It's kind of a corner of the internet that people don't consider as a serious business, but it is very serious. This is new media in a very real sense.

Entrepreneur: *Tell me about the day-to-day at the office.*

Huh: The entire network is driven by user-generated content. It's user-sourced and user-filtered, and we basically moderate it. We have 600 square feet of office space, and there are a lot of people in here writing code, doing [paperwork]—it's very much like an internet startup operation.

Entrepreneur: *How do you find employees?*

Huh: They come to us. You have to do something sort of oddball for us to notice you or say something interesting. But what we're looking for doesn't show up in a resume, and most people who have "it" are people who don't have jobs or can't really hold one down.

Entrepreneur: *But you welcome them.*

Huh: And we welcome them.

Entrepreneur: *So part of your success is because you're not one of those people you want to hire.*

Huh: Yes. Some people will say I'm the indicator of what's going to go mainstream. By the time I find something funny, it's a little too late in terms of hipster cred. When I find it, the rest of the world is going to find it. But there's a roomful of people here who are a lot hipper than I am. So they lead me. They'll say, "You don't understand. This is really funny." And I'm like, "OK. We'll see."

Entrepreneur: *So you aren't just being modest when you tell people you aren't on the cutting edge of humor.*

Huh: No. Seriously, I've never gotten a LOLcat on the homepage of my own damn site. My internet browsing history looks like any other corporate American schlep's.

Entrepreneur: *Is a picture of a cat with misspelled captions inherently funny?*

Huh: It is. Humans like to ascribe emotions to animals, and cats have faces that emote really well. We've done it for a long time. Actually, the first LOLcat was created more than 100 years ago. We found a postcard this company was selling back in the 1800s with a picture of a cat dressed up in a high chair, looking up and asking "WHERE IS MY DINNER?" in all caps. I kid you not. We haven't come that far in 100 years. I was like, "Oh, my God, if you just added a [misspelled word] somewhere, we'd have an actual LOLcat." But the prototype was pretty darn close to what it is today.

Entrepreneur: *Paul Krugman, who won the 2008 Nobel Memorial Prize in Economic Sciences, used a LOLcat in his blog for* The New York Times. *What does that make him in your eyes?*

Huh: It makes him supercool. You'd be surprised who enjoys this. We have a pretty large following at *The New York Times*, apparently.

We were highlighted as one of the more interesting influential sites on the internet by their tech guy, David Pogue. I need to find that article and frame it. [pause] Oh, hold on, here it is. Pogue calls us an "important internet culture website."

Entrepreneur: *Do you agree?*

Huh: I totally agree, but I can't believe he said that about us. That's awesome! [silence] I'm sorry, I'm busy printing this right now [laughs]. I'm sorry, I know this is not how they tell you to behave in an interview.

Entrepreneur: *That's all right. I've seen some interviews of you wearing a cheeseburger hat, and I meant to ask you if it means something.*

Huh: No [laughs]. It was a gift. It was given to me by one of the founders of ICanHasCheezburger, who got it from someone else; maybe his mother.

Entrepreneur: *I just thought maybe you wore it when you were in boss mode.*

Huh: Ha, I should. I should threaten people when I wear it so they associate the hat with bad news. Whenever I'm wearing it, I'll yell at someone so they say, "God, no, he's wearing the hat!"

Entrepreneur: *Do you have any parting thoughts?*

Huh: We'd like to continue to do what we do: Build bigger communities and just kind of evangelize the idea that the user is great at creating excellent content. The market is far more efficient than any one company will ever be. We've applied that theory to economics, but we haven't applied that theory to content. And I think that actually needs to change.

Cheap Tricks with FrugalFun.com's Shel Horowitz

FrugalFun.com

Shel Horowitz, Owner and Founder
Location: Hadley, Massachusetts
Year Started: 1996

Want to see a simple site that also makes money? Check out FrugalFun.com and its sister sites—FrugalMarketing.com and PrincipledProfit.com. No doubt about it: They are frugal—really

▲

cheap, in fact—but their developer and owner, Shel Horowitz, says the sites produce a steady stream of income, mainly from sales of his books, among them *Grassroots Marketing: Getting Noticed in a Noisy World* (Chelsea Green Publishing), but also from ads, consulting/speaking services, and affiliate links. To keep the traffic flowing, Horowitz serves up generous portions of freebies—tip sheets on frugal living and inexpensive travel tips on the FrugalFun.com site, and reams of low-cost marketing tips on FrugalMarketing.com.

PrincipledProfit.com is a business ethics website that highlights another book Horowitz has written called *Principled Profit: Marketing That Puts People First* (AWM Books). Horowitz has two additional sites, ShelHorowitz.com, which directs visitors to the most appropriate of his websites, and AccurateWriting.com, which promotes Shel's marketing and copywriting services. Read on to find out more about why his sites are successful.

Entrepreneur: *What were your startup costs?*

Shel Horowitz: I went online in 1994 with an AOL account. When I set up FrugalFun in 1996, I registered a domain name [$70 for two years] and started with a $45-per-month account covering email, web hosting, web surfing, and site updating, then switched to an $18-per-month ISP/web host. Several years ago, I outgrew that host and separated hosting from my internet access. Since I went online, I have spent $60 on ads hawking the site. My first two site designs [for FrugalFun] cost me nothing—the first version was done by an intern, and the second was a barter deal. The site was up for over three years before I paid anything for site design. Oh, yes, and I had to renew my domain name when the time was up. I am currently operating nine domains; most of them are hosted by httpme (httpme.com).

People started telling me in early 1995 that I needed a website. In my field, marketing, I was shooting myself in the foot not having one. I thought for several months about what the site would contain, did a lot of preplanning, and found an intern who wanted to learn HTML. She coded the first 40 pages, which went up in April 1996. She also taught me what she'd learned. A year later, I bartered with a website designer for the template I used for the next three years. That design, dating from 1997, became somewhat tired. In 1999, I paid a high school student to redesign the page, but it was left unfinished. So, in 2000, I hired a woman I'm still working with, who has redesigned FrugalFun twice and created FrugalMarketing using a similar design. PrincipledProfits uses a template model. I couldn't achieve the look I wanted, but a friend set up a better template for me.

Entrepreneur: *How do you attract visitors and market the site?*

Horowitz: I have done quite a bit to market the site. I participate actively in many discussion lists, and my sig [email signature] draws people to the site. I use some

30 different sigs, depending on what I want to emphasize. I do radio talk shows as a guest about 20 times a year, and I always mention the URL and a reason to visit. For example, [I'll say], "On my site at FrugalFun.com, you can find out how to have a wedding for $300," or "One of my tip sheets has a really good article on trade shows. You'll find the back issues archived at FrugalMarketing.com." These days I also promote through blogs (my own and others'), social networks, and, of course, my speaking and writing.

Also, for the book *Principled Profit*, I'm starting a reseller program, which should spread my reach to many other sites. I am hoping that resellers will account for a high percentage of sales for that title and perhaps with some spillover to sales of another one of my titles—*Grassroots Marketing: Getting Noticed in a Noisy World*.

I've also started attracting significant attention to the book through an international Business Ethics Pledge campaign, with a goal of changing the world by getting 25,000 business leaders to run their businesses according to the values in the book. This has resulted in some very good press, excellent contacts, and a higher caliber of client projects.

Also, I actively solicit book reviews and editorial coverage, and most mention the URL. Search engines draw a fair amount of visitors, but they're mostly in to see a particular page of the rather diverse content. They'll find one article that interests them, and then they move on. If they're looking for marketing info, they stay a while. I've been averaging 45,000 to 55,000 visitors a month—with spikes as high as 110,000 for FrugalFun.com lately. The other [sites] are much less heavily trafficked, something I'll be working to change in the coming months.

Entrepreneur: *What's your look-to-buy ratio?*

Horowitz: Low, but I am not real concerned about that, because the people who need what I have seek me out.

Entrepreneur: *How big is the average purchase?*

Horowitz: I have two kinds of buyers: those who buy books, who spend $8.50 up to $120 or so, and those who buy marketing services, who spend between $155 and several thousand dollars over time. Because of the integrated nature of my business, it's hard to separate revenues. It's not an uncommon pattern, for instance, to have someone visit the site to order my marketing book and then

Smart Tip

Listen up when Shel Horowitz tells you how he markets his site on the cheap. Maybe you don't have books that will win reviews, but you do have email. Are you using your "sig" (signature) for maximum impact? Keep it short at around four to six lines. Then, get busy on the social media and Tweet, post on Facebook, "Like" other people's postings, and network with other entrepreneurs on LinkedIn.

some weeks or months later come back to look over the pages about my marketing services—and then they buy.

Entrepreneur: *Is your site profitable?*

Horowitz: This site, while not bringing in megabucks, achieves a very high return on investment, in my estimation. I sell a fair number of books directly from the sites, and I secure a number of lucrative marketing clients from the sites. I also now have more than 12,000 subscribers to three tip sheets—*Frugal Fun Tips*, *Frugal Marketing Tips* and *Positive Power of Principled Profit*—so I have a way of marketing to my visitors.

How's that for a cheap, effective website? Of course, I've written three books on cheap marketing and one on cheap fun, so I am a very good shopper, but pretty much anyone could duplicate my success.

37

Security Holes, Fraud, and More Bad Stuff

It seems too simple: Put up a website, and you're on the road to a successful business. Guess what? There are plenty of potholes in that road. While touting the possibilities of the web, experts also acknowledge the dark side and the many ways in which things can go wrong, often before you even suspect there's a problem.

According to Wally Bock, author of "How to Create a Profit-Building Web Site" and a consultant on business in the digital age, "Today, many websites are bad. They don't answer the questions or solve the problems that visitors have. They are hard to use, and many simply don't work the way they should."

Fledgling online entrepreneurs need to know the problems this industry faces, from visitors who look but never buy to wholesale theft of your most sensitive information.

One major issue, discussed earlier, is security. While you can post policies explaining how you will protect your costumer's personal information, you also need to do everything you can technically to hold true to your word.

Security

According to the experts, security fraud and theft remain a big issue today despite firewalls and encryption technology that scrambles a customer's credit card information. The problem remains that as fast as the good guys can improve ways of protecting online data, the hackers (aka the bad guys) are also busily finding ways to get around such road blocks. It can happen to the largest of companies, and has on occasion. For example, a federal indictment was reported in the summer of 2013 alleging that five Russian and Ukrainian nationals hacked into major U.S. banks and retailers and collected 160 million credit card numbers, causing hundreds of millions of dollars of thefts using stolen passwords, user IDs, and so on.

The cure? Work with security experts and never let your guard down. Usually, inexpensive solutions can be implemented that safeguard data. But they must be updated regularly.

In a survey by Webroot Software, 70 percent of online shoppers said they

Beware!

What's your vulnerability to hackers? While you likely already have the best antivirus and anti-malware software on your company computers (or damn well should!) and keep them up-to-date, some of the most popular and successful threats today depend more on hacking the humans than on hacking the technology. Train yourself and employees not to fall for scare tactics like "ransom-ware," which try to explain (or threaten) that due to some new law or policy your sensitive information will soon be released to authorities or a third party unless you send money. More insidious tactics include unsolicited warnings that your computer has already been infected or is "running slow" and you should approve the installation of some secure-sounding software to fix it. When in doubt, contact your computer technician or check out a reputable website like www.Snopes.com to debunk such claims.

A Lose-Lose Situation

According to a 2009 Lexis Nexis study, "The True Cost of Fraud," merchants in the United States alone are losing approximately $190 billion a year to credit card fraud, much of it online. Banks lose $11 billion and customers lose about 4.8 billion, so merchants lose almost 20 times as much as banks. Despite greater awareness, the numbers have not dropped. In fact, the following year, fraud was up nearly 14 percent. As of 2012, online fraud cost eretailers about $3.5 billion.

are quite comfortable with entering their credit card numbers on an internet site. However, experts still warn consumers about entering personal data in unsecured wifi areas like coffee shops, airports, or other public locations, as well as on iPhones and other mobile devices that are also becoming a major target. Unfortunately, that does not stop many people from doing so. Apparently, people either don't know or don't care how fragile they are online—until they become victims. But by then, it's too late.

Cases of identity theft, credit card fraud, and phishing, where impostors lure victims into submitting personal information, are all too common. While you cannot prevent customers from ignoring warnings, you can do your utmost to focus attention on having a very secure site.

Outages and Other Problems

Even eBay has had outages, and so have many of the online stock brokerages. The inevitable result is a flood of bad publicity as daily newspapers rush to slam a faltering web business. Sometimes outages are flukes—bugs that surface in software or during a site upgrade, an unexpected server outage or even a hacker—but often the problem stems from poor planning at the beginning.

More troubling still is the fact that outages often happen exactly when a website begins to catch on. For example, a site that works fine when there are 100 visitors a day may show strains at 1,000 and go into meltdown at 10,000 visitors because the site's server cannot handle that much traffic. Sites need to be built to scale as traffic increases, and, frankly, doing that requires nothing more than planning. Always ask, "If traffic goes up tenfold, how will we handle it?" If you don't know the answer, make sure your technical consultants do and that your servers are up to snuff. Often, this work can be assessed and accomplished at the same time as security implementation. And if you can, address the issue before launch— because when a website catches fire, it often becomes a wildfire.

Fraud

What better place to use stolen credit cards than under the relative anonymity afforded by the internet? Most e-business owners flatly refuse to talk on the record about their losses from fraud, but know that every site has had to battle with crooks.

What are some things to look out for? Experts say you should watch out for orders with different "bill to" and "ship to" addresses, as well as orders coming from other countries.

Tip...

Smart Tip

Well-funded ecommerce businesses install system-wide redundancy (aka backups). If the whole setup were to collapse, for example, an exact copy is ready to stand in and do the job. Most website hosting providers offer web businesses a range of backup and failover options for a small additional fee. In addition, anything stored on your business's local computers, like customer data, should be regularly backed up to a rotation of external hard drives and kept off-site. Why off-site? Losing your backup files as well as your originals in a fire, flood, or hurricane is a nightmare you'll want to avoid. If off-site storage is too much of a hassle, use a fireproof and waterproof safe.

According to iOvation.com, the top five countries showing the most cyber fraud in 2011 (as a percentage of the transactions originating in that country) were:

1. Ghana
2. Nigeria
3. The Philippines
4. China
5. Israel

Many others followed, with high rates of cyber fraud.

For a comprehensive list of things you can do to reduce credit card fraud, check out ScamBusters.org, a website and free electronic newsletter designed to help people protect themselves from internet scams, misinformation, and hype.

Here are some tips on fighting off cyber fraud:

1. Along with providing credit card information, ask the customer for additional information such as address and phone number. Check the card

verification number as well. This can help weed out stolen credit card numbers. Having this information will also allow you to use an address verification service to match credit card numbers up with whom they belong to. You'll notice in the brick-and-mortar world that many gas stations are asking credit card users to enter their ZIP codes to ensure against the use of a stolen credit card. It's the same principle, getting more information.

Beware!
When it comes to preventing credit card fraud, the e-business owner's conundrum is that you don't want to lose a sale to a valid customer due to cumbersome security clearances, but you also can't afford to get ripped off. Instead think about it like this: It's better to lose a sale than it is to become a victim. Always look for ways to improve your security as well as the customer's shopping experience, but keep an eye firmly on the till at all times.

2. Use your computer only for business activities and another computer for social media or any interactions and downloads. Make sure the computer has the latest in malware, spyware, and antivirus protection, and is updated regularly. This is your dedicated business computer and should not be jeopardized by other types of transactions or online activities.

3. If you have employees, make sure they have passwords to the computer(s) and have them updated often.

4. Do not get careless with a paper trail. Printouts and hard copies are good to have for when computers are not working properly, but they need to be in the right places, such as locked file drawers if customer data is on such hard copies. While we are a society becoming more acutely aware of online thefts, we often forget that many thefts come from printed matter, such as credit card information or other personal data carelessly left lying around.

5. Look for deliveries such as large orders needed immediately by your customers or orders with different billing and shipping addresses. Sites like AnyWho.com can help you match up names, businesses and different addresses. Ask what the shipping address is: a warehouse? Store? Private residence? Even though someone can make up an answer, it's a question that might throw off a would-be scammer using a bogus address.

6. Make sure all confidential information remains confidential; this includes alerting your staff to exactly how to keep such data under wraps.

7. Look online for news stories, or recent reports, about the latest online scams and stay up-to-date on common tricks being used by scammers.

8. You may also want to get business insurance against such fraud and should definitely train anyone working for you to watch out for orders that seem unusual. Also educate your customer service reps about any scams that may involve getting a replacement product, or part, or a scam in which items are returned.

Is this dark side of the web so gloomy that you should rethink your enthusiasm for this business venue? Nope, because the upside is the potential of fantastic wealth—the payoffs scored by the founders of, say, Amazon, Yahoo!, and eBay.

38

A Tour
of the Web

Sam Walton, the legendary founder of Walmart, loved to shop, especially in competitors' stores. He did not necessarily buy anything, but he delighted in roaming the aisles, noting prices and observing unique, eye-catching ways to display merchandise. Why? Every shopping trip turned into an exercise in competitive intelligence, and whenever Walton caught a competitor doing something right, he looked for ways to do it better in his Walmart stores.

You would be wise to do the same, and that means routinely surfing the web, visiting pace-setting ecommerce sites, and learning everything you can about what people are doing right. Don't think of surfing as goofing off. When you are doing it so that you can become a better ecommerce business owner, it's some of the best work you can do. Jeff Bezos, founder of Amazon, has been known to keep his Tuesdays and Thursdays open whenever possible to give himself time to surf the web in search of cool ideas.

Here's a yardstick: You are doing valuable work when, after every surfing session, you have specific, concrete ideas for improving your site. If you're not getting ideas, you're surfing the wrong sites or not thinking hard enough. Want to know how to look at websites? On the following pages, many name-brand websites are critiqued. Some win generous praise, but throughout, the emphasis is on what we can learn from these sites. And next time you put in a surfing session, ask yourself the kinds of questions you'll see in these site critiques.

River of Dreams

Amazon.com Inc.
www.amazon.com

Amazon founder Jeff Bezos named his website "Amazon" because that river is bigger than any other river on earth—or so the story goes. And Bezos' aim from the get-go was to build the web's biggest store.

Bezos came up with the idea when, as an employee of a New York financial firm, he was asked to run numbers on various possible web businesses. When he hit upon book sales, all the lights went on and Bezos knew he had a winner. Just a couple of distributors stock pretty much every book in print, and it seemed simple to set up a business that amounted to a website with no inventory. As orders came in, books could be purchased from distributors, and whoosh—profits would roll in. Bezos took the numbers to his bosses and asked them to join in funding a startup, but the verdict was *no way*. So Bezos quit, moved to Seattle, and began building what just may rank as the web's crowning etailing achievement.

There is a lot to learn from Amazon, such as the simplicity of "1-Click" buying. Like a book? A registered Amazon user can, with a single mouse click, buy it. It's that fast and that simple (so much so that tests showed users didn't believe it could be so easy. In fact, after a purchase a screen pops up that says the deal has been done).

Beware!

Amazon has filed patents on various bits of its site operation, and although nobody is clear about what Amazon intends to do to assert its rights, wary site designers are treading softly when it comes to closely imitating Amazon. This will not likely be a worry for you, both because your operation will be smaller and your technology will not be nearly as robust as Amazon's. But if you find yourself exactly duplicating the "1-Click" purchase tool, back up a few steps and try another approach.

It doesn't work only on books, however. Anything Amazon sells can be bought with a single click, and nowadays that includes TV sets, videos, CDs, power saws, toys, and much, much more.

Amazon collects and retains a buyer's key information for sales purchases such as billing and shipping addresses and what the customer last searched for in case they have come back to purchase that item. They do not waste time with extraneous information or make customers go through a long checkout process. They also include excellent landing pages so that when customers are looking for a product, it becomes very simple to know all they need to know.

The takeaways from Amazon for any ecommerce site are: ease of navigation, making it simple to make a purchase, and great landing pages. They have also done a wonderful job with customer service.

But didn't Bezos risk diluting Amazon's message by expanding into so many diverse product lines? Remember the company's name: Bezos envisioned expanding into other product lines from the start.

Amazon also features personalization features and services including extensive customer and editorial product reviews, gift registries, gift certificates, wish lists, restaurant and movie listings, travel, and photo processing. They will also make offers and suggestions based on your buying patterns.

Although personalization is hard for a low-budget site builder to incorporate, any site builder can insert "Today's Deals," just as Amazon does.

Why pay attention to what Amazon is up to? From the humble beginning in Bezos' garage, Amazon is now the world's biggest online retailer, and as the fall of 2013, the tenth most-visited website on the planet

Smart Tip

Tip...

Always compare your site with competitors', and do this ruthlessly and without an iota of favoritism. What do your competitors do very well? If you cannot list half a dozen things, go back and look at their sites more closely until you come up with at least half a dozen. The only way to make your site the best it can be is to study competitors, see what they are doing well, and then do it better.

according to Alexa, and the only retail site in the top 25. Amazon ranks number five in the United States. They also have separate websites for several countries, including Canada, United Kingdom, France, Germany, India, Italy, Spain, Brazil, Japan, and China.

The multibillion-dollar company produces their own Kindle e-book readers and their Kindle First tablet computers.

And if you want to think really, really big, consider that Amazon has, in the past 15 years, acquired Internet Movie Data Base (IMDB); Book Serge, a print-on-demand book company that is now their own publishing arm called Create Space; Brilliance Audio, the largest publisher of audiobooks in the country; Zappos; Kiva Systems; and various other businesses.

Beautify Yourself

Estée Lauder Inc.
www.Esteelauder.com

Yes, a business that was around well before the web can cash in and enjoy great online success. Example: Estée Lauder Inc., which was founded by Estée Lauder and her husband Joseph in 1946.

Selling beauty products, skincare, fragrances, and more, the site represents what the company offers in stores worldwide. To make it work, however, there is web content of interest to the Estée Lauder customer including: style guides, Skincare and Foundation Finder, Virtual Makeup Tools, guest blogs from beauty experts, and more. The key is to impart knowledge so that customers feel as if they have a personal shopper with whom to consult on all their needs. Estée Lauder Companies Inc. also owns a number of well-known brands, including Clinique, Prescriptives, M-A-C, Tommy Hilfiger, Donna Karan, Michael Kors, and Ermenegildo Zegna, all of which are represented on the website with their own links. In addition, they have their own sites.

The idea of making it simple to buy all beauty and skincare needs in one place with easy navigation doesn't replace shopping the cosmetics counters on the main floor of a leading department store where you can spray or dab on what you like, but it does increase sales for the millions of potential customers who can't get to the nearest Estée Lauder counter very easily or very often.

Free shipping is also a big plus.

What Estée Lauder does to increase the website potential is utilize online pinboards on the popular (and visually oriented) social media giant Pinterest, which caters largely to a female audience. By doing so, they are not only leading customers to purchases from their pinboards, but also getting them to check out the website and expand their possible buying options. Such cross promotion is very much in vogue today with social media leading to an increase in website visitors.

Pushing the Envelopes

Staples Inc., Office Depot Inc., and OfficeMax Inc.
www.staples.com · www.officedepot.com · www.officemax.com

The three office supplies chains—Staples, Office Depot, and OfficeMax—slug it out online every bit as vigorously as they do in the brick-and-mortar world.

In many types of retail, shoppers enjoy the physical shopping (buying shoes, clothing, or fine jewelry, for example), but with office supplies, it's no problem simply ordering from a catalog or, in this case, from a website.

Unsurprisingly, all three of these office supplies giants take essentially the same route. They all provide well-organized listings of the primary office essentials and more, which in today's business environment includes a wealth of products.

The concept is to make it easy to find the products that business clients need, with prices clearly listed and special deals presented often. All of these sites offer free shipping at some price point and are well stocked.

What can we learn from these giants? In this case, it's clear that more than one big fish can swim in the same pond, as long as there is a large pond, or in this case, a large market. In this case the market is "businesses that use office supplies," which is huge. If you are selling products or services that are very much in demand, you can survive in a crowded marketplace as long as you remain competitive (in regard to pricing and product selection), as these three sites do.

You'll also see how important it is to be up-to-date on the latest in new products as they come out. While office supplies may not be sexy, they are vital to the daily activities of all sorts of companies that rely on having the best products available. These three companies are also leaders in the field because they update their sites and their inventories often and provide cost-effective prices. They also have great customer service.

It's in the Mail

Stamps.com Inc.
www.stamps.com

The biggest challenge in selling is convincing people to do something new, something they have never done before.

Just look at Stamps.com, a site that has been around for several years but offers a service many people may have never used before: postage and shipping labels on demand.

Of course you understand postage, but the way it has always worked is that you've gone to the post office with money and walked out either with a sheet of paper stamps or with credits entered into a postage meter. Stamps.com has changed that for many online customers.

If you look closely at Stamps.com's homepage, you'll see that the primary goal is to show you how simple the process really is rather than trying to sell you immediately. In fact, they even have a video you can click on which will guide you through the buying process. Is that putting priorities in the wrong place? No, because you won't be convinced that you can buy stamps online until you see it's safe and easy. Remember, the smartest, fastest, best way to induce you to try it is to make it fast and simple to use.

Everything about this front page aims at achieving that goal, and that makes this a well-designed site. It's a lesson website designers should absorb. Sometimes the web merely offers new ways to do old things, but in other cases the web is about wholly new things to do, which is the case with Stamps.com.

Clearly, offering a new and simple way to do something online, such as buying stamps and labels, is an advantageous way to launch an e-business. With 450,000 monthly subscribers, Stamps.com has been widely successful serving small business and the steadily growing number of homebased businesses. They have also legitimized their services even more by establishing

Smart Tip

How can you make your customers' shopping easier? Are there "ready-made lists" you can create? How about lists of the most ordered items? Can a customer save his or her own wish list and then forward it to a family member or friend? Face it: No matter what any techie says, web shopping lacks the buzz and fun of a mall (although it has other strong advantages). Build in tools that make shopping go fast, and your customers will thank you by spending more money in your store.

partnerships with Avery Dennison, Microsoft, HP, Office Depot, the U.S. Postal Service, and other well-known brands.

The Right Dose

Drugstore.com Inc.
www.drugstore.com

Who likes shopping for aspirin, soap, razor blades, prescription medicines, and the rest of the stuff that takes us to drugstores? Almost nobody, and that's why an early niche targeted by trailblazing etailers was the drugstore category. Imagine if you could save yourself a half-hour—maybe more—weekly by eliminating those shopping trips and instead clicking a mouse a few times.

That's the value proposition put forth by Drugstore.com, a category leader that has won a variety of awards and accolades over the years. There is much to admire on the Drugstore.com site: pages that load quickly; numerous tools for personalization ("Your List"); a well-organized store directory where you can shop by category, such as "vitamins," "beauty," and "top sellers"; five-star reviews; and a search engine, which makes finding the necessities on your shopping list a snap. Plus, there are extensive customer reviews posted for products on the site, which help shoppers determine the best item for their needs. Special offers are also highlighted on the front page, which is always a favorite with consumers.

Drugstore.com prides itself on transparent drug pricing, making it easy for consumers to comparison shop for their prescription medications.

The other distinguishing feature about Drugstore.com is that it's leveraged upon joint marketing arrangements with well-known, brick-and-mortar businesses; its homepage, for example, highlights the GNC brand in the "vitamins" category. They also do cross promotion with leading brands of beauty products. They figure that having models wearing various brands of makeup is more aesthetically pleasing than bottles of

Smart Tip

Tip...

With whom can you forge alliances? Which companies will dress up your pages and build higher levels of visitor trust in your business? Make up a list, and start knocking on doors. For an online startup, these kinds of partnerships can spell the difference between a fast ramp-up into success or a swift plunge into failure. A few partnerships are plenty; put too many on your page, and you risk blurring your message and losing your identity.

pills and other drugstore items. Since the website is the window to your business, dress it up and make it eye-catching.

In Plain Sight

1-800-Contacts
www.1800Contacts.com

Who would have thought that contact lenses would be a hit online? But they are. The Utah-based business 1-800 Contacts opened online in 1995 and in ten years was bringing in $327 million annually in revenue. Today, it's the largest contact lenses store in the world. And why shouldn't it be? Clearly, contact lenses have become so refined over the years that they are now an easy-to-buy commodity. Customers need only fill in their contact lens prescription from the handwritten prescription provided by their doctor or on the contact lens box. They can then choose from a number of major brands including Johnson & Johnson, Vision Care, Ciba Vision, Bausch & Lomb, and CooperVision.

In June 2012, WellPoint acquired 1-800 Contacts from Fenway Partners. The business model has not changed, as they continue filling a void with fast delivery of contact lenses for nearly half a million regular customers. They have filled more than eight million prescriptions thus far.

In an attempt to cover the often-asked question about whether or not they take insurance, 1-800 Contacts makes it easy for people to use their insurance even if they have an out-of-network contact lens benefit in their vision plan.

In this business, like many others, customer retention drives sales. These are customers who will return again and again for lenses if the service is prompt and reliable. With this in mind, the company has more than 350 customer service agents trained and at the ready to answer any questions. As posted on the 1-800 Contacts website, "Customer retention is what drives us. The real value in this business is the reputation we build. Contact lenses are just the product we deliver. What we really sell is service."

It also doesn't hurt that the site is easy to navigate, focuses on one product, and offers free shipping.

Smart Tip

Tip...

While we can give you a brief tour of some of our online favorites, only you can find the sites that most inspire you to create the type of ecommerce website that best meets your needs. With that in mind, look at sites in your industry, not only competitors, but also other sites that loosely relate to the type of business you will be running.

▲

Start Your Engines

AutoZone
www.Autozone.com

Why does a company with 5,000 locations that sells auto parts need a website? Customers can't drive their cars onto the site and have it repaired. But they can get a lot of knowledge from articles and checklists that inspire them to order the parts they need. For example, AutoZone sports a "How-To" section that provides a wealth of easy-to-understand data even for the car novice. Content drives business, not cars, and it can drive an auto parts business by creating smarter customers. Heck, there's even a do-it-yourself video library plus vehicle repair help! The more they know, the more customers will buy from the site to repair or accessorize their vehicles.

From replacement parts to tools and equipment to accessories and more, the products are carefully categorized, and free shipping on orders of $75 or more is offered.

The auto parts giant opened as a store called Auto Shack in Arkansas in 1979 with a one-day sales total of $300. The name was changed in 1988, and the website was launched in 1996. In 2012, the company had revenues of $8.6 billion.

Like the office equipment giants, the idea is not to provide a host of great photos of auto parts but instead to let customers know what they have and where to find it. Pricing also must remain competitive, so AutoZone.com has regular discounts and stays on top of what the competition is doing, which is always advisable.

There is also the opportunity to sign up to get special offers and sales via email. This is always a great way of drawing customers into your business by making them feel privileged and important. Also by keeping your name in front of them regularly you can stay in the forefront of your buyers' minds so that when something seems wrong with their car, yours is the website or location they will go to first. Again, it's about repeat business, and in the auto industry (like so many industries) such business can make or break you.

Keeping It Fresh

FreshDirect Inc.
www.freshdirect.com

The odds were certainly against it, but FreshDirect Inc. (freshdirect.com), a New York-based online fresh-food retailer, is a hit.

What is making this company succeed when other cybergrocers, such as Webvan and Kozmo, were among the most well-known dotcom flops? Well, for one thing, those companies were straightforward grocery distribution companies with hubs located all over the nation. FreshDirect, on the other hand, is really a fresh-food and meal solution company that just happens to deliver its products to New York customers.

The company, conceived in 1999 by Joe Fedele (a New Yorker who has started gourmet supermarkets), shortens the supply chain by purchasing fresh foods direct from the source and processing orders in a 300,000-square-foot manufacturing facility just outside New York City, using batch-manufacturing processes. Then it delivers its products to customers in parts of New York and New Jersey.

Its food-friendly facility lets the company do much of its own food preparation, like roasting its own green coffee beans, dry-aging its own prime beef, and baking its own breads and pastries. It also sells specialty foods and popular grocery brands. And because it doesn't have a retail location, FreshDirect doesn't pay expensive rent for retail space. These factors help keep food fresh and costs low and allow the company to pass the savings on to its customers. As a result, FreshDirect says it can save customers up to 25 percent compared with local retail markets. The company is expanding rapidly and currently serves most of Manhattan and locations in Queens, Brooklyn, Staten Island, and the Bronx, as well as parts of New Jersey, Westchester, and Nassau County.

As a FreshDirect customer, you can shop anytime from work or home, and the company brings everything directly to you in a FreshDirect refrigerator/freezer truck so the food is protected all the way to your door.

The competitive advantage of Fresh Direct is a vast network of professionals that find fresh food. As FreshDirect co-founder David McInerney notes on the website, his team of food experts "go from Pennsylvania to Patagonia (by way of Alaska) to find our most spectacular fresh foods. You'll get to know the people and places behind the products we're most excited to bring you."

There are numerous reasons for the company's success. One is the concept itself—fresh food sold at low cost and delivered to your door. Another is the company's focus on providing a robust shopping experience for incredibly fresh foods and meal solutions.

Another reason for its success is its easy-to-use website. FreshDirect's online store is a cinch to use and is loaded with

> ### Smart Tip
> A key to FreshDirect's success is its graphics. It shows all its products in a clear and very appetizing way. Are you selling products that would bene-fit from appealing graphics? If so, spend the bucks, and make sure they look good. It really makes a difference to consumers. The bet-ter, more appealing something looks, the more likely people are to buy it.

great information. Learn about what you're buying. Compare products by price, nutrition, and flavor. Get recommendations for foods to suit your taste. When you come back, the company remembers what you ordered last time so you can reorder in minutes.

When you visit the homepage, you'll see that it highlights its delivery information, which is important, especially since it must get many calls and questions from people about this important part of its business model. It also asks you to find out if the company is delivering in your neighborhood. All you have to do is enter your ZIP code.

Smart Tip

Tip...

Navigation is key to a website. Can users find what they're looking for on yours in a glance? Major corporations actually test and time users as they poke around early renditions of websites. You can do the same. Ask employees, friends, or neighbors to navigate your site, and listen to their feedback. It does no good if you hide your gems. They need to be readily visible, even to casual lookers.

FreshDirect will even let you know, on the homepage, if you aren't located in an area where they deliver. You can still browse the site and enter your email address to receive a notice if FreshDirect will be coming to your area.

FreshDirect's homepage is designed to make navigating its vast product offerings very simple. The homepage includes Daily Produce Quality Ratings, Chef-made Entrees, and Easy Family Meals, plus other catchy headlines that attract attention and provide food-friendly ideas. Departments such as "Fruit," "Dairy," and "Meat" are clearly listed. Once you are in each department, you are treated to more graphics and details so you can easily click on the exact item you'd like. Prices are clearly listed here as well, which is a plus.

As a new ecommerce entrepreneur, you can learn a lot from FreshDirect. The website is clearly built around what customers want: numerous product choices, easy navigation, assurance of fast delivery, and competitive prices. The company meets a need, serving people in a vast metropolitan area that may not have the time to get out and shop as often as they would like. For busy executives (and there are many in the New York City area), as well as seniors and individuals with disabilities, FreshDirect serves them well.

They have built their business around a geographic area in which such a business model works, recognizing that delivering food to people in rural areas or farmlands with vast resources and easy access to fresh foods would probably be less lucrative than delivering to those in the big city who have less access to freshly grown foods.

You may also find that your business model works best in a specific city or region that is underserved.

Get Connected

PC Connection
www.pcconnection.com

Founded in 1982, PC Connection has grown into a trusted source in the highly competitive computer industry. Bringing in roughly $2 billion in annual revenue, the site works by offering thousands of products from more than 1,500 manufacturers, all while providing excellent customer service and IT consulting.

A key to being a smaller player in a very competitive industry is offering more service and imparting more knowledge. By staying ahead of the always changing high-tech learning curve, PC Connection has been able to provide answers, custom configurations, strategies, and solutions that some of the larger players don't have the time to offer.

Another key to the success of PC Connection is that they not only serve small and large companies but also work with government organizations and schools from K-12 to higher education. By positioning themselves in these arenas they can provide expertise in meeting the needs of these large buying markets.

The site itself features easy-to-find products and brands and simple checkout tools. There are also key sections for professional IT services, a Solutions Center, and Technical Resources. The goal is to maintain the infrastructure throughout the IT lifecycle.

Just like the folks at PCConnect.com, you can also build your site around the needs of your audience, provide as much service as possible, and seek out other large buying markets, whether that means the local government, schools, or seniors. Expanding your market to those who need your products and services is a marvelous way to gain a large chunk of additional business.

If the Shoe Fits

Shoebuy.com Inc.
www.shoebuy.com

Shoebuy.com is one of the largest retailers on the internet focused on all categories of footwear and related apparel. Shoebuy has partnerships with more than 400 manufacturers and offers more than 600,000 products from top brands, including Dockers, Florsheim, Keds, New Balance, Reebok, Skechers, Tommy Hilfiger, and many more.

Simplicity is the guiding principle of the Shoebuy.com website. There are several ways to find your shoes of choice quickly and easily, and they are clearly listed on the Shoebuy homepage: You can browse departments for men, women, teens, or children, or sale shoes; browse by collection, such as "boots" or "bridal shoes"; or browse by brand. A search button at the top of the page also allows users to search by brand, size, wide shoes, or narrow shoes. There is also an "Advanced Search" button.

Shoebuy.com also offers a 100 percent price guarantee. If you find a product for a lower price on another website, it will refund you 100 percent of the difference between the lower price and Shoebuy's price. It will even refund the difference if it lowers the price at Shoebuy. Plus, the company has been offering free shipping on all orders since January 2000, when its site was officially launched. This freebie is prominently displayed throughout the site.

The CEO and co-founder of the company, Scott Savitz, has said that he didn't want to enter into this business if he couldn't sell a product that offered free shipping because he believed it was part of the whole value proposition. He felt that just because Shoebuy.com was offering a product on the internet, that alone wasn't enough for somebody to make a purchase.

Of course, in the shoe business (*and there's no business like shoe business*), free return shipping can make or break you since the biggest consumer fear is whether or not the glass slipper will fit. Shoebuy offers free return shipping.

Shoebuy.com, Amazon.com, Drugstore.com, and nearly all these companies, plus many more, are using free shipping promotions to encourage people to buy online. And why not? Experts have said that they lure more mainstream buyers to

Dollar Stretcher

How can you give away shipping and not go broke? While FedEx and its competitors negotiate highly favorable rates with big shippers, they won't necessarily do the same with small businesses. But that doesn't mean only big-bucks options are left. Use UPS standard delivery or the post office. Both are cheap. A one-pound package can be shipped cross-country via the post office for around $4.60, and that buys two-to-three-day Priority Mail delivery. If that gets you a buyer who becomes a repeat customer, isn't it some of the smartest money you've ever spent? Don't be too quick to say you can't afford to offer free shipping for the right order amount.

the internet—such as shoppers who are more price-sensitive, have lower incomes than frequent online shoppers, and are more used to the brick-and-mortar world than surfing the internet. But there are some downsides to free shipping, and a major one would be cost. So before taking the free shipping plunge, run the numbers and make sure it won't have a devastating impact on your bottom line.

These are just a few of the many online businesses you can visit. Remember to search often and learn from other sites.

The Future
of Ecommerce

Where is ecommerce heading? Tough topic, but to gain insight into the future, I asked Bruce Weinberg, chair of the marketing department at the McCallum Graduate School of Business of Bentley College and a visiting scholar at the McCombs School of Business of the University of Texas at Austin, for his thoughts.

A writer and thinker about the net, with particular expertise in online shopping and online consumer behavior, Weinberg is both a tough critic of present-day etailing and a bona fide optimist about the role of ecommerce in tomorrow's retailing mix. You may not always agree with the opinionated Weinberg, but his thoughts are well worth pondering.

Entrepreneur: *What's the best etailing site on the web?*

Bruce Weinberg: Amazon is still *numero uno*. eBay remains a great alternative for many buyers and sellers; although, the shine is off this rose a bit. In addition, I want to give a shout out to local merchants and wholesalers who have extended effectively to online retail and are providing value to customers by offering information online and/or items for sale.

Some key aspects of their approach to constructing and operating a business are:

- Enabling customers to develop high degrees of trust in the exchange process, which, theoretically and practically, is critical for long-term success in any business. As 1972 economics Nobel Laureate Ken Arrow said, trust reduces the friction in commerce.

- They each offer great value by making it easier for customers to find a wide variety of items through a one-stop shopping experience. The notion of value in a one-stop shopping process in an online environment may sound strange given the ease with which you can switch from one website to another. However, some factors at play that make this plausible are that time is relative and loyalty is an investment that keeps on giving.

Time Is Relative

If I told you that you could be physically transported to the aisles of your favorite bookstore in 5 to 10 seconds, you would be elated. Normally this could take on the order of 5 to 30 minutes. However, waiting 5 to 10 seconds for a web page to download would drive you nuts (assuming the use of a high-speed internet connection). Normally, a web page loads in one second or less with a high-speed connection. In the physical world, one to two seconds is really fast; however, in the web world, one to two seconds is not so fast—it may even be annoyingly slow to some people. So time is relative. The few seconds it may take to type in another URL or search for another online store to visit may not be perceived as quick when operating in an online state of mind (with apologies to Billy Joel). One-stop shopping saves online consumers time.

Loyalty

The investment that keeps on giving. On average, consumers continue to view shopping online as a risky activity. This risk is reduced when consumers find a trustworthy and reliable merchant (or merchants, in the case of eBay). Consumers believe that the majority of online purveyors are untrustworthy, so when they find one they can trust, they are surprisingly likely to stick with it. One good experience after another increases customers' trust and loyalty. Consumers are investing their shopping hearts and minds into the online merchant. This results in a cycle that is difficult for a competitor to break. The loyal and invested customer is more likely to consider and value alternative offerings, such as those that could be offered in a one-stop shopping environment.

In general, a website—and the processes set in motion based on customer interaction with a website—should do the following six things:

1. *Allow customers to move through the buying process better than is possible through other means.* If the purpose of the site is to provide information, then it should provide information either more effectively or more efficiently than was possible before the firm offered a website. If the site allows customers to order products, then it should enable a better experience in some meaningful way. For example, catalog retailers should make the online ordering process either faster or more convenient than ordering via telephone.

2. *Clearly describe a product* so that consumers know exactly what they are considering (check out a camera review at Dpreview.com, and you'll see an example of a site that leaves little to the imagination).

3. *Put forth a sincere effort to truly understand a customer* through communication and sincere interest.

4. *Provide full and accurate information upfront about what is being offered.* For example, don't make customers go through the checkout process in order to find out whether an item is in stock or to find out the full cost of an order (which includes the costs of the product, sales tax, and shipping).

5. *Keep promises.* Say what you mean and mean what you say. For example, deliver the next day when a customer pays for next-day service. And don't call something next-day service unless it means the product will be delivered to the customer on the next day.

6. *Respect customers' privacy and security.* Consumers have serious concerns about these issues. Once a person overcomes them to buy from you, do everything in your power to maintain the promised and expected levels of privacy and security.

Entrepreneur: *Do you have a personal favorite website?*

Weinberg: My favorite sites tend to be the ones that help me find effective solutions to my problems.

I'll mention two particular sites here, but I'll note a couple of experiences that speak to the general notion of a "favorite" website that helps me find effective solutions. For online shopping, my most preferred site is eBay, the online auction site. At eBay, I almost always find what I want, when I want it, at a price that I find reasonable (as I play a role in setting the price when bidding in an auction). In addition, I get a thrill from shopping at eBay; it is an affect-rich shopping and buying experience. First, there is the excitement associated with finding an item that I thought I would never find anywhere (e.g., a Rolls-Royce key case, a brand-new unit of an old version of a handheld solitaire game). Next, there is the delight associated with interacting with other bidders (though some would call this the rush of competition). Then, there is the agony of defeat or the thrill of victory (with apologies to *ABC's Wide World of Sports*). Finally, I don't buy items on eBay; I win them. I love the feeling of getting a great deal when I win. But on eBay and other online auction sites, you should be careful of the winner's curse (in essence, paying too much for an item) and of the potential for addictively "chasing losses." Researchers at Harvard Medical School have observed some similarities between gambling and auction bidding with respect to human behaviors and emotions.

I also enjoy using Google. Two to four years ago, it probably would have sounded strange to have a search site as a favorite. Now, however, I suspect that Google is a favorite site for millions of people. In both my professional and personal life, I frequently find the need or desire to search for information online. Google typically leads me to information that will help me "find" what I am looking for or solve a problem, either now or down the road. For example, I easily reconnected with a long-lost friend from Sweden by "Googling" him. His name appeared in a few web pages, one of which included his email address. We got together in Boston for dinner and I'm now arranging for my family to visit his home in Sweden.

Google has also helped me find websites that addressed pressing problems for me. During the summer of 2005, my central air conditioning compressor unit stopped working. Most people would probably call an air conditioning repair company. Well, I was not sufficiently confident that I would easily find one that would act mostly in my best interest (and pocketbook). A new unit could cost thousands of dollars! So I hit the internet looking for, and finding, a place where I could learn how to diagnose and, as it turned out, repair my central air conditioning unit. I visited the "Cozy Community" of CozyParts.com, an independent Lennox dealer in Oklahoma.

Similarly, I had a problem getting my radio to work in my 1993 Lexus LS400 after I had disconnected and then reconnected a battery cable. I believe a Lexus dealer would have charged upward of hundreds of dollars to "help me out." In the end, I found a solution within a community of car owners at CarKB.com, which cost me a few minutes of my time in the end. My approach to resolving a problem may not be effective for everyone, as I can be a bit of a do-it-yourselfer type.

Entrepreneur: *What's wrong with all—or virtually all—ecommerce sites today?*

Weinberg: Tough question. I'll stop short of saying that certain problems are associated with all ecommerce sites. But I will highlight some areas where firms should seriously reconsider the status quo.

First, I believe many sites could benefit from a greater appreciation of the consumer buying-decision process. The process has been the same for centuries, and it is unlikely to change in the foreseeable future. It details precisely what consumers do when engaged in the process of buying. They: 1) recognize a problem or need, 2) may search for information to reduce the risk associated with the buying decision to be made, 3) may evaluate alternatives and come to a decision about which one may be "best," 4) make the purchase, and 5) carry out a variety of post-purchase activities, such as consuming the product, spreading negative or positive word-of-mouth, returning the item, and so forth.

Second, businesses should realize that humans engage in exchange and that the internet, the web, computers, and other technologies are exchange tools for humans—not the other way around. Model your approach for exchange based on this simple and important principle. eBay brings together buyers and sellers. Match.com brings together people who want companionship. World of Warcraft, an online game with about 10 million subscribers, brings together people who like to interact through and explore fantasy worlds.

Third, scaling [growing your business] is a great way to garner more profits per dollar invested; however, scaling works only when a successful process remains a successful process in its scaled form. Don't assume that every business process that can be automated and scaled up in some way should be automated and scaled up. For example, using a Help/FAQ section as a means for scaling the availability of customer service may not be enough. Sometimes the customer or the situation requires more assistance than what is offered by a set of FAQs. Even mighty Amazon learned this lesson, as it now offers customer service over the phone.

All this being said, there are situations where scaling online may be extremely effective. For example, consider the case of viral marketing, or getting others to pass along your message or some message that will bring customers to your door. The internet can be extremely effective in this regard. In addition, the web is a great way to scale the number of interactions with a person and the number of people with whom you have an interaction. For example, you can have interactions through an electronic newsletter. This can effectively support a permission-marketing program.

Entrepreneur: *What business principles hold in ecommerce?*

Weinberg: Tried-and-true business principles hold in ecommerce. If your value proposition is weak, then your appeal to customers will likely be weak. In addition, to survive in ecommerce, it is critical to have a clear vision and reasonable plan for success, determination and discipline in execution, and the ability to understand and satisfy consumers. You must not only have a great idea, but also be able to "make it happen." There is a long history of entrepreneurs who developed "greater mousetraps" that did not result in everyone beating a path to their door. In addition, understand that consumers, in both B2C and B2B, have more "power" and expectations.

> **Smart Tip**
>
> Tip...
>
> Where do eBay and Amazon excel? By enabling customers to develop high degrees of trust in the exchange process, offering great value by making it easier for customers to find a wide variety of items through a one-stop shopping process, keeping promises, and respecting their customers' privacy. Do you do these things? If so, you're on the right track to success.

Entrepreneur: *What niches have yet to be fully attacked by etailers?*

Weinberg: I currently see a lot of opportunity in online (video) games. Some massive multiplayer games have been successful, such as World of Warcraft and Everquest, and many have failed, such as The Sims Online. However, I see the stars aligning in terms of consumers' experience with mobile devices and relevant technological advances in wireless devices and service delivery, and game development. The line between physical reality and virtual reality is going to increasingly blur. Consumers will be doing more, and spending more money, in virtual/digital contexts.

Entrepreneur: *What will the next-generation sites offer that today's sites don't?*

Weinberg: Sites in the future will offer increases in speed, fidelity (e.g., the ability to feel items and speech recognition), ease of use, and access for the physically or psychologically challenged. In addition, sites will facilitate or carry out decision making. The web has become a terrific place for acquiring information; it will evolve into a great place for not only this but also for using/processing that information, such as making decisions or evaluating/judging emotions for you.

Entrepreneur: *What are two bad ecommerce sites? Why?*

Weinberg: Pick any two that make your blood boil or bring out frustration. The most common causes are grounded in content (e.g., limited product information, limited product availability), functionality (e.g., navigation, checkout, customer service), and privacy or security. A site that bothers me is that of Hermès, one of the world's leading luxury good brands. The site provides an irritating shopping experience. Navigation is neither intuitive nor pleasant, and information is minimal.

Entrepreneur: *What has fundamentally ailed the prevailing B2C website business models?*

Weinberg: I see many problems. Here are a few:

- Systems should be structured [according to how] consumers think and behave.

- Great ideas are wonderful things. They stimulate other great ideas. A great idea, however, is not enough to build a sustainable enterprise.

- Many firms got hung up on giving product to consumers. Some initial promotions effectively generated awareness and trial. At some point, however, these promotions should have stopped. Aside from credit card fraud, shipping charges are one of the most-mentioned [negatives] for those who have not shopped online (and even for some who have shopped online). If organizations were to provide free or flat-rate shipping and drop the ridiculous promotions, I bet sales would do just fine and profits would be improved.

- Websites lack personality; they can be sterile. Let's see some faces or caricatures on these sites. Provide cues that bring out human affect—we humans like emotion.

- Word-of-mouth is the most powerful and persuasive form of communication. Organizations should more actively look for ways to integrate this into their websites, and they should utilize the social media through their presence on Facebook, Twitter, and so on. Allow customers to share their opinions/ratings and reviews, to read those of others, and to interact with one another. Sure, it means giving up some control, which can be frightening. But it can also be liberating and improve the customer experience and the bottom line.

Entrepreneur: *Is Jeff Bezos still the smartest etailer around? Why or why not?*

Weinberg: Two years ago, I wrote that, in my opinion, he and Meg Whitman [eBay] were the smartest online retailers and marketers who were leading internet companies. Jeff Bezos has primarily earned his reputation through Amazon. He was an ecommerce groundbreaker and has inspired and taught millions of people to engage the internet as buyers, sellers, surfers, etc. I see great nerve and genius in what he has done. Jeff cleverly helped Amazon evolve into more of an etailing platform provider where, like eBay, it leveraged its technology and understanding of the marketplace to bring buyers and sellers together while outsourcing much of the physical (and harder-to-scale) aspects of the buying/selling process.

Entrepreneur: *Are any small etailers safe from Amazon now that Bezos has extended his retailing empire into more new categories?*

Weinberg: Amazon can flow on and on. I love its model of involving everyone and helping him or her get a piece of the online pie (e.g., individuals, small companies, affiliates, other leading retailers). The internet is partly about creating connections, sharing information, helping people identify their passions and realize their dreams, getting people involved to use their brainpower and voice, and providing access. I believe that Amazon does most of this reasonably well.

Entrepreneur: *If ecommerce is different in the near future, how will it be? How will it be the same?*

Weinberg: I mentioned multichannel marketing before. Many aspects of ecommerce will be integrated into the ways business gets done and customers are served. It will no longer be perceived as a process that dominates the entire way a firm does business; rather, it will be considered an element in an overall business process. The government will play a greater role in regulating ecommerce and will more effectively enforce laws that are violated in an ecommerce context. Issues of privacy and security, particularly identity theft, will remain important. I expect to see a huge increase in the number of "digital" security companies. In the physical world, American life transitioned from a time where people left the front door open to one where you'd be crazy to leave your house or car without setting the alarm. I expect the same to hold in the virtual world. Digital security will become increasingly complex and lucrative as more aspects of our lives become connected online/electronically, such as the home, cars, and—yes—people. A variety of devices will begin to get connected via the internet. Think back to the 1967 movie *The*

> ### Smart Tip
> Tip...
>
> Remember: Amazon offers many ways for you to succeed by helping it get more successful. There are auctions, the low-cost shops—instant storefronts with fixed pricing—and, of course, the slick Amazon affiliates program. By all means, Jeff Bezos wants to be the top dog on the net, but he is shrewd enough to see that your success can forward his goals. So do as Bruce Weinberg suggests and find ways to help yourself while helping Amazon.

Wireless Wonders

In the movie *The Graduate*, the future revolved around plastics, or so the young grad was told. Today, the future definitely revolves around wireless and mobile technologies. Find your niche in mobile technologies, and you are on a very fast track to success.

Graduate and say the word "wireless" instead of "plastic" (see "Wireless Wonders" in this chapter).

One big change I see is the powerful force of large players dominating various aspects of ecommerce and internet media. For example, just as ABC, NBC, and CBS were dominant when TV broadcasting was emerging and maturing, I expect to see Google, Yahoo!, Microsoft, and, perhaps, in some shape or form, eBay, dominating internet information/functionality delivery. These sites, in many respects, have become one-stop gateways for consumers' internet needs.

Appendix
e-Business Resources

Here's the blunt truth about ecommerce: Most of what you need to know will not be printed in books or even in magazines and newspapers. One medium that is successfully tracking the rapid developments online is the web itself. When you want to know more or need answers to questions, log on to the web and go searching. The information you crave is rarely more than a few clicks away. Here you will find sites that deserve tracking.

Blog Software

Blogger: blogger.com
Typepad: typepad.com

Wordpress*: wordpress.com*

Competitive Intelligence

Fuld & Co.'s Internet Intelligence Index

Fuld & Co., a research and consulting firm in the field of business and competitive intelligence, has compiled a comprehensive index of information from a wide variety of sources in an effort to help businesses stay abreast of the competition and be prepared to overcome competitive challenges. Fuld uses customized, proprietary research, analysis, and consulting to help their clients. www.fuld.com

KnowX

The savvy engine ferrets through public records and reports on bankruptcies, liens, judgments, and such against individuals and businesses. Reports typically range from free to $29.95. www.knowx.com

Thomas Register

This sourcebook on U.S. and Canadian companies has been around for 95 years. You can find the book in print or on CD or DVD, and it is free to companies in the United States and Canada, not including shipping and handling charges, plus the content on the website is free as well. www.thomasnet.com

Yahoo! Finance

This all-inclusive website has everything from up-to-the minute market summaries to stock research to financial news—and much of it is free. www.finance.yahoo.com

Consumer Websites

BBBOnLine

The Better Business Bureau's ecommerce monitoring site. www.bbbonline.org

Internet ScamBusters

This is a website and a free electronic newsletter designed to help people protect themselves from internet scams, misinformation, and hype; much of the information focuses on internet merchants and consumers. www.scambusters.org

SafeShopping

Created by the American Bar Association, this site bills it as "the place to stop before you shop." www.safeshopping.org

Stop Fraud

This is a government site at which you can report fraud, including cyber and computer-based fraud. www.stopfraud.gov

WebAssured

An etailer evaluator. www.webassured.com

Direct Marketing and Mail Order

The Direct Marketing Association

This association's website offers lots of great information for companies starting out online or in mail order. www.thedma.org

National Mail Order Association

Longstanding organization providing marketing information for direct marketers and web marketers. www.nmoa.org

Domain Name Registrars

1 & 1: 1and1.com

All Domains: alldomains.com

GoDaddy: godaddy.com

iWantMyName: iwantmyname.com

Name: name.com

Namecheap: namecheap.com

Network Solutions: networksolutions.com

Register.com: register.com

Ecommerce Solutions

Amazon's WebStore

Create your own store and use Amazon's payments system. www.amazonservices. com/webstore

eBay

Offers successful auctioneers a storefront within eBay stores. ebay.com or pages.ebay. com/storefronts/start.html

Intuit Solutions

Set up your own store through http://quickbooks.intuit.com/qb/products/pos/pos_ storefront/pos_storefront_benefits.jsp and sell up to 100 products.

osCommerce

Open-source online ecommerce solution with 7,000 add-ons. www.oscommerce.com

ProStores

Ecommerce solution owned by eBay; users can run their stores independently or list their inventory on eBay as well. www.prostores.com

Web.com

A full suite of tools for building and hosting a complete ecommerce storefront. www.web.com

Yahoo! Merchant Solutions

A simple and fast way to get an ecommerce store up and running. www.smallbusiness.yahoo.com/ecommerce

Global Commerce

GlobalEDGE

Michigan State University's International Business Center's vast library of world trade resources that includes an outline of the business climate, political structure, history, and statistical data for more than 190 countries; a directory of international business resources categorized by specific orientation and content; and much more. globaledge.msu.edu/resourcedesk; www.globalcommercesolutions.biz/index.shtml

Miscellaneous Ecommerce Information

Constant Contact

A leading email marketing service provider targeting small businesses; the company helps set up and run an email list. www.constantcontact.com

Keynote NetMechanic

For checking your site for bad code and broken links. www.netmechanic.com

LinkShare

For signing up for affiliate status with name-brand etailers. www.linkshare.com

Microsoft Business Hub

A great resource for anyone starting a new business, with technical and business solutions. www.microsoftbusinesshub.com

ReveNews.com

A leading blog that covers topics such as affiliate marketing, online marketing, contextual advertising, search marketing, online publishing, and spyware; the blog has very knowledgeable writers that offer fresh commentary on current events. www.revenews.com

Online and Offline Publications

Business 2.0: http://money.cnn.com/magazines/business2/

E-Commerce Times: ecommercetimes.com

Entrepreneur **magazine**: entrepreneur.com

Internet Retailer: internetretailer.com

Mashable: mashable.com

MIT Technology Review: techreview.com

Wired: wired.com

Payment

Authorize.Net: authorize.net

Cubecart: cubecart.com

Cybersource: cybersource.com

PayPal: paypal.com

PrestaShop: prestashop.com

Shop Factory: shopfactory.com

Search Engines

Bing: bing.com

Google: google.com

Google Adwords: adwords.google.com/select

SearchEngineWatch: searchenginewatch.com

Yahoo!: yahoo.com

Shopping Bots

BidFind: bidfind.com

BizRate: bizrate.com

BottomDollar: bottomdollar.com

eSmarts: esmarts.com

Google Product Search: google.com/products

mySimon: mysimon.com

RoboShopper: roboshopper.com

Social Networking

Facebook
Originally for college students, this juggernaut is now one of the top two websites in the world (along with Google). www.facebook.com

Google Plus
Google's attempt to compete with Facebook; however, many members are included by simply utilizing other Google services. https://accounts.google.com/

LinkedIn
The social networking network for businesspeople. www.linkedin.com

MySpace
The granddaddy of social networking sites is revamped but remains a shell of its former self. www.myspace.com

Ning
Online service that allows you to create, customize, and share your own social network. www.ning.com

Pinterest
A very quickly growing visual platform where businesses, and consumers, set up pinboards with photographs, many of which are outstanding. www.pinterest.com

Twitter
A headline-driven, fast-paced social network where users post up to 140 characters (more on occasion) from their phones or computers. www.twitter.com

Software

Dreamweaver CS3
Popular, higher-end web design software

Download.com
Powered by cnet.com, the site allows users to download trial and full versions of software.

Photoshop Elements 11
Consumer-friendly "light" version of Photoshop. www.adobe.com

Website Building Software
(found on various sites selling computer software)

Intuit Website Creator

Web Studio

WebEasy Professional

WebPlus

Yola Silver

ZyWeb

Statistics and More

ClickZ
Net-related stats in a readable format. www.clickz.com/stats

eMarketer
A great news source with an ecommerce focus; lots of stats. www.emarketer.com

Traffic Reports and Ratings

Alexa
Measures the most popular sites on the web. www.alexa.com

comScore Media Metrix
This features the audience measurement division of comScore Networks. It offers an internet audience measurement service that reports on website usage. www.comscore.com

Internet Traffic Report
Measures router volume at various points around the world. www.internettrafficreport.com

Nielsen NetRatings
A leader in internet media and market research. www.nielsen-netratings.com

Venture Capital and Angel Information

Angel Capital Association
An organization of angel groups with listings to browse. www.angelcapitalassociation.org

Angels Den

Features a variety of ways to connect entrepreneurs with angel investors including SpeedFunding™, Angel Clubs, and Custom Emails. www.angelsden.com

Entrepreneurship.com

A website from the well-known Ewing Marion Kauffman Foundation that can be tapped for timely, practical information on how to start, manage, and expand your business.

National Venture Capital Association

This association's website contains industry statistics and lists of venture capital organizations and preferred industry service providers. www.nvca.org

Funding Post

A source for information on pitching and accumulating funding, also runs nationwide meet-ups and conferences to bring entrepreneurs and investors together. www.fundingpost.com

Golden Seeds Angel Network

One of the nation's largest angel networks, Golden Seeds has more than 280 members who evaluate funding and help new businesses through the investment process. www.goldenseeds.com/angel-network

VFinance.com

A directory of venture capital resources and related services; a good site for getting info on who's who in the VC world and how deals get cut. www.vfinance.com

Web Art

Clip-Art: clipart.com

Free Graphics: freegraphics.com

FreeRange Stock: freerangestock.com

iStockPhoto: istockphoto.com

New Vision Technologies: nvtech.com

The Open Photo Project: openphoto.net

Stock.xchng: sxc.hu

Stockvault: stockvault.net

Web Hosts

1&1 Internet: 1and1.com

ANHosting: anhosting.com

Blue Genesis: bluegenesis.com

Bluehost: bluehost.com

Compare Web Hosts: comparewebhosts.com

DreamHost: dreamhost.com

FatCow: fatcow.com

Globat: globat.com

GoDaddy: godaddy.com

HostGator: hostgator.com

HostMonster: hostmonster.com

Hostway: hostway.com

iPage: iPpage.com

Ipower: ipower.com

JustHost: justhost.com

Midphase: midphase.com

Top 10 Website Builders: Reviews of top web hosts. http://web-hosting-review.
   toptenreviews.com

TopHosts: Another web host comparison site. www.tophosts.com

Web.com: web.com

Westhost: westhost.com

Website Building Tools and Help

TechRepublic
www.techrepublic.com

123 Webmaster
More than 4,500 free resources for web development. www.123webmaster.com

W3Schools
Free source for web-building tutorials. www.w3schools.com

WebDeveloper.com
One-stop shopping for advice and tools for building better websites, with links to web design tutorials, affiliate program guides, and more. www.webdeveloper.com

Webmaster Tools Inc
Directory of webmaster resources. www.webmastertools.com

Wireless Web

Open Mobile Alliance
This organization is designed to be the center of mobile service standardization work, helping the creation of inter-operable services across countries, operators, and mobile terminals that will meet the needs of users. www.openmobilealliance.org

TagTag
A one-stop shop for web-ready mobile content. www.tagtag.com

Glossary

Advertising network: a company that connects advertisers with publishers that want to display ads.

Affiliate program: a program that allows companies to earn revenue by advertising and selling the products of another company.

Angel investor: a private individual who invests his or her own money into an entrepreneurial company; angels can be affiliated (meaning they are familiar with you or your business beforehand) or nonaffiliated.

Angel network: a group of angel investors who team up and invest together.

Antivirus: software that helps protect computers from viruses.

Beta site: a test site, usually erected in the authoring phase of a website.

Blog: a running archive of entries typically on a specific subject. Many sites have blogs on them.

Bot: a robot, or software program, that automatically does specified tasks.

Brick-and-mortar: a term describing traditional businesses with a physical storefront rather than a cyberbusiness.

▲

Browsers: programs that let you view web pages and websites including text, graphics, sound, etc. Popular browsers include Microsoft Internet Explorer (often called IE), Mozilla, Safari, Opera, and Chrome.

Business to business (B2B): companies that market to businesses, not consumers, as customers.

Business to consumer (B2C): companies that market to consumers.

Clip art: off-the-shelf images anyone can use; website authoring programs usually include lots of clip art.

Common gateway interface (CGI) script: a simple program that runs on the net; guest books, for instance, often are CGI scripts.

Cookie: data created by a web server that's stored on a user's computer to identify that user on return visits to the website.

CPC (cost-per-click): a method of advertising that pays money to website publishers only when an online ad is clicked on by a site visitor.

CPM (cost-per-thousand): a method of advertising in which advertisers pay website publishers a certain amount of money for every 1,000 ads displayed on their website(s).

CRM: stands for "customer relationship management."

Domain name: the name that a company or individual registers to use as a location on the internet; it's what comes before the ".com," ".net," or ".edu," all of which are known as top-level domains.

File extension: letters at the end of a file name that indicate the type of file. For example, .txt is for text and .jpg or .gif are often used for photos.

File transfer protocol (FTP): the system used to transfer files over the internet. You FTP files to your host.

First-mover advantage: the built-in advantage of being the first business in a particular category.

Flash: multimedia technology that allows you to add interactive and animated components to a website.

Fulfillment: the process of honoring and sending out product orders.

Host: a company that provides space for storing (hosting) a website (aka hosting service).

Hyperlink: a connection between one object and another; also known as a link.

HTML (hypertext markup language): code that creates web pages.

Internet service provider (ISP): the company that provides the connection that lets a user connect to the net; typical connection methods include DSL, wireless broadband, dial-up, ethernet, and cable modem.

JavaScript: the very popular scripting language on the internet, developed by Netscape, that lets you add special effects to your website.

JPEG and JPG: graphic formats for storing compressed images.

Keywords: terms that advertisers bid on through PPC (pay-per-click) ad programs like Google AdWords. Keywords are also terms used on a web page that factor into its search engine ranking.

Log: a record of all visits to a website; a log usually gives a click-by-click report on a visitor.

Metrics: a system of measurement used to evaluate web data, such as web traffic.

Podcasting: recording audio or video files and making them available online so they can be downloaded and listened to rather like an "on-demand" radio show.

Pure play: a company that does business exclusively on the web (it has no brick-and-mortar stores).

ROI: an acronym for return on investment, which means how much you are seeing in revenue from your web marketing expenses (or investment).

RSS feed: RSS is a family of web feed formats, specified in XML and used for web syndication.

Search engine: a website that exists to help users find other websites; Google (google.com) is the most popular.

SEM (search engine marketing): the process of increasing traffic to a website through paid methods, such as pay-per-click ad programs AdWords and Bing Ads.

SEO (search engine optimization): the process of optimizing the content of a website, including its use of keywords, in order to improve its listing in search engine results organically.

Shopping cart: a program that lets users shop and buy products or services at an online website by adding items to a virtual cart and paying or "checking out."

Social media: community-oriented websites that allow users to create their own homepages, "friend" other users to create social networks, interact with one another, and join communities of interest; for example: Facebook.com and LinkedIn.com.

▲

Spam: unwanted, unsolicited commercial email.

Spider: also known as crawlers or web spiders, search engines use spiders to find web pages.

Template: a predesigned document; a web page template, for instance, requires the user to simply fill in some blanks to produce a publishable document.

Term sheet commitment: a written offer from a venture capitalist that sets out how much money the firm will invest in a startup in return for a percentage of ownership.

URL: an acronym for universal resource locator or, more simply, a web page's address.

Venture capitalist (VC): a professional money lender who seeks out high-potential startups to fund and usually receives an ROI via the startup's IPO or acquisition.

Web analytics: the measurement, collection, analysis, and reporting of internet data for purposes of understanding and optimizing web usage as well as marketing.

Web designer: someone who creates the graphics and the content that contributes to the look and feel of a website.

Web developer: someone who builds a website using programming languages; he or she is responsible for the framework behind the content you see on a web page.

Widget: miniature web application that allow users to view information such as news headlines or weather forecasts, view photos, and play music and video.

Wiki: a collaborative website that allows readers to add content on a subject, which can also be edited by others; for example: Wikipedia (http://en.wikipedia.org).

Wireless application protocol (WAP): the standard underlying programs that run on cell phones.

Wizard: a help tool (usually in step-by-step format) that steers the user through to completion of a task.

WYSIWYG (what you see is what you get): when the computer screen reflects exactly what the final output will be for a printed page or a web page.

XML (extensible markup language): a markup language that was designed to transport data, as opposed to displaying it, as HTML does.

Index

A

ad networks, 137
AdSense, 115. *See also* affiliate programs
advertising, 27, 113–118, 136–138, 156–158, 182. *See also* word-of-mouth
AdWords, 115, 136, 156–157, 199
affiliate IDs, 118
affiliate programs, 113–118
Amazon.com, 24, 114, 136, 200–201, 210–211, 230–232, 241, 248, 249–250
Amazon's WebStore, 32–33
analytics, 143, 157, 198–200, 202, 205
Angel Capital Association (ACA), 98, 101
angel investors, 97–103
anti-virus protection, 224, 227
Association of Strategic Alliance Professionals Inc. (ASAP), 122–123
auction sites, 136. *See also* eBay
audience, 9, 58–59, 117, 136, 157, 162, 186, 197–206

Autobytel, 77–80
Autozone.com, 237

B

B2B ecommerce, 69–75
Backcountry.com, 3–4
backing up data, 63, 226
Bailey, Maria, 57–60
bandwidth, 40, 63
banner ads, 137
Bezos, Jeff, 114, 200–201, 230, 249–250
Bhatia, Sabeer, 93
Blinds.com, 129–131
blogging, 25, 41–43, 64, 82, 113, 137, 150, 214
BlueSuitMom.com, 57–60
bounce rate, 153. *See also* sticky websites
Bowen, Craig, 145–147
BowlingConnection.com, 179–182
Bresee, John, 3–4
brick-and-mortar stores, 15–20, 119–124
broken links, 31, 48

▲

browser compatibility, 26, 29
Burke, Ken, 121
business plans, 3, 12, 89, 91, 92, 95
business-to-business (B2B) ecommerce, 69–75
buying-decision process, 247

C

CarKB.com, 246–247
catalogs, print, 8, 18, 82, 126, 145–147
CGI (common gateway interface) scripts, 43–44
chats, online, 134–136
ChocolateVault.com, 4–6
click-and-mortars, 17–20
Cobb, Eliot, 125–126
Cobb, Peter, 125–128
collateral for loans, 89
commercial lines of credit, 89–90
common gateway interface (CGI) scripts, 43–44
Compaq, 2–3
competitive research, 229–242
Constant Contact, 140
contact information, 4, 48, 82, 200
content, 35–36, 39–45, 142–143, 150–154, 232, 237, 248
cookies, 204–205
copyright, 30
copywriters, 140
Corporate Toners Inc., 105–108
cost-per-click (CPC) advertising, 115
coupons, 20, 43, 114, 142, 143
Craigslist, 136–137
crawlers, 152, 153, 156, 158. *See also* search engine ranking
credit card fraud, 225, 226–228
credit card payments, 32, 167–173, 185
credit lines, 89–90, 168–169
credit scores, 89–90, 172
cross promotion, 18, 232–233, 235
crowd sourcing, 200
culture, company, 84–85, 122
customer data, protecting, 202–206, 224–225, 227
customer emails and comments, 201–202
customer loyalty, 82–83, 107, 143–144, 244–245. *See also* customer retention
customer retention, 6, 83, 107, 130, 224, 236, 237, 241. *See also* customer service

customer reviews, 163, 235
customer service, 4, 35, 63, 82–84, 107–108, 177, 191, 207–211. *See also* customer retention
customers, knowing your, 197–206. *See also* targeting markets
customs charges, 184

D

daily website content, 45
data backup, 63, 226
data collection and analysis, 197–206
data storage, 62
data tracking, 143, 157, 198–200, 202, 205
data use policies, 202–206
Dell, 2–3
demographic audience, 9, 58–59, 117, 136, 157, 162, 186, 197–206
DHTML, 154
Diez, Esther, 145–146
Direct Marketing Association (DMA), 141
directories, 155–156
discussion groups, 27, 134–136. *See also* forums
domain names, 63–64, 65–67, 153, 186, 194, 220
dotcoms. *See* ecommerce
Drugstore.com, 2, 161–164, 235–236, 241

E

eBags.com, 125–128
eBay, 74–75, 136, 244, 246, 248
eBay Stores, 32
e-businesses. *See* ecommerce
eCoast Angels Network, 98
ecommerce
    advantages, 2–3, 7–9, 22
    assessing potential for success in, 17–20
    brick-and-mortar stores and, 15–20, 119–124
    disadvantages, 9–10
    early, 1–2
    future of, 243–251
    readiness for starting, 5
    reasons for failure in, 12–14
    shortcomings in, 249
    status today, 2
    success stories, 3–6, 230–242

eHolster.com, 165–166
elevator pitches, 94
email, 64, 141–142, 204
email lists, 138, 140–142
email marketing, 138–142
email services, 140
email signatures, 134–135, 220–221
encryption, 118, 170, 205, 224
engagement, 142–144, 247, 249
EsteeLauder.com, 232–233
exchange process, 75, 244, 247, 248
exit strategies, 12–13, 59, 91, 122

F

Facebook, 49–50, 135–136, 139, 200, 202–203, 249
Facebook Ads, 136
Faith, Mike, 51–55
FAQs (frequently asked questions), 208, 210, 247
feedback, 9, 44, 116–117, 200, 208, 211, 239
financial management, 12
flat-rate shipping, 249. *See also* free shipping
Forrester, Gary, 179–182
forums, 27, 44–45, 134–136
fraud, 225, 226–228
free online store, 34
free shipping, 82, 83, 127, 163, 236, 237, 241–242, 249
frequently asked questions (FAQs), 208, 210, 247
FreshDirect.com, 237–239
Fridgedoor Inc., 193–195
FrugalFun.com, 219–222
fulfillment, 8, 111, 187
funding sources, 87–103
  angel investors, 97–103
  bank loans, 89–90
  personal funds, 88–89, 90
  SBA loans, 89–90
  venture capitalists, 3, 83–84, 91–94, 95, 99–100, 101, 102
FundingPost.com, 94, 98

G

Garage Technology Ventures, 92–93
gateway accounts, 168, 172–173

Geer, Walt, 70
GiftCertificates.com, 123
GiftTree.com, 145–147
Google, 246
Google AdSense, 115. *See also* affiliate programs
Google AdWords, 115, 136, 156–157, 199
Google Analytics, 143, 157, 199
Google+, 135–136
Gore-Scott, Rhonda, 17
GotChef, 94
graphics, 27–30, 35–36, 39–40, 48, 127, 142–143, 238. *See also* videos
groups, 27, 134–136. *See also* forums
growing your business, 247
Gust.com, 98
Gwynn, Chris, 193–195

H

hacking, 170, 205, 224, 225. *See also* hijacking
Headsets.com, 51–55
Hermès.com, 248–249
hijacking, 118. *See also* hacking
Holland, Jim, 3–4
Horowitz, Shel, 219–222
hosted ecommerce solutions, 31–33, 171
hosting services, 23–24, 26, 31–33, 61–67, 171, 226
Hotmail, 93
Houck, Gail, 22
hours of operation, 8
Hsieh, Tony, 81–85
Huh, Ben, 213–217

I

ICanHasCheezBurger.com, 213–217
images, 27–30, 35–36, 39–40, 48, 127, 142–143, 238. *See also* videos
information, offering, 142–143, 163, 177, 244, 245
international markets, 183–188
internet businesses. *See* ecommerce
introductions, website, 39–40, 48. *See also* graphics
investors. *See also* funding sources
  angels, 97–103
  exit strategies for, 12–13, 91
  venture capitalists, 3, 83–84, 91–94, 95, 99–100, 101, 102

J

JavaScripts, 44
Juneja, Kapil, 105–108

K

Kawasaki, Guy, 92–93
The Knot Inc., 120

L

landing pages, 24, 158, 231
Lee, Jonas, 123
Lepore, Dawn, 161–164
LinkedIn, 135, 139, 221
links, 31, 48–50, 116–118, 134, 136, 139,
    153–154, 156
Liquidity Services Inc. (LSI), 72–73
loans, 89–90, 168–169
logos, 30, 49
logs, web server, 200
loyalty programs, 143–144. *See also* customer
    loyalty
Luthi, Bernard, 175–178

M

Macy's, 120
Mail Chimp, 140
mailing costs. *See* shipping costs
mailing lists, 138, 140–142
mailing services, 140
marketing, 3, 73–74, 113–118, 120, 139, 155,
    198. *See also* social media
marketing materials, 134
marketing plans, 13, 151
MarketLive, 121
marketplace sites, 136. *See also* Amazon.com
May, John, 98, 101–102
May's department stores, 120
McCann, Barbara, 4–6
McCann, Jim, 4
McQuilkin, George, 98–101
merchant accounts, 32, 168, 171–172
metrics, 143, 157, 198–200, 202, 205
Michael C. Fina jewelry, 120
mistakes in web design, 47–50
mobile devices, website compatibility with, 26,
    29
MyRide.com, 78

N

Nakagawa, Eric, 213–214
navigation, 49, 153, 231, 239
Netscape, 1
New Vantage Group, 98, 101, 102
Newegg.com, 175–178
newsletters, 44, 138–142
niche markets, 4, 16, 18–19, 127, 248
Nordmark, Jon, 125–126

O

OfficeDepot.com, 233
OfficeMax.com, 114, 233
1-Click buying, 230–231
1800Contacts.com, 236
online discussion groups and chats, 27, 134–
    136. *See also* forums
online sales. *See* ecommerce
open-source online store, 34
operating costs, 8, 88
opting out of mailings, 138, 140, 204
osCommerce.com, 34
outages, 225–226

P

paid placement, 156–158
Panera Bread, 210
partnerships, 59, 118, 119–124, 235
passwords, 227
payment gateway accounts, 168, 172–173
payment options and issues, 32, 167–173, 185,
    225, 226–228
PayPal, 169–170, 172–173
pay-per-click (PPC) advertising, 156–158, 182
PCConnection.com, 240
permission-based email, 141–142
permits, 8–9
personalization, 67, 209, 231, 235
Phenix Direct, 70
photographs, 27–30, 35–36, 39–40, 48, 127,
    142–143, 238. *See also* videos
Pinterest, 136, 139, 232–233
podcasting, 43. *See also* videos
Polis, Jared, 189–191
polls, 41, 201
pomexpress.com, 16
PPC (pay-per-click) advertising, 156–158, 182

presentations, 94–95, 101
privacy policies, 202–206
problem solving aspects of websites, 245–247
ProFlowers, 189–191
protecting online data, 63, 118, 170, 202–206, 223–228, 250
purchase experience, simplifying, 231, 234, 238–239, 244
purchasing-decision process, 247

Q

Quarterman, Scott, 165–166

R

Radio Flyer, 110
Rand, Sherry, 16
ranking, search engine, 27, 36, 150–158
redundancy, system, 63, 226
RedWagons.com, 109–111
reliability, 20
repeat business, 6, 83, 107, 130, 224, 236, 237, 241. *See also* customer service
restaurants, 18
retailers, 16–19
return policies, 16, 18, 82, 83, 127, 211, 241
ReveNews.com, 114
revenue models, 12
Riesenbach, Jim, 77–80
robots.txt files, 158
Roeder, Tony, 109–111
R.R. Donnelly, 121
RSS (Really Simple Syndication) feeds, 42–43

S

safeguarding online data, 63, 118, 170, 202–206, 223–228, 250
sales tax, 184, 245
Salesforce, 140, 143
SBA (Small Business Administration) loans, 89–90
scaling, 247
scams, 118, 226–228
search engine marketing (SEM), 155
search engine optimization (SEO), 27, 36, 150–155
search engine ranking, 27, 36, 150–158
search engines, 149–159

security, 118, 170, 202–206, 223–228, 250
Segil, Larraine, 122
self-motivation, 10
SEM (search engine marketing), 155
SEO (search engine optimization), 27, 36, 150–155
servers, 40, 48, 64–65, 159, 170, 200, 225–226
shipping costs
    flat-rate, 249
    free, 82, 83, 127, 163, 236, 237, 241–242, 249
    international, 184–185
    reduced, 72
Shoebuy.com, 241–242
shopping carts, 24, 33, 36, 159, 169, 170
sitemaps, 153
Small Business Administration (SBA) loans, 89–90
social media
    building awareness with, 19, 50, 59, 83, 221, 249
    customer feedback with, 200
    discussion groups and chats on, 134–136
    linking from websites, 49–50, 136, 154
    profiles on, 139
    relationship building with, 139, 202, 249
    traffic generation with, 135–136
spam, 141–142, 204, 206
spiders, 152, 153, 156, 158. *See also* search engine ranking
sponsored search, 156–158
Stamps.com, 234–235
Staples.com, 233
startup costs, 8, 13, 87–88, 166, 176, 180, 194, 220
startup seed funding, 11. *See also* funding sources
Steed, Frank, 125–126
Steinfeld, Jay, 129–131
sticky websites, 45, 142–144, 153
storage, data, 62
surveys, 41, 191, 200–201
Swinmurn, Nick, 81
system redundancy, 63, 226

T

Target Club Wedd gift registry, 120

targeted mailing lists, 140–142
targeting markets, 9, 58–59, 117, 136, 157, 162, 186, 197–206
testing websites, 29–31, 48
The Knot Inc., 120
third-party merchants, 168, 172–173
Today's Deals, 231
tracking data, 143, 157, 198–200, 202, 205
trademarks, 30
Trader Joe's, 210
traffic generation, 39–45, 133–144, 199, 201
translation services and tools, 185, 186
transparency, 48, 203, 235
travel agencies, 17–18, 19
trust, 244, 245
Twitter, 135–136, 139, 200, 249

U
Unebasami, Kari, 213–214

V
value propositions, 248
value-added tax, 184
venture capital, 3, 83–84, 91–94, 95, 99–100, 101, 102
videos, 27, 29, 40–41, 43, 63, 234. *See also* graphics
vino2u.com, 17
virtual servers, 65. *See also* servers

W
walk-in clientele, 17–18
web analytics, 143, 157, 198–200, 202, 205
web businesses. *See* ecommerce
web sharing, 64–65
websites, 21–50
    advertising on, 27, 113–118
    bounce rate for, 153
    compatibility with browsers and mobile devices, 26, 29
    contact information on, 4, 48, 82, 200
    content for, 35–36, 39–45, 142–143, 150–154, 232, 237, 248
    critiques of successful, 230–242
    designing, 24–25, 26–30, 47–50, 154–155
    determining your purpose for, 22–23
    directories, listing in, 155–156

functionality, 24–25
generating traffic to, 39–45, 133–144, 199, 201
graphics on, 27–30, 35–36, 39–40, 48, 127, 142–143, 238
growth potential, 25
hosting services, 23–24, 26, 31–33, 61–67, 171, 226
for international markets, 185–187
landing pages, 24, 158, 231
links, 31, 48–50, 116–118, 134, 136, 139, 153–154, 156
loading time, 142–143, 244
membership capabilities on, 28
music and sound on, 28
navigation, 49, 153, 231, 239
necessity of, 20
page titles on, 154
payment/checkout features on, 24, 27, 33, 36, 159, 167–173, 185
search engine ranking, 27, 36, 150–158
search engine submission, 151–152
site builders, 21, 23–26
social media and. *See* social media
sticky, 45, 142–144, 153
testing, 29–31, 48
updating, 31, 36, 49
videos on, 27, 29, 40–41, 43, 63, 234
web developers/designers, 34–37
WebStore on Amazon, 32–33. *See also* Amazon. com
WeddingChannel.com, 120
Weinberg, Bruce, 243–244
Whitman, Meg, 249
wine stores, 17
word-of-mouth, 139, 166, 182, 195, 208, 247, 249

Y
Yahoo! Auctions, 136
Yahoo! Merchant Solutions, 31–32
Young, Andy, 125–126

Z
Zappos.com, 81–85, 211